The Intimate Room

The Intimate Room provides an original exploration of psychoanalytic thought, showing how contemporary psychoanalysis seeks to answer the challenges raised by today's postmodern culture.

Offering a deeply personal and insightful reading of Bion, this book acts as a stimulating guide to the development of the psychoanalytic field and both its technical and clinical implications. As such topics of discussion include:

- the concept of the internal setting
- the rhetoric of interpretation
- the 'subversive' notion of Nachträglichkeit
- the role played by characters in analytic discourse
- the bi-personal field as Virtual Reality
- new concepts of transference.

Allowing the reader to engage with the inner space of analysis, *The Intimate Room* will be of interest to psychoanalysts, psychotherapists and all those with an interest in the field of psychoanalysis. It will also be a useful tool in psychoanalytic and psychotherapeutic work on a day-to-day basis.

Giuseppe Civitarese is a psychiatrist with a PhD in psychiatry and relational sciences. He is a Full Member of the Italian Psychoanalytic Society (SPI) and of the International Psychoanalytic Association (IPA). He lives and works in Pavia, Italy.

GW00566835

THE NEW LIBRARY OF PSYCHOANALYSIS
General Editor   Dana Birksted-Breen

The New Library of Psychoanalysis was launched in 1987 in association with the Institute of Psychoanalysis, London. It took over from the International Psychoanalytical Library which published many of the early translations of the works of Freud and the writings of most of the leading British and Continental psychoanalysts.

The purpose of the New Library of Psychoanalysis is to facilitate a greater and more widespread appreciation of psychoanalysis and to provide a forum for increasing mutual understanding between psychoanalysts and those working in other disciplines such as the social sciences, medicine, philosophy, history, linguistics, literature and the arts. It aims to represent different trends both in British psychoanalysis and in psychoanalysis generally. The New Library of Psychoanalysis is well placed to make available to the English-speaking world psychoanalytic writings from other European countries and to increase the interchange of ideas between British and American psychoanalysts.

The Institute, together with the British Psychoanalytical Society, runs a low-fee psychoanalytic clinic, organizes lectures and scientific events concerned with psychoanalysis and publishes the *International Journal of Psychoanalysis*. It also runs the only UK training course in psychoanalysis which leads to membership of the International Psychoanalytical Association – the body which preserves internationally agreed standards of training, of professional entry, and of professional ethics and practice for psychoanalysis as initiated and developed by Sigmund Freud. Distinguished members of the Institute have included Michael Balint, Wilfred Bion, Ronald Fairbairn, Anna Freud, Ernest Jones, Melanie Klein, John Rickman and Donald Winnicott.

Previous General Editors include David Tuckett, Elizabeth Spillius and Susan Budd. Previous and current Members of the Advisory Board include Christopher Bollas, Ronald Britton, Catalina Bronstein, Donald Campbell, Sara Flanders, Stephen Grosz, John Keene, Eglé Laufer, Juliet Mitchell, Michael Parsons, Rosine Jozef Perelberg, Richard Rusbridger, Mary Target, David Taylor and Alessandra Lemma, who is Assistant Editor.

ALSO IN THIS SERIES

TITLES IN THE NEW LIBRARY OF PSYCHOANALYSIS TEACHING SERIES

THE NEW LIBRARY OF PSYCHOANALYSIS

General Editor: Dana Birksted-Breen

The Intimate Room

Theory and Technique of the Analytic Field

Giuseppe Civitarese

Translated by Philip Slotkin

Routledge
Taylor & Francis Group
LONDON AND NEW YORK

First published 2008
by Edizioni Borla, Italy
Title of the original Italian edition: L'intima stanza:
Teoria e tecnica del campo analitico

First published in the UK 2010
by Routledge
27 Church Road, Hove, East Sussex BN3 2FA

Simultaneously published in the USA and Canada
by Routledge
270 Madison Avenue, New York NY 10016

Routledge is an imprint of the Taylor & Francis Group, an Informa Business

© Edizioni Borla 2008
English Translation © 2010 Philip Slotkin

Typeset in Bembo by RefineCatch Limited, Bungay, Suffolk
Printed and bound in Great Britain by TJ International Ltd, Padstow, Cornwall
Paperback cover design by Sandra Heath

This publication has been produced with paper manufactured to
strict environmental standards and with pulp derived from
sustainable forests.

British Library Cataloguing in Publication Data
A catalogue record for this book is available from the British Library

Library of Congress Cataloging-in-Publication Data
Civitarese, Giuseppe, 1958–
[Intima stanza. English]
The intimate room : theory and technique of the analytic field / Giuseppe
Civitarese ; translated by Philip Slotkin.
p. ; cm.
Includes bibliographical references.
ISBN 978–0–415–57509–6 (hbk) — ISBN 978–0–415–57510–2 (pbk.)
1. Psychoanalysis. I. Civitarese, Giuseppe, 1958– Intima stanza. English. II. Title.
[DNLM: 1. Psychoanalysis. WM 460 C582i 2010]
BF173.C496 2010
150.19′5—dc22

2010004055

ISBN 978–0–415–57509–6 (hbk)
ISBN 978–0–415–57510–2 (pbk)

For Silvi, Rocco and Giorgio

Contents

Foreword

Antonino Ferro

For some time now, the concept of transference has been complicated by that of relationship, which in turn assumes a number of different forms as interpreted by authors ranging from the post-Kleinians to the intersubjectivists. Furthermore, an additional level of complexity has been imparted to it by the notion of the field, which has itself developed in fits and starts.

Not many authors would be able to negotiate a path through this complex, progressively expanding universe while at the same time maintaining a holographic and multidimensional vision of psycho-analysis. Giuseppe Civitarese is surely one of the few – the *very* few – who have this capability. Furthermore, he makes a contribution of his own in the form of a looming fifth extension of the field concept – namely, the implications of virtual reality, considered as the space accorded to dreaming in the analytic session.

In so doing, the author remains firmly rooted in a profound know-ledge of Freud's thought and an increasingly passionate and personal rereading of Bion. That in itself would assure him of great appreci-ation, but he also demonstrates a natural propensity for abstract reflec-tion, based on his familiarity with the disciplines of philosophy and semiotics; and, if that was not enough, he exhibits unusual narrative skill in the way he enables us to enter the analyst's consulting room and come into contact with even the most delicate of clinical vicissi-tudes. So, whereas he is admittedly not an 'easy' author (precisely because he is complex), he nevertheless makes it easy for the reader to follow him, by taking the reader by the hand and leading him along difficult pathways, many of them never before described, and thus mapping out routes through as yet tangled undergrowth.

The subjects addressed in the book are from the outset those most central to contemporary psychoanalysis. While the first chapter sets off reassuringly with the Freud of the 'Further recommendations on the technique of psycho-analysis' (1913–14), it immediately takes wing by advocating the 'rigorous adoption of the dream paradigm in the session' and confronting the thorny and highly controversial issue of (external?) reality in analysis. Bravely espousing an especially radical stance as befits our analytic métier, Dr Civitarese sees the session as a dream; that is not to say that everything else is unimportant, but that the significance of other aspects lies elsewhere. As with one of those equations that can only be solved by 'making the absurd assumption that x equals . . .', so in analysis we can work only by making the absurd assumption that what the patient says belongs to the analytic field. As Bion, Ogden and Grotstein remind us, our work involves the development of the 'dreaming ensemble' which allows the 'symptom $\leftrightarrow$ oneiric-transformation-capacity' oscillation to be shifted towards the latter of these two poles.

As an anecdote, let me mention that Giuseppe Civitarese 'donated' the title of the multi-author book (the contributors to which included myself) *Sognare l'analisi* ['Dreaming analysis'], a title which powerfully asserts that it is not a matter of denying external or historical reality (heaven forbid), but that the analyst knows that he can work only by developing the patient's – and his own – capacity to dream so that unelaborated sensory inputs and proto-emotions are not evacuated, thereby giving rise to symptoms, but can be alphabetized, metabolized and hence forgotten, stored in the form of memories, and used as memories for the purpose of thinking.

All this is presented in a manner solidly anchored to psychoanalytic theory and with detailed, precise and convincing clinical examples that reveal the author's ability to play – an ability which is in my view one of the most important qualities needed by an analyst.

Dr Civitarese is, of course, bound to take an interest in one of the most significant present-day challenges to psychoanalysis: do the areas 'beneath' those of psychosis concern us? An in-depth consideration of Bleger, Marcelli and Ogden seems to afford intriguing glimpses of the very foundations of mental functioning. Indeed, it is precisely the book's alternation of theoretical parts and clinical narrations that enables the reader to assimilate concepts such as the agglutinated nucleus or the sensory floor, which are thus in effect rejuvenated.

The culture of semiotics makes a powerful entry into the text in the third chapter, at first in the form of literary and cinematic narrations. Next, the interplay of characters and the narration, as well as the significance of the analyst's bursting in person into the text (by way of transference interpretations that disrupt a certain narrative frame), is illustrated by other examples drawn from fragments of sessions which demonstrate the author's ability to combine theoretical and clinical aspects without doing violence to either, and indeed his constant capacity to adopt a fresh clinical approach that is then placed on a new and firm theoretical foundation.

In the fourth chapter, field theories are enriched by the metaphorical potential of virtual reality, of possible worlds and of characters as holograms. Further concepts borrowed from narratology, such as transparency, mapping and accessibility, are also adduced. In one unforgettable section the author presents the impressive case of Alessia, in which interpretation becomes a means of escape from *The Matrix*. Here interpretation is seen to assume a variety of forms: explicit or non-explicit, interactive or immersive, saturated or unsaturated. This chapter clearly demonstrates the remaining untapped potential of the fruitful encounter between psychoanalysis and narratology. One need only consider the increasing frequency with which contributions on the subject are now appearing in the *International Journal of Psychoanalysis*.

In addition, one is bound to admire the author's ability to navigate skilfully and creatively among highly condensed, complex and sometimes ambiguous concepts, whose historical development he maps clearly and which he places within their individual psychoanalytic geographies, on each occasion finding an original perspective. Sometimes he displays an enviable – and playful – capacity for synthesis, as in his apt summing up of the evolution of the concept of transference in the United States: 'the transference is born of spectres, becomes a spectrum of concepts, and, lastly, might well end up as the spectre of a concept.' Giuseppe Civitarese in fact has a particular taste for the history of concepts, whose roots he always considers in great depth – after which he succeeds in surprising us with his own personal view.

The account of the Reed/Schachter controversy cannot fail to excite even an analyst disinclined to concern himself with theoretical problems, for intricate notions are treated with a lightness of touch and metabolized as if by an aboriginal tribesman beating a path through a forest who, however, is also a graduate of MIT and possesses a satellite navigation unit – a perfect synthesis of a surveyor and Dersu Uzala in Kurosawa's eponymous film. Similarly, although having a firm, declared and clear-cut position of his own, the author is able to engage in a dialogue (without any trace of fanaticism) with the British, French, North and South American brands of psychoanalysis.

A consistent thread that runs through the entire book is the author's sense of humour (exemplified in the splendid anecdote of the two cats), as well as his lightness of touch in tackling even subjects that are anything but easy – qualities perhaps best displayed in the brilliant pithy comments of 'The restricted field'.

This, then, is a many-sided book, which at one and the same time comprises a clear approach to the complexity of psychoanalysis and its multiple models; a historical and geographical survey of many of its key concepts; a means of access, by way of the wealth of clinical material presented, to the *inner space* of analysis and the mind, enabling the reader to share in the intimacy of the analytic relationship; a guide to the ways in which the concept of the field (which is so central and yet so unknown) has been enriched; and, lastly, an introduction to narratology by means of all the connections it enables us to make, and to the realms of metapsychological and philosophical theorization.

The atmosphere one breathes, which is not immediately noticed owing to one's total immersion in it, is an atmosphere of 'intimacy': one is with a friend, led by the hand through fascinating landscapes such as the Brocken, a mountain known for its weird diffraction phenomena, with sometimes difficult deconstructions and demanding philosophical arguments, which, however, never discomfit the reader, but instead make him feel that he is in the presence of a guide who is passionate about explaining things in simple terms and assuring him of safe passage through areas that are as yet in darkness and remain unexplored.

An attempt to accommodate Giuseppe Civitarese's book within Bion's Grid would yield a very odd result: the image that occurs to one is of a billiard ball rebounding from cushion to cushion at every possible angle and with every possible geometry. From the most abstract rows to those of dreams and myth, as well as to the most concrete rows, it would bounce between A and F, and then follow a zigzag path from Column 1 to Column 6 and beyond, each time exerting its particular influence on the reader. This is a book which, as Bion might say, constantly uses the language of Achievement.

The only other book with which I could possibly compare it, in terms of its depth, richness of content and opening of horizons, is James Grotstein's recently published *A Beam of Intense Darkness* (2007).

For the time being, Giuseppe Civitarese is an analyst who is better known abroad than in his native Italy. Among the few to have had several contributions published in the *International Journal of Psychoanalysis*, as well as in other journals in English, Portuguese, Spanish and Russian, he is an author characterized by the complexity of his thought, the depth of his cultural roots and the simplicity in which he clothes himself and his work. Let us not tell him so too loudly, but he is one of the most promising authors on the international psychoanalytic scene, and – as they said when the events of May 1968 were unfolding in France – 'this is only the beginning.'

Acknowledgements

Chapter 1 is based on 'Fire at the theatre: (Un)reality of/in the transference and interpretation', *International Journal of Psychoanalysis*, 86: 1299–316 (2005).

Chapter 2 is based on 'Vincolo simbiotico e setting', *Revista de Psicoanálisis*, 50: 117–48 (2004) and *Rivista di Psicoanalisi* (APA, Buenos Aires), 63: 427–456, 2006.

Chapter 3 is based on 'Metalessi ovvero retorica dell'-interpretazione di transfert', *Rivista di Psicoanalisi*, 53: 5–28, 2007.

Chapter 4 is based on 'Immersion versus interactivity and the analytic field', *International Journal of Psychoanalysis*, 89: 279–298.

Chapter 5 is based on 'Note su memoria e causalità psichica a partire dalla teoria della funzione cerebrale di Edelman', *Prospettive psicoanalitiche nel lavoro istituzionale*, 14: 356–369, 1996.

1

Fire at the theatre
(Un)reality of/in the transference
and interpretation[1]

In 'Further recommendations on the technique of psychoanalysis', Freud (1913, 1915a), with his usual inventiveness, successfully embeds a number of key metaphors for portraying the structure and dynamics of analytic work. Here they play an even more important role because, through the narrative and rhetorical turn sharply dramatizing the theoretical discourse, they seem to repeat a chapter in the history of psychoanalysis (and, in a word, of every analysis). If Freud (1913) begins with the reassuring image of a game of chess, evoking the order and precision of a sophisticated intellectual exercise, then, dealing with transference love (1915a), he presents a coup de théâtre: in its subject matter first of all, an 'untoward event' (1914a: 12), and then in the figurative elements chosen to represent it. The irruption of passion, the transformation of the patient's 'affectionate transference' into an 'outbreak of a passionate demand for love' (1915a: 162), is equated to the screams provoked by the outbreak of fire in a theatre. Behind this lies the episode of Anna O's passion for Breuer, which induces him to abandon his patient (just as a similar feeling would distance Dora from Freud), but which leads to the formulation of the theory of sexual aetiology of neuroses and founds psychoanalysis.

In 'Observations on transference love', Freud (1915a) tackles a point that created a scandal for the new cure and his public reputation, now defused and encapsulated in one of the commonplaces about psychoanalysis, although not on a theoretical level. Here, instead, the problem of the nature of the facts of analysis and the type of 'objectivity' that belongs to it continue to be 'scandalous'. The fire in a theatre

1

is an incident, a real element that irrupts and causes the play to be stopped; it is a complete change of scene, a particularly surprising image. Indeed, in this passage Freud is not referring, as we might expect, to events in the external world or to facts of material reality, which might be so urgent and dramatic as to necessarily annul the *as if* functioning of the setting's device, but rather to the flaring up of transference love, something that he now places *inside* the framework of the cure, after initially considering it an impediment. At this point, they are no longer real fires in play, but those within the analytic relationship and the setting; or, better, within the analyst's internal setting (which can be defined as the capacity to hold oneself at a level of listening specifically directed towards understanding the patient's unconscious). Then, in the following lines, the question becomes even more involved: on the one hand, Freud advises dealing with such an intense (and risky) transference manifestation as unreal; on the other, he acknowledges that its nature of a *real*, in other words not illusory, passion cannot be denied. In a few incisive lines, we thus find a series of complex themes: the nature of the transference and its constituent duality, the ambiguity of what is 'real', and the prerequisites for defining the setting.

The concept of transference can thus be considered as Freud's solution to the problem of the relationship between external reality and the setting's internal reality (a theory of knowledge can also be glimpsed here), between the stories of the patient's present and past life and their transposition or re-edition, mediated by unconscious phantasy, on the analytic stage. Some contemporary ('sceptical') theoretical developments emphasize the 'reality' of the transference, indicating its rootedness in the patient–analyst relationship and no longer only in the *definite, true reality* of childhood history. In this way, the transference, displaced towards the existing and the present, interpreted in a wide sense, loses resolution as a concept, becoming unfocused and aspecific (Blum 2003; Smith 2003).

This happens, however (at least in some currents of psychoanalysis), within an area where the two polarities of the real and the imaginary, already contained in Freud's discourse (reassumed in the image of the theatre on fire), remain in tension. It occurs within models that radicalize the 'dream paradigm' to different extents in their idea of clinical interaction, that consider the session as a dream (Langs 1971; Lothane 1983; Meltzer 1984; Kern 1987; Boyer 1999; Ferro 2002a; Ogden 2003a) and the analytic process as 'symbol-poiesis in situation'

(Bezoari 2002). When the transference inclines towards the relationship, the reduced specific weight attributed to psychic reality on the one hand finds itself balanced on the other by the fact that in the dream of the session external reality – but also the analytic situation – by definition appears first of all under the form of the day's residues; these, as in the night dream, are 'nothing more than elements or signs used by the unconscious wish' (Laplanche and Pontalis 1967: 96) and by the phantasy.

The theoretical hypothesis of this chapter is that rigorous adoption of the dream paradigm in the session (an obvious Freudian principle, but which only finds in Bion's extended idea (1962) of 'waking dream thought' a fully applicable field) succeeds in combining the radical antirealism expressed in the postulate by which all the patient's communications concern the transference – as displacement and projection of the patient's psychic elements – with the 'reality' of the transference and with the conviction that the facts of the analysis are codetermined by the patient–analyst dyad. It is moreover misleading to think of being able to separate the phantastic component from the real component in the analytic relationship, at least on an 'entrance', 'horizontal' level, for example, in nominalistic terms, with the simple fact of presupposing the transference/relation distinction. In other words, to separate it from all those aspects of the interaction that cannot be reduced to the basic idea of transference as misunderstanding and 'false connection'.

For example, the perspective pertaining to a model of the analytic field – adopted in this chapter – considers on principle *any element* of the patient's discourse as potentially 'transfigured' by the dreamwork and by the rhetoric of the dream; in short, filtered by psychic reality and by the transference. The intersubjective dimension, which is also intrinsic to this model, accounts instead for the analyst's participation in the transference and in the patient's realistic reactions to the analytic situation. So, in the patient's interaction with the therapist, it will be possible to deduce, mostly a posteriori, the emotional quota bound to the transference – understood here in its narrowest meaning – from the quantitative disparity in answer to stimuli. It will be possible to find the mark of the transference in the outsize, excessive, eccentric, disproportionate effects, which it will in the end introduce into the cure (Imbeault 1997).

In my opinion, this is a satisfactory solution for a debatable point: what one includes in the transference and what one does not. Since

Freud does not see any reason (not any more, at least) for abandoning the theatre in the case of transference love, what are, if they exist, those *real elements* that interrupt the setting? Those elements that cannot be taken back to the self-observing, virtual regime of the analytical device? What 'facts' belong instead by right to empirical reality and to what extent is it meaningful to maintain a setting even in their presence? This chapter would like to answer that the therapist's inner setting is set on 'fire' every time the irreducible ambiguity or para-doxicality of the transference is defensively and exclusively resolved either in the patient's external or intrapsychic imaginary reality.

Insomnia

'I am ready to tell the *facts*. Pure facts. The insomnia perhaps started before, but my memories only go back to when I began going to nursery school. *Not able to sleep and not able to dream* or to play, but only and always to stay on the alert . . . keep watch . . . all night long . . . look at my parents' door, then the corridor . . . convinced that they might go away and leave me alone. And then, after a bit, just seeing their bodies was no longer enough to reassure me, I needed to hear their voices . . . my mother's voice. And every five minutes I used to wake her up to tell her that I loved her. I could only manage to keep my eyes closed for five minutes. Then, our roles changed. The sentinel was kept under surveillance. My mother began to observe my insomnia, stretched out on the floor beside my bed. Exasperated. Judged to be a naughty whim, a deviance to repress and correct, I was slapped and shouted at for a long time. And in the morning, taken to nursery school . . . there I was effectively abandoned; a *tragedy* because *I absolutely didn't want to be left* and threw myself on the ground crying . . . Because this was the second of my unshakeable convictions: that they would leave me there. For me, every goodbye . . . every time . . . was as though it was the last.'

'For a child, separation can be a terrible thing,' I say to Alberto (in his second year of analysis, three sessions a week), and my words seem to alleviate the tension and produce a first change in the emotional climate of the session, as his reply shows.

'It *immediately* went *much better* at elementary school,' he says. 'From the first day *I changed*. I had a *gentle, loving*, very affectionate teacher, a minute classroom, almost half the size of *this room*, all girls except for

4

me; there were only six of us. Then, in the *third year* [an allusion to today's session which, being Friday, is the third and last of the week, and to what happens every time he separates from analysis?] the teacher changed and everything began all over again, no discipline, and so on, until – and my mother still remembers this – I said, giving up: "Okay, if things are like this, from now on I will pretend to be a machine, disciplined and punctual!" And I added something horrendous: "But I will also pretend that the teacher is a machine too!" So I did, and I stopped being a problem for my parents.'

This is an extremely vivid, overbright, clearly traumatic, frozen memory belonging to the patient and to his story: a factual account of how a radical fracture was established in his being. But the patient's insomnia is also for long stretches the insomnia of the analysis, ensnared in a dizzying, immobile vigil of intelligence and reflective logic, lacking – except in some rare moments – imagination, playfulness and humour.

Alberto brings a dream to the next session – Monday – which, although conserving the same glacial and suspended atmosphere, represents something new in the analysis. In the old house, in the dark, he is a child while looking at the road through the cracks in the shutters. His parents are also at home, by now resigned. All are living in the expectation of being 'killed'.[2] In the dream, he says, 'It's impossible to sleep.' He wakes from his nightmare in the grip of terrible anxiety.

The patient dryly, like an 'insomniac', relates his dream at the beginning of the session, as though he was expounding an abstract concept, a sort of theorem derived from various basic postulates: what he considers to be objective traumatic situations suffered in childhood, an old accident (concussion), scholastic 'persecution'. I think that he is also talking about how he might have experienced the separation of the weekend and I tell him, to help him make contact with his emotions, that this dream is perhaps the real thread (much more violent) or at least the more subtle one hidden behind the fear of being left at nursery school (and I mean that separation for him is like dying), which he had talked to me about the session before.

Meanwhile, an earlier event returns to my mind. On beginning sessions after the Christmas break, just a few weeks ago, Alberto related a childhood memory: once, his mother, very angry, had lost control of herself and had hung him *upside down* because he did not want to leave his parents' bedroom, and he had angrily grabbed on to the doorframe and nearly unhinged it. After a moment's silence, he

5

then talked to me at length about a friend who was in therapy with a renowned, respected analyst and we had laughed together about the complaints that he had been told in an ironic but affectionate tone about this colleague. The next session (having perhaps sensed the anger contained in a hypothetically depreciative element rather than an eventual 'oneiric' self-reference and an indication of how important it might be for him to refind the analysis!) I 'forgot' to close the door on entering the room while he was settling on the couch, arousing his protests. In fact, to myself, I thought it might have been an unconscious answer to what I had experienced perhaps as a provocation of his, along the lines of: 'I don't need you! You aren't anybody!' Arriving at the next session, a couple of days later, he placed what looked to me like some sort of strange instrument on a second chair (beyond the one the analyst sits in), visible to both and obviously *empty*. At a certain point I phantasied that it could be for recording our conversation. Then again in the next session – and I am still referring to the initial period of the year to which my mind had returned during the Monday session – distracted by unease and curiosity about the peculiar object (perhaps a new model of a mobile phone), ritually placed in the same place by the patient just before lying on the couch, I had inadvertently left the door open. A few seconds later . . . and both of us burst out laughing! Despite this, Alberto, pained, expressed his distress at my acting, repeated on two occasions, which he interpreted as an unconscious desire of mine to show him the door.

This sequence of events reported in an extremely synthetic form shows how the envelope of the analysis – and also the material arrangement of the setting – can be 'breached' when emotional contents that are too intense in a given moment do not meet a container capable of receiving and metabolizing them. However, one can ask oneself: what more enlightening representations (realized by inducting the maternal 'role' into the analyst, and by repeating the old 'expulsion' on the stage of the setting) and more effective communic/a(c)tions could be given of the intensely persecutory experiences that can be found at the origin of the patient's obscure ill?

The working through that followed this double crisis allowed the setting to be 'repaired', to represent with greater precision the intersecting plane between past history and present transference, and to advance an 'allegorical' reading of the same childhood memory (being thrown out of his parents' bedroom) with respect to a lack of perhaps more primary care. Alberto was also able to positively see himself in the analyst's same obviously imperfect humanity and obtain a 'reward of humour', without in any way feeling his old anxiety, set in motion by what had happened between us, devalued.

But it is only in the session of the dream – after a lapse of time – that I feel able to understand the significance of this episode of the analysis (which had occurred immediately after the holidays) and to outline sufficiently clearly, a posteriori, an *acting* → *memory* → *dream* sequence as elements of a progression – even when the contents are of the same emotional tone – towards an increased capacity for symbolization (and towards a consequently greater intimacy of the analytical relationship). These moments present themselves like the successive layers of old writing on parchment, each recursively throwing light on the preceding ones.

On the stage of the setting, patient and analyst interpret – also as spectators and critics – roles from a script that both take part in writing in the very moment they act it, each drawing from his own life. The plot unfolds against the background of the patient's story (of his actual reality) and alludes to it – in a relationship of reciprocal involvement that decides the preliminary conditions for understanding it – but does not exactly reproduce it. As in a play, it reflects the author's existential path, but at the same time it functions or it does not function, compared to the expressive aims declared, on the basis of its own internal dynamics, the observance of determined dramaturgical rules, and the quality of the stage set.

With regard to the clinical vignette described, the priority of the cure lies not so much in tracing Alberto's insomnia or infantile neurosis to abstract phantastic nuclei, or to 'deviances' in a biography, but rather in allowing him to assume first in analysis and then in the theatre of his life new roles and viewpoints; to be able to *dream*. But, for him to be able to dream, he must feel sufficiently safe: it is necessary to look in his words and perceptions for the sense of the emotions that are activated in the reality of the meeting and from there move to lay the premises for possible transformations.

Alberto has been able to dream – certainly more of a nightmare than anything else in the sequence of sessions considered here, an 'interrupted dream'. He was able to pass from the induction of acting in the analyst to the memory and then to the dream (which I consider also in its condition of second-level memory, more 'real' precisely because it is protected and indicated as fictitious by a further narrative frame) because many small transformations from 'keeping vigil and punishing' to 'gentle, loving teacher' must have occurred in the meantime. Many small moments of synchrony must have been lived, like the liberating burst of laughter that had opened the way to expressing a true feeling of sadness, something the 'machine' he had decided to become in order to hide his true self would not have been able to do. These moments were responsible for gradually improving his ability to sleep (it is a paradox – and at the same time a valuable example of the formation of a new awareness of the self – that the patient in sleep says 'it is impossible to sleep'!) felt as a painful discontinuity of being, like the impossibility of immersing oneself again in a temporary state of fusion with the object.

This clinical vignette is useful for allegorically illustrating the paradigm behind the analytic work, that of dreaming. The 'facts', the 'pure facts', are in the first place the facts of the analysis. In the dream of the session by definition, external reality appears above all as the day's residues.

To sum up, after the holiday break, and for several weeks afterwards, Alberto does nothing but tell of his disorientation and pain for the absence of the other. He does this (a) through the moving memory of being thrown out of his parents' bedroom and through the induction of acting. The crucial moment is the instant when the analyst's listening becomes 'suspicious'; it turns to external reality – the patient's friend in analysis, the other therapist – and opens the path for the persecutory phantasy of the recorder, in a temporary suspension of the analyst's own internal setting: *the fire at the theatre*. These 'facts of the analysis' are only partially metabolized, remaining as semi-processed products, which is enough, though, for the patient to be able to narrate after a few sessions, in a flow of unreachable memories up till then, (b) the 'pure facts' (the sleepless nights) of his childhood. Then a further transformation – we will think of it as produced by the appearance/s of the 'gentle teacher' character who indicates a new function in the emotional field – enables him to recount (c) the anxiety dream of the shutters. At this point – and resonating with the dream, which, so to speak, is even more intrinsic to the emotional field than the more neutral childhood memory – the analyst too recovers the earlier event of the two sessions in which he had left the door open, in what can be considered true reverie and not a violation of the Bionian precept about memory and desire. The effects of integration are evident and placed at various levels. For example, and to mention only one, the analyst's feeling of being threatened experienced in the moment of his acting, already connected – in the last of the four sessions described, at the start of analysis after the Christmas break – to the image-memory of Alberto 'head down' (evoking *Paradise lost* and the abyss of the *inferus* world), can now really be 'felt' as the emotional equivalent of what was/is set off in the patient every time he experiences an 'expulsion from the room' as the execution of a sort of verdict of non-existence on the part of an authoritative, punitive parental couple, and can prepare the ground for greater interpretative closeness.

For obvious reasons of space, the description of Monday's session, limited to a few initial minutes, must stop here. But, from this experience of the unexpected sharing (Bolognini 1995) of an affect that so pervades the patient's internal world, the emotional atmosphere of the cure has changed considerably, and with time more room has been won for play and creativity.

Literature has always linked life and dreams in an equivalence, which is nothing but a corollary of the *topos* of the *theatrum mundi*. In psychoanalytic theory, the nearest equation, thought = dream, unfolds to its greatest extent in the theoretical ideas of Bion (1962), Langs (1971), Meltzer (1984), Ogden (2003a) and in the elaboration of the model of the emotional field (for which see the various essays in the publication edited by Gaburri 1997).

In Langs (1971), widely inspired by Bion, the Barangers and Searles, we are already on the way to a 'strong' involvement in the concept of analytic interaction of the dream paradigm with the systematic reabsorption of fragments of external reality in the setting and the possibility of deconstructing the dream-transference work – based on Freudian mechanisms of condensation and displacement – directed to show the patient how he has unconsciously answered the analyst's interventions stimuli.

Already with Bion (1962), dreams were no longer considered mere protectors of sleep but also of the waking state. Being able to dream, that is, to have a functioning alpha-function capable of transforming beta-elements (raw sensory-emotional data) into alpha-elements and dream thoughts, guarantees the 'production' of both the conscious and the unconscious. What varies in the mind's different states is only their reciprocal involvement and equilibrium on a quantity level; an involvement regulated by the relative permeability of the alpha screen or contact barrier, surrounding and defining their respective fields.

The metaphor of the dream as insanity decays and becomes the opposite: 'the dream emerges as the first evolutive stage of symbolic thought' (Riolo 1983: 71). If anything, the accidental disintegration of the contact barrier, replaced by the beta screen, will cause massive infiltration of the conscious by unconscious elements and with it psychosis anarchy (expressed clinically in the hypersaturation of the analytic relationship with projective identifications). To preserve or repair the contact barrier would then mean for the analyst 'transforming the emotional participation in the patient's psychic experience into an *imaginative* participation [. . .] dreaming the emotional experience while it happens' (p. 74); in short, implementing the capacities for symbolizing.

After Bion the dream-theory revolution continues with Meltzer. From spurious products, delegated to protecting sleep, considered by Freud himself, according to Meltzer, 'of little significance other than as a patchwork of day-residues and distortions' (1984: 161), dreams increasingly become the weft itself of thought, a constant activity of the mind, both in sleep and in waking life, transforming and assimilating emotional experiences. Consequently, psychic suffering is seen as an undigested build-up of proto-emotions, which can only take the path of evacuations that are more or less dangerous for the subject.

So the meeting of two minds becomes essential for the cure: two 'dreamers', one less able to symbolize and the other ready to make his own alpha-function or dreaming capacities available. The common aim is to encourage development of the patient's alpha-function, or, more generally, his mental growth. This aim can be pursued through repeated transforming emotional experiences, a 'gymnastics of words' – as one of my patients expressed himself – but of words that are 'full' or 'incarnate', in which the analyst dreams the patient's dream or 'carries it out'.

The therapy is thus reassumed in a series of consecutive symbolic transformations – from more elementary to more complex forms, and, as in poetry, interwoven with emotions, sensoriality and feelings – that take place in the transference–countertransference area and that aim to produce new meanings and an increase in *narrative competence*. The game of interpretation does not so much clothe the patient with the analyst's truths but helps him to develop his own creativity; moving pieces of the jigsaw puzzle (Meltzer 1984), adding a pencil line to a squiggle (Winnicott 1971a), or a child's building block to the patient's construction (Ferro 1996).

Clearly in the face of this *game*, less importance is given to historical reconstruction – so central to the archaeological or heuristic model – as a specific therapeutic factor, or to the identification of a constellation of unconscious phantasies, which inevitably tends to be stereotyped and, so to speak, fixed and atemporal. Meltzer's position here is unequivocal: the 'reconstruction of the patient's life history is left as a byproduct of interest but not, in my opinion, of therapeutic importance' (1984: 145).

The analyst's attention shifts to the development of the patient's symbolic thought *in the session*. In this light, the patient's dream, in either a narrow or derived sense, and the analyst's reverie mark the zenith and nadir of the analytic work. Here reverie stands, in the words of Di Chiara, for the capacity to receive 'the patient's pre-verbal or verbal mental communications; all those emotional messages that are resolutely directed towards finding "the Other" ' (1992: 26).

Waking dream thought receives and elaborates perceptive and emotional stimuli 'live' and gives an immediate account of them, filtered by the rhetorical mechanisms of dreaming, in the form of narrative derivatives (Ferro 2002a). Just as directional and global positioning systems (GPS) for navigation permit a boat's position and speed to be calculated at any moment and to a few metres, so the dream function activated in the field detects climatic conditions in real time, oscillations of the pair's mental functioning and variations in the relative capacities for taking in and elaborating emotions. Naturally, unlike the GPS – which during stormy moments at sea takes second place to a skipper's experience and instinct – consulting the system of emotional observation is anything but easy, since it is in large part unconscious.

Abyss

It is the last session before the summer holidays. Carla (in her third year of analysis at three sessions a week) arrives and says she is sorry that she has to talk about something that happened the day before; she is upset about having a session like this today. The evening before, she had been at the seaside with some friends. They swam in the sea at night. It was rough and very dark. Everyone went in and so did she. She lost control. The waves swept her away and submerged her. She was frightened she wouldn't make it, that she'd drown. Then, she managed to shout for help. She saw a hand stretched towards her that pulled her out of the water. I am lost for words. Then I manage to express my amazement and regret. I say it must have been terrible. For a while, Carla recounts all the details, repeating over and over how it had happened, attempting to work off the shock she had felt, that still persists. In front of the others, she had pretended not to be too frightened, but they hadn't been taken in. She cannot understand how it could have happened. And there were so many of them, and she had always been very confident in the water. They tried to play it down and she began joking about it too. 'Obviously guardian angels exist,' she says, less frightened and with a bit more voice, and 'He must have said it wasn't time yet.' I am moved. I imagine a gesture, putting my arms around her as the only way to comfort her; I feel her so much like a child still trembling with fear. I gradually perceive the tension lessening, and even signs of slight euphoria in her words, perhaps in reaction to her distress, I think, and I say in a voice that I discover slowed down as though marred by bitterness, 'It would seem that going on holiday might be dangerous.' She replies that she has booked a sailing course this summer, but there she will have a *lifejacket*. She adds that she certainly couldn't tell her father anything like this. And again she regrets the session, today, *the last one*. I tell her that at least she can tell it here . . . that luckily we are here to talk about it. She really believed she would die: 'The dark . . . the water . . . I said to myself . . . if I can hold my breath for another three seconds . . . and in fact the wave rolled away and I saw that hand.'

'You did it,' I say, and meanwhile the film of the scene passes before my eyes. 'You didn't let yourself get sucked down by the waves.'

'And then, perhaps,' she starts up again, 'I might have frightened myself. The others let themselves go with the waves. How irresponsible I was!' We slowly touch on the subject of what might have led to underestimating the danger, and what the event might tell us of 'messengers' from the darkness and lack of responsibility. Only when the session is about to end do I feel able to tell her that, perhaps, our session of today was for her a little like a session on the edge of an abyss, but that once again she would seem to have found a helping hand.

The beginning of the session is dominated by the enormity of the event, almost indescribable, unprecedented. Then the tension gradually lessens. The fact itself – such a serious irruption of external reality, but also a death phantasy, the most terrible of all – begins to be able to be 'worked on' in a symbolic sense, although always using an evocative, open, elliptical language. Thus, an objective, traumatic event such as a serious life-threatening situation lends itself to being inserted into the meaningful weft of the analytic relationship. The abyss of the sea is transformed into the abyss of the absence of the other, of separation, in the fear of being submerged by the waves of ill-being and depression. The phrase that Carla manages to say – 'I might have frightened myself' – already shows a certain distance, the recovery of a perspective, control over the event, as well as the perception of a possible emotional factor. The 'irresponsible' in her story appears immediately afterwards. Capacity for containing the anxiety can originate and be developed from this point. Carla does not give up the sea or sailing, but she promises she will always wear, at least for this summer, a lifejacket (and will take with her a guardian angel! One of those which – according to tradition – know the secret thoughts of men), perhaps the memory of our conversations.

Some authors are concerned that a psychoanalytic model based on the dream paradigm, on the one hand, and on the relational–intersubjective paradigm, on the other, is too self-centred; that the asymmetry between the patient and the analyst disappears; that history, normally burdened with the weight of genetic reconstructions, remains only, eventually, as a story and the past of the therapeutic relationship. In clinical work excessively focused on its own internal phenomenology, the 'real', the instinctual and the individual identity would not find adequate recognition. Other authors express doubt that listening to the patient's unconscious derivatives as a comment on the analyst's interpretations might almost provide for a deliberate exclusion of contents and themes regarding the past and factual reality; and that it may not, instead, be only a decentred, but respectful and attentive, listening of this other level of reality, of the facts of material life, and also of the intrapsychic organization of the subject. The same centrality of the idea of reverie is indicated as a possible instrument for toning down and defensively sterilizing the patient's painful truth.

On the other hand, it is difficult to disagree with Meltzer (1984), who considers historical reconstruction an epiphenomenon of the analytic relationship. If the dream is the foundation and by extension the paradigm of the analytical work, keeping to material reality would be like waking up from the dream; abandoning exploration of unconscious levels of communication to become rooted in consciousness. When this happens, I believe it really is because we are

13

shielded as therapists (fortunately too, it is necessary to add) from the unconscious contents of the patient's communications that carry excessive quotas of anxiety. It is as though a certain level of awareness were tolerable only for a while; as though an economic principle would intervene each time to restrict the amount of responsibility that can be assumed in the relationship.

In Gill's opinion (1982), psychoanalysis is not generally practised at a good technical level and analysis of the transference in particular is widely disregarded. Important testimony on this point, expressed about confirmation ratings of the interpretation (and, after all, of the process) is provided by Etchegoyen, author of the most recent and authoritative manual of psychoanalytic technique: 'Few think, like me, that such associations also include a judgement on what we have just interpreted' (2000: 39). Analysts too can unconsciously share an attitude of denying psychic reality. In her acclaimed work on transference as a 'total situation', Joseph (1985) points out how extratransference understanding of the 'material' relative to the patient's life experiences can have the sole function of preserving the analyst from disturbing events. Puget (1995) identifies a form of distraction in the analyst, who stops functioning in an analytic way – on the basis of evenly suspended attention – precisely when interrogating himself or herself about the objective reality of a given event.

To play the game of the setting then – that 'playing of the unconscious', a new capacity and form of pleasure that Bollas (1999: 194) indicates as one of the results of analysis – is still, one might say, rather scandalous; it is disturbing on the emotional level and disorienting on the logical-discursive one. The paradigm of the dream is hardly ever assumed in a radical way; it is set up only partially inside the setting. Whether from inertia, habit, the natural ingenuous realism that is our practical philosophy, at times for gaps in the theoretical models that guide our clinical work, the prejudice that leads us to enhance factual reality achieves the result of weakening Freud's inspired idea. This idea lies in overturning the oneiric into the 'reality' of the patient's internal world and, through *transference work*, reality into the virtual situation of the analytic relationship, and also in bringing reality to a psychic on which concreteness and effectiveness are conferred equally. This, in fact, becomes a true ' "realization" of the psychic' (Le Guen 1995), to which the state of experimental and controlled de-realization of 'evenly suspended attention' corresponds on the part of the analyst. Indeed, if there is a specific quality in analytic listening, it lies precisely in the radical *epoché*, in phenomeno-logical terms, of reality outside the setting. For as long as a setting is required, the rule should be both to coherently assume the illusional dimension pertaining to the theatrical stage of analysis and to rigor-ously suspend judgement on reality, so that everything the patient brings to the analyst's room is considered to have something to do with the relationship. If this postulate is accepted, the attention paid to material reality in an extratransference perspective emerges as a tech-nique suspending the setting or a symptom of the dysfunctioning of some element of the analytic device, if it is not conditioned by the more or less conscious adoption of a supportive attitude, obviously present in every analysis.

The Siren's song of the external world in fact almost always serves the analyst's antalgic collusion and defensive splittings. Facts, under-stood as external events that only 'belong' to the patient, lend them-selves to functioning as his 'thermal shields' (Ferro 1992: 107, 2003a), indispensable naturally when dealing with incandescent material. Clinical experience reveals, instead, surprising effects every time the demarcation line between setting reality and external/historical reality is gone over, even when extremely difficult, unavoidable and traumatic realities are being dealt with: other possible meanings of the relation-ship open up and the relationship becomes more immediate and vital. From a fixed photographic image, one passes in an instant, as in cer-tain films, to a whole animated scene in which the characters grad-ually begin to move and talk, thus making themselves knowable. In this way, a sense of the real and of truth as emotional experience (Ogden 2003b) is recovered, but what matters most is to keep firmly in mind the connection between the actuality of the relationship and the facts of the session in every minimum detail, as this seems to be the vertex that allows maximum trust in the modifiability of psychic facts.

Encounter

An antecedent

The week before the one preceding the summer break, Anna (in her first year of analysis at three sessions a week), arriving breathless in the studio, was convinced that it was the last-but-one session. She was

15

amazed at her mistake. Together, we thought it might be like a game of hide and seek, making me disappear only to find me straightaway.

Seven days later

She arrives, sad and almost in tears. She announces bad news. Her father has written a few short lines saying he cannot take any more. He has decided to leave home. Her mother is devastated, stunned by the unexpected event, even if there had been warning signs. She cries. She asks for advice about how to help her mother. I feel myself cornered. It is difficult not to lean towards a more supportive attitude, focusing attention on the 'objective' fact. I fumble a bit. I remember one of her earlier dreams in which the analyst's studio appeared in her grandmother's house, and the associations expressed a mixture of trust and fear of intimacy. Anna pictured herself as 'cautious' in front of her boyfriend, represented as a detective with a pistol (which aroused her curiosity) and handcuffs (of dependency: between prison and erotic games), in front of perhaps an analyst still a bit too much in the 'uniform' of his professional role, a policeman of meaning. So I abandon the idea of interpreting the transference or of investigating the 'pure facts'. Instead, I choose to focus on the characters of the session and try to reply simply, saying that it is a very sad situation, that perhaps her mother is the one who is suffering most now, that I would ask myself how I could help her mother. And, in fact, I ask her, after a few minutes of silence, what can be done to help her. Anna replies that she doesn't know, that she had advised her not to push her luck, that sooner or later it would have ended like this . . . that *he would have left her*. And she regrets having helped almost inadvertently to reveal proof of her father's infidelity to her mother: small things, a message, an email saved on the computer, sent secretly but almost with an obvious impulse to confess. She moves on to say she has seen R again, her ex, who had left her some months earlier. The encounter had been less awkward than expected. *Some objects had been returned* (and I think of her need to disinvest from analysis in order to be able to face the separation). They asked each other again whose fault it had been, each immediately denying it. 'Perhaps I still love him,' she says. Then she remembers a dream from last night in which another boy let her know that he still loved her, and she was embarrassed, because now she was with someone else. (The pain of separation begins to become more tolerable, I think to myself. Despite having returned various objects, she still feels 'in love' and a vague sense of being at fault. But the problem is still there.) 'So then,' she asks, 'how can I help my mother?' I tell her that she could stay close to her and listen to her (and I believe I help her in this way to express her own sadness at the break in the analysis). 'But I don't want to come between those two!' she says.

'It's not necessary,' I reply (as I say to myself that perhaps Anna is afraid of not being able to manage her own emotional ambivalence). 'Listening to someone does not mean taking one side against the other.'

'Because *I love my father very much*', she continues, emotionally, '*and even if he is irresponsible in wanting to leave* . . . and I am frightened for his health . . . and for now he has said that not having anywhere to go he will get his own meals and do his own washing . . . You know, when I saw R, it was a bit like in Guccini's *Incontro* [Encounter], the song . . . which goes, "and running he met me on the stairs".' (The song is about refound friendship.)

Positive results can be achieved by speaking the language of reality, while accepting the illusionistic statute of the session's characters (who transport emotions not yet recognizable) and still maintaining the specifics of analytic listening, without 'breaking' the framework by interpreting the transference. (Anna would have received that with diffidence and pain in such a moment, and would have taken it as a sign of insensitivity.) This allows resources for self-soothing and the ability to think to be reawakened in the patient herself. It also allows her to tolerate jealousy for her former boyfriend, now with someone else, and to live parting from the analyst through the reverie of Guccini's song. The separation that can no longer be postponed is now characterized by depressive working through – from PS to D, one might say, – by tenderness and awareness of a lasting bond, just like in the song. To get back to the internal vertex of the setting, after every slide into factual reality, to bear the near-scandal of continuing (starting again) to think even in front of particularly dramatic and urgent facts, thus becomes an anti-splitting mechanism that allows Anna (the abandoned mother), in her turn, to reintegrate in herself in such a difficult moment in her life both maternal and paternal identification.

The next session

Her mother had been to the doctor who gave her Effortil®,[3] and she is now a little better. *She has started sleeping again.* For the weekend, she will stay with a girlfriend.

'Today is the last time I'm coming here and I wonder . . . what if something happens? . . . I'm not a compulsive shopper, but . . . right now I'm really keen on underwear.[4] And I say: 'This . . . and then this, I really need it! And then my boyfriend goes: "*Neeeed* ?!?" [she laughs]. For this weekend at the sea . . . when I go, I always take a bag full of things for every occasion.'

'That's a heavy bag to carry,' I comment, in an 'open' way, 'giving up the need for *intimissimo* for a while . . . but, with a little Effortil® . . .'.

'I wouldn't do it,' replies Anna (who thus decides, *herself*, to put herself in some way on a transference plane, with an unexpected change of rhythm and 'narrative' level), 'but, if I really should need to . . . can I make a phone call? . . . I wanted to tell you that, in any case . . . since I have been coming here . . . I go a bit less to Don Armando.'[5] And I believe she is telling me that she can lower her guard a bit and trust a bit more ('loving') the intimacy of the meeting.

Keeping to empirical reality can be a conscious tactical choice for reaching the patient. The analyst can be sufficiently alerted to the transference level of the interaction and therefore take up the paradigm of the dream correctly, even if he clothes his interpretations in referential language. He can therefore intervene, or comment, on the factual reality, without denying the intersubjective, virtual dimension of the meeting, with narrative, unsaturated, weak, indirect, displaced, '*in* the transference', and so on, interpretations.

And then, not all 'ills' are harmful. External reality acts like a *great attractor* which permits opportune splittings (and oscillations in the analyst's mental functioning), without which the analytic work would stagnate. As well as being inevitable and frequent, temporary interruptions of the analyst's internal setting and of the theatrical space of the cure are necessary because, once identified and resolved, as far as possible, they are more often than not fruitful for the progress of the analysis.

The problem of how to consider external reality in the analytic space is often posed in an ambiguous way. It is obvious that the anamnesis, biography and family history are crucial in the subject's psychopathology, but the point is another: the use the analyst makes of these elements in the session (and not when he reflects, writes or communicates a case to his colleagues). If the analysis functions like a dramatizing mechanism (Petrella 1985), or imaginary space (Viderman 1979), or illusionary/*as if* area (Winnicott 1971b) – to the extent that, for some, it is troubled by 'hyperrealistic' transferences or by not triggering off the transference neurosis – everything that disturbs this functioning, or 'suspends the representation', can be considered to emerge as a break in the setting. Even the plot of a play at the theatre takes its meaning from a background that can only be that of life itself, and there too the bracketing of external reality is only partial (likewise, during oneiric activity the sensory channels are obstructed up to a certain threshold level). But, as long as it is worth maintaining a setting, continuing with the play, the lights must necessarily illuminate the stage, and not the stalls or the square in front of the theatre itself.

The theoretical option forming the background of this chapter (here only a few distinctive features can be outlined) could be defined as a 'radically antirealist', if one draws on the field of contemporary philosophy. It is in line with changes that are being outlined in psychoanalytic thought relative to the order and specific weight of the various therapeutic factors. A correlate of the value attributed to the analytic situation as co-defined reality and interpersonal relationship can be seen in the importance given to what Fonagy (2003) reassumes in a specific 'way of being with another', Stern *et al.* (1998) in the 'moments of meeting', and others with the Bionian 'being in unison'. For Ferro (1996), the most important thing for the patient is not that the analyst finds a depth of interpretation or a truth to communicate to him – which would originate in that case only from one mind and, however 'true' and thought, it would always be, for the patient, a minus K – but to be on the same affective wavelength and 'elaborate' with him, in the today of the meeting, whatever happens in the emotional field that is created.

The objective of the therapy is not so much to arrive at those discriminations for which the blank-screen analyst model was held to be functional, but to reduce the patient's anxiety, improve his capacity for symbolizing, and to increase therefore indirectly also the appropriateness of his reality test and the consistency of his life story. From specific symptom, expression of resistance to the cure, the transference thus becomes diffused, immediate, aspecific, less referring to a one-person psychology and less contaminated by 'radioactive waste' (in that it creates a distance) of an objectively traumatized past (or of a present), and therefore implicitly not transformable. On the one hand, the analyst himself takes part in the patient's transference; on the other, the patient's transference can contain an entirely appropriate assessment of the analytic situation. From unreal, in the sense of vehicle of distortions, the result of his childhood neurosis, it becomes gradually more real. Think of the credit conceded now to the analysand's unconscious perceptions, and of the prestige of concepts such as the patient as his analyst's *best colleague, supervisor, interpreter* (Hoffman 1983) or *therapist* (Searles 1975). External reality loses importance, increasingly absorbed into the dream of the session, reduced to a day's residue. The transference, which appears more opaque, is only more pervasive and the establishment of the oneiric paradigm preserves it – together with the patient's story life, of which one presumes transference is the transposition in the analytic setting through the intermediation of the unconscious phantasy – from being flattened to mere interaction in the here-and-now.

To think of the past or present empirical events of the patient's biography as concrete data, not mediated by waking dream thought, can therefore mean colluding with the defensive mechanisms that he has used to construct the rigid plot of his own story. The dream of the session and a posteriori reworkings of memory come to a halt. The patient's trauma becomes the trauma (the 'insomnia') of the setting. Attention to reality/history then risks being frozen by hyperrealist immobility, that is denying – in the very act of trusting in the pseudo-justifications of a material reality as a reassuring simulacrum and therefore a counterfeit – 'reality' as the true sense of life. The analyst can oppose this ideology of reality through constant interrogation of himself with the patient; a permanent, by definition open and irreconciled, investigation of a reality pervaded by the shadow of the dream and the unconscious: of what else if not psychic reality?

I realized only after having written this chapter that the headings chosen for the three main sections could suggest identical moments that appear in every analysis: *insomnia* as the laceration of symbiotic–fusional tissue on which the feeling of the self's continuity is based and as a lack of symbolization; *abyss* as crisis, but also, playing on the ambiguity of this word, as the device of the setting – the 'dream of the cure' seen as a scene *en abîme* – which allows one to look out on to the emptiness of the insignificance of existence without falling in; *encounter* as an experience of unison and synchrony with the other, like that which makes the void or absence thinkable, and – however painful – the secret of 'usual illusion',[6] which the patient takes with him on parting, tolerable.

2

The symbiotic bond and the setting

The two principal sources for the modern theory of the setting are Winnicott (1956a) and Bleger (1967a). However, whereas the former author is universally known for having maintained that the setting is more important than interpretation as a component of the analyst/ environment system in cases of primal deficiencies of the ego, the same cannot be said of the latter. For this reason, I wish to compare Bleger's conception of the setting, and in particular of its underlying theory of a primitive mode of mental functioning called the *glischro-caric position*, with certain later conceptual developments of the post-Kleinian school. I postulate that, by tracing the course of this 'karstic stream'[1] of psychoanalytic thought, we shall be in a better position to identify a posteriori its extraordinary significance for defining the therapeutic factors in the treatment.

The problem is relevant to the present situation, as witness the many contributions which, oddly enough, correlate turning points in an analysis with breaches of setting. Among the authors who have addressed this subject, Modell (1989) occupies an important position. Denying that therapeutic change can in any case be based on the transference neurosis or on insight, he instead stresses the element of the *frame* and, drawing attention to Bleger's study with its characterization of non-process and of the constants within which analytic therapy unfolds, presents the intriguing hypothesis that the main function of interpretation lies not so much in making the unconscious conscious as in preserving the setting.

On the basis of this area of more general interest, the specific idea for this chapter stems from Bleger's (1967a) view that the setting constitutes an ally of the patient's psychotic part. This formulation can readily be deconstructed into its component parts. In it, Bleger in effect presents a simplified version of the topographical model of the psyche as commonly applied in analytic practice – a model in which psychotic and non-psychotic parts of the personality are contrasted – and, not without first inverting the terms in which it is usually expressed, derives the military metaphor of an alliance from it. His contribution is in itself already a paradoxical and indeed bewildering text. What kind of alliance can ever be forged with an entity (the psychotic part) against which one is fighting, and which one therefore seeks to defeat, and no longer, or not only, with the healthy parts of the ego? Again, if the two opposing camps are not to be deemed totally irreconcilable, as one is to suppose, and if a channel for diplomacy, albeit concealed, is kept open, how are we to conceive of splitting, the basic functional element in such an organization of the mind? Lastly, what recommendations on technique can be derived from Bleger's characterization of the setting?

The meta–ego

Bleger's paper on the setting (*encuadre*) can be regarded as an application of his manifestly Bion-inspired theory of the 'psychotic part of the personality' and of symbiosis as a developmental stage and mode of relating. At birth, the individual is in Bleger's view not isolated. There is already a relationship, which is primitive in nature but not objectless, between the ego and the world. Hence the starting point of human development is a state of primitive fusion on the structural level, which always includes the subject and the environment, albeit not as clearly differentiated entities. On the phenomenal or behavioural level, this state can also be described as symbiotic. Such a relationship results from a form of experiencing reality that Bleger calls the 'glischro-caric position' (*gliscros-karuon*: the expression, borrowed from Eugène Minkowski, literally means 'viscous nucleus').

The idea of a third 'position', due to Pichon-Rivière, is developed by Bleger in an original way. Prior to the Kleinian paranoid-schizoid and depressive positions, the glischro-caric position is seen as corresponding to a stage in which the ego is not distinct from the object, which for this reason is called an agglutinated or glischroid object, and is characterized by the presence of specific anxieties (of a catastrophic/confusional nature) and specific defences (splitting/projection/immobilization). The 'agglutinated object' was only later

23

to be renamed the 'agglutinated nucleus', in order to emphasize its nature as a relationship that is not truly with an object but instead based on a primary identification, in Fairbairn's (1952) sense of the term, between the object and the part of the ego linked to it – or rather on multiple identifications, which are so numerous that this primitive ego must be deemed 'granular'. What matters is that, from this first developmental phase, the subject can gradually evolve the sense of reality and define itself in terms of identity.

With the activation of the paranoid–schizoid position, part-objects (both good and bad) make their appearance, and the ego gradually differentiates and becomes more coherent at the expense of the first agglutinated nucleus, which, however, persists to some extent, albeit in slowly and progressively discriminated and fragmented form. The glischro–caric position in fact lies at the root not only of primitive symbiosis, but also of the residues of symbiosis to be found in the mature personality, and which can be observed in any psychoanalytic treatment. These residues mostly remain silent, but on occasion they may invade the personality for internal or external reasons. A given subject's degree of need for symbiotic dependence is thus correlated with the persistence of the agglutinated nucleus, or rather with the *relative dimensions* of unresolved archaic residues of undiscriminated fusion of the ego with the object.

The corresponding part of the personality, which, in the adult, Bleger calls the *psychotic nucleus*,[2] is that which constitutes the background to, or the foundation of, the more differentiated or neurotic ego. That is why Bleger calls it the *non-ego* or *meta-ego*, by analogy with the terms used in describing disorders of the body schema. It is in fact an essential, but not perceptible, level of psychological organization. It is the set of 'steady or motionless relationships (the non-absences) [which] organize and preserve the non-ego, and serve as a basis for the building up of the ego according to frustrating and gratifying experiences' (Bleger 1967a: 512). These 'psychotic' levels of the personality, which are characterized by intense symbiotic needs, are assigned the task of protecting the subject from separation.

To return to the setting, Bleger's main contention is that the analytic relationship, which can in itself be broken down into process-related and non-process-related (i.e. variable and constant) phenomena, is essentially symbiotic, or rather that it is called upon to make up for an absent or distorted symbiosis, and that therapy consists in a gradual process of de-symbiotization or reduction of the agglutinated nucleus. It is the organization of the setting that enables the primitive and undifferentiated relationship with the object (or rather, the part of the personality which, as its heir, corresponds to it) to take the stage once more so that this developmental process can take place.

The setting, defined as 'the role of the analyst, the set of space [. . .] and time factors, and part of the technique' [Bleger 1967: 511], includes the unchanging elements of the relationship. By virtue of the sense of security stemming from the set of rules that define it, the setting is the part of the analytic situation most suitable for serving as the 'depository' and guarantor of symbiosis. In addition, by virtue of its stability,[3] it can be regarded as an institution and, like any institution, it constitutes the fundamental – in most cases silent – nucleus of the personality. In the analytic relationship, the setting takes the form, vis-à-vis the process, of an indifferent background element of non-absence, just as the meta-ego is, for the ego, that which is non-experienced, in the sense of non-reflective, as opposed to experience that can be assumed by consciousness, and the foundation of its very structuring. Moreover, it is precisely the equation 'setting = symbiosis = institution = nucleus of identity' that lies at the heart of Bleger's thesis. The key point in his argument is that, whereas the therapeutic alliance is indeed forged with the neurotic (i.e. healthier) part, 'this is true of the process but not of the frame. In the latter, the alliance is established with the psychotic (or symbiotic) part of the patient's personality' (ibid.: 516).

The clinical manifestations of the agglutinated nucleus swing between excessive control (symbiosis, affective blockage, hypochondria or violent reprojection) and loss of control (various degrees of alteration of consciousness due to massive invasions of the ego). Two forms of psychotic dissolution lie at the two respective extremes: (a) loss of agglutination with dispersal of the agglutinated nucleus; and (b) destructuring of the more integrated ego. This outline clearly demonstrates the importance for mental health of a good dynamic equilibrium between the 'psychotic part of the personality' and the more differentiated ego.

Before continuing our consideration of Bleger, let us compare his theory of the steady, 'viscous' nucleus of identity with those of other authors whose models of early mental functioning are in certain respects similar – in particular, Marcelli (1986), who postulates the existence of an 'autistic position' at the beginning of mental life, and Ogden (1989), with his hypothesis of a generative matrix of the ego's 'sensory floor'.

Touching

Two decades on from Bleger's study, a few years prior to Ogden's first paper (1989) on the subject, and following the contributions of Tustin (1972) and Meltzer *et al.* (1975), which are based on considerations of psychopathology, Marcelli (1986) describes an autistic position, which he regards also as a transitional phase in the normal development of newborn and very young babies – i.e. in the first three months of life. His theory derives from the study of the deficiency of symbolization observed in autistic children, who fail to exhibit the typical gesture, at age 12 to 18 months, of pointing at an object with a finger. Stemming from a failure of the motor act of gripping something, pointing eventually assumes the role of a precious instrument of communication when the mother intervenes to confer meaning on it and to transform it into the word for the object pointed at. Pointing is therefore an essential stage in the acquisition of language, representing in effect an unparalleled presymbolic idiom in that it involves an initial recognition of the boundary between ego and non-ego. In Kanner-type autistic children, who are considered to find it difficult or even impossible to accept this first boundary, there is instead first a refusal of language, and second the characteristic gesture of using an adult's hand for reaching an object, in a mode denoted by the concept of adhesive identification.

Having devoted an initial contribution to the problem of the absence of pointing, Marcelli (1983) considers whether or not such behaviour falls exclusively within the purview of psychopathology. After all, the absence of pointing, together with the presence of a particular type of adhesiveness, also seems to be characteristic of a phase of ontogenesis in the very earliest period of a baby's life: 'the hand of a newborn that clasps its mother's finger or clings or attaches itself to the breast can be said to represent, at a very early stage, the mechanism of adhesive identification through which libidinal cathexis of the skin can perform a limiting and containing function' (Marcelli 1986: 28, translated).

It is then but a short step to postulating a similar fusional/symbiotic level in normal infant development, with an underlying early type of mental functioning. According to Marcelli, the adhesive identification and dismantling described by Meltzer *et al.* (1975) in infant autism are present at a very early age and constitute a stage in development that is necessary in order to permit the tracing of an initial boundary of the self. In the earliest phases of life, these two mental mechanisms have the function, on the neuropsychological level, of effecting a perceptual simplification for the baby, which they protect from an excessive flow of sensations. They help the baby to familiarize itself with an environment that has been made less complex and more easily assimilable. In other words, they serve the purpose of development. This strategy of the autistic position has its counterpart in the information-filtering function expressed in Freud's concept of the protective shield against stimuli. It therefore appears reasonable to assume the existence of a normal 'adhesiveness', which serves for the perception of a boundary and for initiating the process of identity construction, and which fails only if it becomes hypertrophic. But how is symbolization arrived at? How does an embryo of intentionality come into being?

At the beginning of mental life, the primitive autistic phase is followed by a symbiotic phase, characterized by the progressive cathexis of exteroceptive sensitivity. This is still a pre-object stage. At a certain point in mental development, a pre-consciousness of the mothering object appears, in the form of an initial distinction between pleasurable/good experiences on the one hand and painful/bad experiences on the other. An essential requirement for the transition from sensory activity to representability is temporality, the rhythmic succession of so-called primitive aggregates (fragments of objects + fragments of affective experience), which may be deemed equivalent to Bleger's agglutinated objects. What matters is the ritualization of maternal behaviour. For the genesis of a first thought, which is a thought about succession and time, along the lines of 'after this there will be something else', time itself must be organized in a circular and predictable manner. In this sense, the increase in meaning is a function of repetition: 'It is not absence in itself that permits thinking and access to symbolic activity, but the regular sensation of absences and presences, of the regular repetition of experiences [. . .]. Rhythmicity appears to be the basis on which the child's activity is constituted' (Marcelli 1983: 65–67, translated). Starting from an initial thought about time and succession, the child gradually acquires the capacity to represent reality to itself.

The experience of discontinuity, of a caesura in the temporal order, has a structuring effect precisely because it permits the coming into being of an embryo of intentionality, an outline of the ego, a state of anticipation, of 'tending towards'. In this way, a 'purely physiological

27

need' is transformed into a wish. The 'founding agreement' on the identity in the process of formation will stipulate that the subject's capacity to wait for satisfaction or the subject's threshold of toleration of frustration at any given time shall not be exceeded.

The autistic position assumes pathological significance when it is no longer in the service of a strategy, and when its retention as a defensive posture becomes the strategy itself. Conversely, 'normal' adhesive identification establishes relationships of continuity that are not conceived as static. For it is reasonable to assume that the line of the bodily boundary comes to be defined gradually by way of the dynamic – sensory – modulation of the contact surfaces. It is only in the case of the autistic object that sensations become fixed, with the consequent disappearance of the sense of a limit, which can arise solely from the possibility of distinguishing and perceiving variations in accordance with an appropriate gradient of tolerability.

Observation of mother–child interaction has shown that pointing in effect acts as a presymbolic organizer, performing a function of communication (the failure of which, as the residue of a gesture, can be seen in various stereotypies), and that the preceding phase of touching is its precursor: might this perhaps be analogous to the dynamic concreteness/sensory nature of the setting? Pointing does not initiate any symbolic interaction, but remains a purely motor act unless it encounters the maternal intentionality or reverie that gives it meaning. In the same way, by analogy, if the analyst's symbolization function is deficient, the setting too becomes an empty ritual, an autistic object (Ogden 1989).

In psychoanalytic treatment, the setting is an important primary guarantor of the necessary rhythm of security, seen as the harmonious distribution and regular, rhythmic succession of tonic and atonic moments, moments of intention or of withdrawal. The material and formal elements of the setting are in my view those which, by virtue of their concreteness, invariant recurrence and non-process character, are best suited to serving as the place where needs for symbiotic adhesiveness can be deposited. A particular function of the setting is precisely that of providing a 'skin' still in adhesive contact, with the role of integration, like that of touching in an infant until it is able to perceive initial, elementary phenomena of tactile discontinuity, micro-areas of space-time of non-contact, thus ultimately leading to more mature and extensive forms of symbolization.

Freud himself had already wondered how a system capable of

satisfying requirements both of preservation and of change could possibly be modelled. That is the fundamental paradox of psycho-analytic treatment, as well as of memory and of the self, poised between confirmation of identity and the impetus for transformation and emancipation, between non-process and process. Repetition confers meaning and order on things. As we know from clinical practice and from life, breaches of or discontinuities in the setting give rise to disorientation and disquiet. They have the consequence of a painful sense of loss of familiarity, a form of vertigo that may descend into actual anxiety. Something alien bursts on to the scene. All of a sudden, a secure place becomes unrecognizable and inhospitable. The entire fragility of the foundations of a subjectivity that cannot but discover itself to be rooted in the encounter with the other is seen to reappear. This is the 'impact of experience' (Berto 1998), when the subject is struck by something that cannot immediately be accommodated within a pre-established horizon, but which gives rise to a profound disturbance, sometimes utterly transforming the affected subject – a phenomenon described by Bleger as the catastrophic effect of the unforeseen loss of the agglutinated nucleus. Yet it is only by exposing itself to these risks that the organism can integrate the new, can change, adapt to and learn from reality, on each occasion establishing a new equilibrium for itself.

The particular interest of Marcelli's ideas lies in his identification of autistic adhesiveness, which can now be represented on the theoretical level by the conceptual apparatus supplied by Meltzer and Tustin, as a necessary stage in the process leading to the development of thought. What limits this notion, however, as will be shown below, is the fact that Marcelli links it strictly to an archaic period of development, rather than seeing it also as a permanent experiential level of the subject.

The sensory floor

The concept of the autistic-contiguous position (Ogden 1989) is a new version and further development of the trends of research pursued by Bleger and Marcelli. Unlike Bleger, Ogden extends his model to the description of phenomena within the realms of both normal and pathological functioning. With regard to the term 'position', the ambiguity of the model used – psychopathological or ontogenetic – is resolved. Pathology is correlated with a hypertrophy or rigidification of the modes of production of experience characteristic not only of an obligatory stage of development but also, later, of normal mental functioning.

The Kleinian notions of the paranoid–schizoid and depressive positions (to avoid terminological confusion, Winnicott [1963] preferred to call the latter the phase of the 'capacity for concern') came less and less to denote developmental stages contained within precise chronological boundaries, and increasingly the components of an elementary affective–cognitive chemistry of the mind, of processes of splitting/analysis and integration/synthesis that form the background to any ideo–emotional activity. It is in Bion's theory of the mind that the Ps ↔ D oscillation ultimately assumed central importance, the two 'positions' having become synchronic dimensions of experience.

Ogden sees the autistic–contiguous position as a third mode used by the mind to generate meaning – that is, to 'test' reality. Complementing Klein's, and later Bion's, dynamic of the Ps and D positions, it in fact represents their necessary premise in so far as it organizes an initial psychic space. For it is only once an initial frontier for the demarcation of a psychic place has been defined that initial projective–introjective phenomena can arise. This sensory floor develops from sensory-type experiences and on the basis of the care received by the infant from birth. In this way a model of the mind that is both structural and dynamic is delineated: the autistic–contiguous position is conceivable only in a continuous dialectical relationship of coexistence/alternation with the other two 'modes', as night follows day and darkness light. In its variable states of greater or lesser equilibrium, this relationship determines the quality of the subject's perception of reality in general and the occurrence of certain psychopathological states in particular.

The autistic–contiguous position, too, is defined in relation to a specific constellation of anxieties, defences, organizations of thought and characteristics of the object relationship. Again in accordance with Kleinian usage, the second term (contiguous) refers to the psychological organization, while the first (autistic) concerns the associated defences. A psychic state corresponding to the autistic–contiguous position is one whose structuring element is a particular type of sensory functioning, stemming from impressions produced predominantly on the level of the epidermis, from contact with sensory surfaces. The mode of experiencing based on 'contiguity' is presymbolic. That is to say, it does not entail any distance from the object, from that which is symbolized, or, consequently, the need for mediation vis-à-vis the object. The essential point for Ogden is that this earliest form of experiencing reality *operates throughout life* 'out of awareness as the experiential matrix [. . .] for all succeeding subjective states' (Ogden 1989: 33n). Precisely because it constitutes 'an even more primitive presymbolic, sensory-dominated mode' (p. 30), it is difficult to represent in words: 'Rather it is a relationship of shape to the feeling of enclosure, of beat to the feeling of rhythm, of hardness to the feeling of edgedness [. . .]. Early experiences of sensory contiguity define a surface (the beginning of what will become a sense of place) on which experience is created and organized' (pp. 32f.).

A psychological and sensory film, a first type of relationship, is constituted by way of experiences of periodicity (originating mainly from aspects of care, such as being held or cradled, or the sound of words), which become the sense of rhythm, of symmetries – a sensory 'going on being' (Winnicott 1956b: 303). These forms of contact or, literally, 'impressions', which are in fact equivalent to the autistic forms described by Tustin (1986), will subsequently come to be associated with ideas of security, protection, relaxation, affectivity and warmth. This leads to a basis for the construction of identity and of the reflective ego, or self-consciousness, a *'barely perceptible* background of sensory boundedness of all subsequent subjective states' (Ogden 1989: 50, my emphasis). The autistic-contiguous position thus comes to represent the matrix within which an initial rudimentary outline or integration of the self comes into being, with the gradual onset of the sense of bodily limits or of an enveloping and containing surface.

The three basic modes of experiencing reality (autistic-contiguous, paranoid-schizoid and depressive) are paralleled by an increasing gradient of symbolization capacity. Development proceeds from the asymbolic/fusional level to the presymbolic level, to the symbolic equation, and ultimately to appropriate symbolization, as expressed in the terminology of Segal (1978). In this sense, every single psychological event is overdetermined, but the balance may be shifted towards one or other of the various modes. A good capacity for thought presupposes an active and flexible interplay between the various positions, while the exclusion of any one of the levels of experience always results in psychological and emotional

31

impoverishment: one and the same depressive mode, sometimes portrayed as the – in a sense definitive – ideal of maturity and balance by virtue of its supposed character of 'integration, resolution and containment [. . .,] if unopposed, leads to certainty, stagnation, closure, arrogance and deadness' (Ogden 1989: 29f.). The compensation afforded by the paranoid-schizoid mode, on the other hand, opens the way to new thoughts and connections, just as, in Bleger's model, it succeeds in fragmenting and discriminating the agglutinated nucleus.

Any sudden discontinuity of form, symmetry, rhythm or intensity in maternal care may have adverse consequences, causing the infant to experience a state of 'non-being'. Each mode of experiencing reality creates, preserves and negates the other. From this point of view, psychopathology:

> can be thought of as a collapse of the generative dialectic interplay of modes of experience [. . .]. Collapse in the direction of an autistic-contiguous mode results in a tyrannizing imprisonment in a closed system of bodily sensations that precludes the development of 'potential space' [. . .]. Collapse in the direction of a paranoid-schizoid mode results in a sense of entrapment in a world of things-in-themselves wherein one does not experience oneself as the author of one's own thoughts and feelings; rather, thoughts, feelings, and sensations are experienced as objects or forces bombarding, entering into, or propelled from oneself. Collapse in the direction of the depressive mode results in the experience of a subject alienated from his bodily sensations and from the immediacy and spontaneity of lived experience.
>
> (Ogden 1989: 77f.)

If obstacles arise to the evolution of these primary forms of containment – if it proves difficult to form a 'psychic skin' – recourse may be had to excessive and dysfunctional solutions, with the aim of avoiding the experience of separation and loss, in the form of a 'second skin'. This is a tendency to search constantly for something or someone to 'hold things together' (in this case, integration of the self is guaranteed by dependence on surface qualities of an external object), by means of forms of adhesive identification and pseudo-relationality (Mitrani 1992). Part-qualities of the object – odour, voice or the visual element – may become a source of sensory stimulation to which the subject can cling. The internal function of containing parts of the self, or the capacity to be alone or to console oneself, may not develop sufficiently.

To recapitulate, with Ogden, Bleger's model ceases to be bogged down in an excessively psychopathological vision. The reconstruction, however hypothetical, of early exchanges between mother-environment and infant is refined. One senses why the function of (re)constructing the sensory floor/foundation that is equivalent to Bleger's meta-ego can be substantially attributed to the elements of the setting (but obviously it is a question of degree, the setting being understood in an extended sense as including the so-called internal setting of the analyst) and to the 'concreteness' of these elements.

Clinical fragments

In accordance with some ideas put forward by Di Benedetto (2000) on listening to the preverbal in psychoanalysis, the setting/environment can in my view be thought of as a multimodal source of sensory stimuli made up of rhythms, tones, intensities and tactile, auditory, olfactory, pressure-related and kinaesthetic sensations, which have in common with music the fact that they constitute a 'language as yet lacking in "vocabulary" ', which is not yet symbolized. As its components gradually acquire order and structure, this environment, like any other that is meaningful, takes the form for the subject of an initial level of sensory integration which, while destined to recede into the background in the process of treatment or of individual development, never completely disappears, nor is it ever drained of its cohesive force.

It is not hard to think of events whereby these normally silent basic/symbiotic levels of the ego, deposited in the setting like a kind of 'phantom world', are made to speak. The following very brief clinical vignettes, while not claiming demonstrative status, nevertheless illustrate situations, atmospheres and stories in which the concepts discussed above seemed to me to be useful for an initial understanding of the patient's emotional problems, or merely as a guide to the formation of some early, provisional impressions.

I shall begin by describing some situations involving a temporary crisis in the setting (in which, as Bleger would say, symbiosis 'weeps'[4]), followed by others in which an increased need for adhesiveness or a symbiotic connection with the analyst can be glimpsed. In all the cases portrayed, the significant element is in my view the implicit reference to silent, 'institutional' levels of the setting (even if the reference is not exclusive – i.e. something that leaves the door open to different interpretations).

Silvia tells me that, *in the last few days of the holiday break* that has just ended, hypochondriacal anxieties resurfaced. When she goes to bed at night (*but also, I observe, on the couch*), *she finds it difficult to find, or refind, a comfortable position*. A kind of tension forces her to arrange her limbs in unnatural postures. It is as if – as she feared – she had caught mad–cow disease, and was feeling the first effects of the dramatic neurological *instability* she happened to see in a television documentary about the affected animals. A partial movement of relatively undifferentiated aspects into the more mature ego, attributable to a crisis in the setting, may perhaps have given rise to confusional anxiety, which was at one and the same time a symptom and a means of self-preservation. In particular, the hypochondria is indicative of an attempt to recover a form of 'framing' on the level of the body. By 'tossing and turning' on the couch, Silvia is of course also telling, in the here-and-now of the session, of the difficulties she is experiencing in repositioning herself in the symbiotic area of the setting and of the relationship.

Owing to an unforeseen problem, I had to cancel Stefano's session with only a day's notice. However, because his mobile phone battery was flat, he did not receive the message I left on his voicemail, so he comes to the consulting room and is confronted by a closed door: 'There *wasn't even a light on* in the corridor!' he tells me later. Next evening, when lying down on the couch, he stumbles and bumps his head against the wall, fortunately without serious consequences, and almost overturns the couch (!). Having recovered, he tells me about the '*earthquake*' caused by the reorganization of shifts at his workplace, and the sense of *void* he experiences in wandering about the city in the afternoons, now that he has an enormous amount of free time at his disposal – 'a weird situation,' he remarks.

We both have a sense of painful discomfort when – one would hardly credit it – the same thing happens again next time. I try to establish the sequence of events: he sits down on the top end of the couch, which is in the shape of a 'horizontal' S and not fixed to the base, so that, by an unnatural twist of the upper part of his body, he can keep his eyes on me for as long as possible (so as not to see me disappear again?).

For the next few months, he consistently arrives about ten minutes late for his session; this arouses a chronic sense of uncertainty in me, and none of my interpretations succeeds in modifying this behaviour. Eventually I conclude that it is a way of 'playing' with absence and of letting me share the feeling of what happens when the floor of the ego 'trembles' – as reflected in the traumas of 'bumping his head' and the (semi-)obscured light of consciousness.

Nora's session is about to end. A few minutes before it finishes, the next patient arrives early for his appointment and rings the bell. I apologize and go to open the door. When I return, I see that Nora has put her coat on and is about to leave, but I cannot help noticing that the adjustable top end of the couch is inclined sharply to one side and *almost in the process of overturning* (!). I wonder, and then ask somewhat nervously, in a low voice, whether the interruption has made her angry, but she seems as surprised as I am at what has happened. The unexpected micro-fracture in the relationship has in effect operated on a sensory level, which cannot be expressed in words, interwoven with as yet unrecognizable emotions – rather like a dissonance in a musical text or a tear in a preverbal, presymbolic connective tissue.

Matteo, a 30-year-old clerical worker who 'always stands bolt upright like a soldier', comes into analysis on account of a depressive state connected with the break-up of his marriage, which he experienced as a rent in the continuity of his identity and self. Now in the fifth month of his analysis, he brings me a dream: he notices that he has marks, which then seem to him to be sores, on his hands, and then also on his arms. He undresses, and finds that they are all over his body. In comes A., his wife, who sees him and then goes away again. He comments that everyone distrusts him and thinks he is ill. In the last few days he has resumed using creams for the psoriasis affecting his elbows, which has recently got worse. He cannot hide the sore places on his hands. They go away, and then come back. His wife knows that they are not catching, but what about other people?

Referring to something discussed in an earlier session, I say: 'So you are still afraid of showing yourself, you are ashamed.' (Meanwhile, I wonder where I might have 'gone away' to and whether some of my recent absences to attend congresses might have contributed to the 'sores'). He answers: 'Yes, because I see it as a failure; I see myself as a marked man: yesterday I was ashamed to go and vote. Everyone knows everything in the country – it's incredible. *Separated*, after less than a year of marriage! Fantastic! A nice one, that! In my imagination I have to bear *this mark impressed on my skin . . . like a leper.*'

35

During the course of this analysis there were numerous images in which he appeared inside a tough protective shell, consisting more than once of a car. In an initial dream brought in his first session, seeing himself in the company of a girlfriend in a Lancia Y10, he had presented his 'genetic heritage', providing a kind of equation representing his affective world. In the analyst's associations, the image had been transformed into that of a patient with a chromosome complement of the type X + 10Y! The *genetic map* corresponded, in the reality of his history – as a little boy he was tormented by a humiliating sense of inferiority because of his slow growth – to his choice of acting as a parachute officer and adopting the associated mental and muscle 'tone'; he assumed the thick hide of assault troops, the first to be sent behind enemy lines, but his skin was also covered in sores and exposed to any and every insult.

The dream helps me to work with a maximum of tact (applying an ointment consisting of the avoidance of any interpretative 'violence'); to respect the patient's needs for rigid self-containment, as expressed in his bearing, his manner of speaking and even in the posture he adopted on the couch, as well as in his hypersensitivity to 'physiological' variations in the setting; and to be aware that any interruption in the link with the analyst/wife reactivates intense feelings of persecution and leaves him feeling alone like a leper (that is, it presents a direct threat to his 'skin' as the psychic integument of the self), hovering between risks of impulsiveness – the Y10 – or of depressive *collapses* which are increasingly difficult to *ward off* or to repair. Matteo has gradually become more 'visible' not only to some friends, to whom he has been able to recount the vicissitudes of his life, but also to myself. As a result, we have witnessed a gradual reduction in the amount of Y, which, as we know, is often greater in violent personalities; that is to say, we have observed an increase in his capacity to manage emotions of which he was previously very afraid.

Alessia, whom I see on a face-to-face basis in our initial interviews, suffers from a kind of inability to find her own way in the world, owing to envy of her friends and intolerance of her mother, as well as to her consuming anxiety about a young man across the Atlantic. She would like to get away from home as quickly as possible – soon, perhaps, as a voluntary aid worker with a humanitarian organization in Albania. She talks incessantly and at each meeting picks up a pencil and plays with it for the entire hour; she goes through the motions of drawing on the wooden surface of the table, but does not leave any mark (suggesting to me the need to fill an affective and relational void by putting herself in contact with, or sticking firmly to, the material medium of the setting). Each time she leaves in haste, just as she came in, as if there were never enough time, or she could never really stop to think – as if, for the time being, she could only tolerate the 'geographical' (affective) confusion and oceanic distance separating her from her love objects by withdrawing into an envelope of sensations, the possible starting point for the reconstruction of a reliable and secure symbiotic bond which she perhaps lacked in the past.

In her first interview, Olga describes to me a devastating state of loneliness, which gives rise to recurring crises of depression and suicidal fantasies. Hunched, short in stature and so awkward that she initially conveys the impression (which soon, however, proves false) of a slight stammer, her face lights up and she becomes secure and uninhibited in her speech when she turns to the subject of her studies in the field of literature, in which she excels. Owing to severe health problems from birth, she had to undergo repeated operations and needed to wear an orthopaedic corset for years. The family environment was equally restrictive, the rhythms of life being governed by very strict rules. While listening to her, I see in my mind's eye the course of a therapy confined within an *orthopaedic corset of intelligence*, but probably lacking for a long time the physicality of emotions and affects.

Paolo, for his part, is tormented by hypochondriacal anxieties and panic states, and for a long period his sessions call for the structuring of an abundant *film of dreams* – complex dreams – which appear fascinating, and are also, I would say with hindsight, characterized by a strong illusion of transparency. He soon develops considerable skill on the level of coherent, winning presentation, accompanying the dream deposited at the very beginning of the session. His confirmation of my interpretative ideas is always equally prompt. After a time, I begin to wonder to what extent all this is, paradoxically, a way of remaining on the surface – of establishing forms of adhesive, imitative, 'ambiguous' forms of contact, necessary at a certain stage of an intense symbiotic transference in order to avoid any movement in the direction of differentiation, which would arouse unbearable experiences of loneliness and abandonment, like those that caused him so much pain in his infancy.

In other situations, the invasive presence of obsessional thought mechanisms or a posture of virtually 'clinging' to the couch, with the patient's hands anchored firmly to its edges, may convey the impression of levels of functioning involving somewhat excessive recourse to adhesiveness, to a second skin – which, however, like an orthopaedic corset, admittedly holds, but also constrains, without permitting much freedom of movement or providing adequate permeability, protection and warmth. This is the case with Bruno. He is very intelligent as long as he remains on the 'operational' level, but has serious difficulties with symbolization, or, as Bick (1984: 352, translated) puts it, with 'grasping ideas'. With great clarity, he describes the stupefying effect – the 'befuddling of consciousness', as Bleger might say – which he seeks in smoking and drinking, as well as, at other less desperate times, in intense intellectual work, to relieve the burden of a chronic sense of emptiness.

The breaches of the setting illustrated in the first few of these clinical vignettes, which are physiological or take the form of a 'forcible entry' and are experienced and suffered in the meta-ego, give rise in the patient to a trauma that is expressed in almost immediate repetition – in a tension, as yet not mediated by words, in the direction of representability and reparation. In this way, through the crisis of space triggered by the interruption of symbiosis, the usually mute sensory floor afforded by the setting/body/environment system, whose existence we can normally only infer, becomes perceptible. These breaches are made up of composite events, probably attributable both to levels of unconscious intentionality, which can therefore be interpreted as enactments, and to more asymbolic stratifications of the ego, or unmentalized experiential planes that emerge together with signs of a laceration; moreover, these signs are never lacking, just as the various modes in which the mind experiences reality are simultaneous.

In the second group of clinical fragments, on the other hand, the common feature is the need, expressed in various ways, for 'hyper-sensory' self-containment, with the probable aim of intense 'deposition' in the setting.

Ambiguity

In the light of the foregoing theoretical and clinical presentations, let us now consider the fundamentals of Bleger's argument. His theory of the glischro-caric position on the one hand paved the way for Marcelli's developmental-physiological thesis and for Ogden's physiological-structural approach, while on the other adopting a paradoxical formula to draw attention to the crisis affecting the very concept of the therapeutic alliance. Bleger thus anticipates and contributes to the change of paradigm from the drive-based to the relational model which, according to Ponsi (2002), underlies this crisis.[5]

The formula of an alliance of the setting with the 'psychotic part' entails a complex conception of the meaning of splitting, which has repercussions at clinical level. Contraposition is superseded by complicity. Surprisingly, the psychotic part appears first as the guardian of a sense of continuity of the self (the meta-ego or 'frame' of the ego), and then as a helper that knows how to manage certain situations which arise when the ego is confronted by the danger of dissolution. This is what Steiner (1993) seems to suggest in stating that pathological organizations of the personality act like a medicine that enables the wounded ego to feel less in danger of disintegration. Consequently, indications of a singular and secret unity of the psyche can be discerned even in the most disquieting manifestations of dissociation. The psychotic and non-psychotic parts can then be conceived in positive terms as 'modes' of generating meaningful experiences of reality. As already argued by Bleuler in relation to dereistic thought, the salient factor may lie in the logic of complementarity that links the 'parts'. These seem to espouse the motto *flectar non frangar* in a dialectic in which one term creates and preserves the other by negating it – the converse also being true – thus linking them in a relationship of mutual necessity.

It now becomes possible to adopt a more problematic, provisional and relativistic approach to the concept of the therapeutic 'alliance', which, at least in certain operational forms, proves to be reductive precisely in the negative, 'demoniac' connotation of the sick part. After all, the military metaphor is limited by its neglect of the factor of *antagonistic solidarity*, the 'play of parts', or secret consonance, and by its emphasis on conflict to the detriment of the concealed pact of mutuality that links the two (or more) parties present in the mind, which appear as opposing and irreducible only if considered in isolation from each other. A clear-cut schematic consideration of this kind runs the risk of relegating the more dramatic phenomena of mental suffering to an area of pre-Freudian opacity and of reducing the space available for establishing or preserving a link with the patient.

The problem seems, on the other hand, to be that of unblocking or reducing conflicts by means of innovative solutions that strengthen the ego without breaking the links with the psychotic part, and, in particular, of adopting an emotional posture allowing the analyst to make contact with the sick parts and to tolerate long-lasting states of seeming non-relationship.

Bleger (1967b: 216) appears to support this model in certain notes; for instance: 'upon the occurrence of highly persecutory situations which the subject cannot face because he would otherwise be plunged into total disorganization or a state of psychotic dissolution, he blurs the contradiction or persecution he is experiencing and regresses to ambiguity.' If, as Freud (1920: 13) states, there 'is something about anxiety that protects its subject against fright [. . .]', mobilization of the agglutinated nucleus constitutes a secondary means of confronting an inexpressible, non-representable terror coinciding with the 'threat to life' (p. 31) presented by traumatic shock, which the assistance of the psychotic part begins to hold back as the 'last line of defence of the shield against stimuli' (p. 31), while at the same time organizing an idiosyncratic world for which a price must be paid in terms of pain, albeit a pain that is already less intolerable.

In Bleger's view, in a sufficiently integrated person the agglutinated nucleus (the psychotic part) remains split off. In a situation of mental suffering, on the other hand, it may come to the surface, and may then assume a variety of forms, all of which, however, can be traced back to the clinical treatment of ambiguity.[6] Ambiguity is seen as the expression of the type of non-discrimination characteristic of the glischro-caric position and of the organization of the primitive ego – a 'granular' ego made up of fragments of different, coexisting identifications, or swarms of syncretic egos. In other words, the sense of the contradictory nature of antinomic terms proper to the paranoid-schizoid position is lacking, as is the possibility of experiencing ambivalence which is characteristic of the depressive position.

Now it seems to me that the 'play of parts' of the personality can be expressed equally well in terms of the clinical manifestations of ambiguity, which, because they reveal the lack of discrimination in identity and in ego/non-ego differentiation, are for Bleger the distinctive mark of the psychotic part. The 'granular ego', the 'kaleidoscope of personalities', inauthenticity or bad faith, mimicry, the proteiform character, permeability with regard to the assumption of varying roles, provisionality and artificiality, or '*Zelig* qualities' – might all these manifestations of regression to the syncretism of the glischro-caric position represent, within limits, not so much malignant degenerations of the ego as life-saving resources?

Unlike Bleger, Ogden does not see ambiguity as resembling Winnicott's *false self* or Deutsch's *as if* personality. He attributes imitation, one of the salient aspects of the ambiguous personality, to the mode of functioning of the autistic-contiguous position, and his theory sees it as a strategy for acquiring a basic cohesion upon which a self will subsequently be able to develop. In a word, he regards it as an important form of object relationship, and thereby offers an example of how a more elaborate theoretical model can be expected to help us distinguish better between different clinical facts and to place ourselves more effectively on the patient's side.

Sensation, memory and the object

As we have seen, a genetic and developmental theoretical structure remains the basis of Bleger's theses, the idea of development in phases being substantially retained. The glischro-caric position is the oldest of these phases and, even if it may reappear in certain stages of both normal and pathological development, is destined to be overcome. It can persist solely in the form of residues of a primitive agglutinated formation, of encystments of immature parts, and deficiencies in personification and the sense of reality are a function of their consistency. Notwithstanding his acceptance that narcissistic transferences – both autistic and symbiotic – are present in every analysis and that narcissistic nuclei exist virtually in any individual, however 'mature', Bleger's theory does not yet fully espouse the conviction of a necessary, continuous and in fact non-eliminable matrix of production of experience 'on that level' (he alternates between the concepts of persistence and regression). This is so even if this very matrix seems in some way to be implied by the concept of the meta-ego and even if, in particular, its finer mechanisms remain unexplained. It is as if the function of the glischro-caric position were exhausted in the very earliest phases of psychic life, and as if the agglutinated nucleus were formed once and for all, although it can change its location in space, shatter or expand.

Developed on the basis of the conceptual instruments of infant psychoanalysis, Marcelli's contribution enriches the concept of a 'third position', transferring it to an original ontogenetic dimension and assigning importance to the aspect of temporality. Its reconstruction of the transition from sensory functioning to representational or symbolic thought is convincing. This transition in fact constitutes the pivotal point between process and non-process, between the invariance necessary for the non-ego and the change that allows the individual to adapt to the demands of reality.

The decisive step taken by Ogden is his demonstration of the necessity of the activation and maintenance of somato–psychic experiential levels, of a presymbolic nature, throughout life. Just as, in Gestalt psychology, a figure can stand out perceptually only against a background, so the ego cannot be differentiated and preserved except as against a non-ego or meta-ego. An appropriate image might be that of walking, which is possible only by applying the feet to a floor or ground that remains sufficiently stable. It can be modified, but only within limits, and only by the slow deposition of variations, otherwise there is a risk of falling – of trauma. Conversely, tolerable elements of discontinuity, which do not exceed the individual's threshold level, in each case represent opportunities for thinkability and for ego development and maturation.

This situation is reflected in a famous passage from Proust. When the protagonist almost stumbles over the uneven cobbles of a Paris courtyard, the sensation of falling evokes involuntary memories of the irregularly shaped slabs making up the floor of the baptistery of St Mark's in Venice, thereby restoring to him a profound and gratifying sense of continuity of the self. No one understood better than Marcel Proust how memory and identity are rooted in the senses:

> And so it is with our own past. It is a labour in vain to attempt to recapture it: all the efforts of our intellect must prove futile. The past is hidden somewhere outside the realm, beyond the reach of intellect, in some material object (in the sensation which that material object will give us) which we do not suspect.
> (Proust 1998 [1913–1927]: 61)

The subject thus apparently needs to experience reality in a 'presymbolic, sensory-dominated' mode (Ogden 1989: 30) – to structure symbiotic bonds and links, even in adulthood, as guarantors of identity. After all, concepts featuring widely in the psychoanalytic literature, such as unison, empathy or identification, surely also refer to this persistent need for contiguity/adhesiveness. Might the setting act in this way as a presymbolic organizer awaiting transformation through the intervention of the analyst's alpha-function and 'apparatus for thinking thoughts' – a 'function' and an 'apparatus' whose molecular level is identified by the 'positions' – in symbolopoiesis, just as touching gradually gives rise in an infant to the gesture of pointing and the attentive mother gives a name to the objects of reality for the first time?

In this way, in adapting or otherwise to the spatio-temporal and dialogic coordinates of the setting, patients in the analyst's consulting room bear witness to the state of this symbiotic life of theirs – their meta-ego – to the humps and bumps of the 'ground', and to the general conditions of solidity and reliability of their 'floor'. In some, the incessant need for reparation proves to be obsessive, given the extent to which this sensory floor is felt to be damaged, energy even being withdrawn from the more differentiated and reflective capacities of the ego – an ego that remains bogged down and blocked on the level of a primitive adhesiveness, which is in fact a hypertrophic agglutinated nucleus.

For example, some patients constantly ask the analyst questions – questions for which actual answers are not expected, other than as signals of the analyst's presence; the answers are therefore not listened to in terms of their content, but have a high pragmatic value. The situations concerned are characterized for long periods by two-dimensional surface functioning, pending the possibility of creation of a psychic space between patient and analyst, and hence in the patient's mind. Conversely, we are all familiar with certain cases, which may even be more difficult to treat because they express firmly established autistic defences, involving an 'illusory transference', in which the apparent rich vein of symbolization rests on a foundation of radical splitting between emotions and thought (Ferro *et al.* 1986). Bleger himself postulates that these clinical pictures, which present as systematized – i.e. pure – neuroses may in reality be based on rigid dissociation of psychotic aspects of the self.

Confusion/emotion

Bleger holds that the task of psychoanalytic therapy is essentially antisymbiotic. The treatment must proceed by 'contamination' in contact with the reality of the differentiated person of the analyst. In choosing this term, which is felicitously 'ambiguous' because it also alludes to the associated risks of corruption and contagion, to denote the cornerstone of the treatment, Bleger (1967b) tellingly conveys its antinomies and vicissitudes. By contamination he means the gradual reintrojection, 'in small doses and at an appropriate rate', of 'chopped-up', fragmented parts of the agglutinated object, which is achieved by exposure to new relationships and by the diversification of links with other objects and other depositories. The analysis must, however, enable the patient to experience the symbiotic bond and to learn from this experience in order to be able thereafter to separate: 'We must make ourselves the faithful depositories of the psychotic part and act as tolerant parents who allow time for growth and do not prematurely overwhelm the patient with problems which his ego is as yet not equipped to tackle' (Bleger 1967b: 88, translated). In other words, we must avoid any over-hasty attempt to force the reintrojection of deposited aspects. This means that we must permit symbiosis to become established and to be secure and reliable. What is guaranteed to the therapy by the setting, the 'ally of the psychotic part', is precisely the security of being able to resume the relationship after each separation; it is this that enables the relationship to evolve.

Whereas, in Bleger's view, symbiosis is the relationship that keeps the psychotic part or agglutinated nucleus immobilized and under control (however, the opposite is also the case: the agglutinated nucleus guarantees the symbiotic links necessary to life), he does not yet seem able to regard it in his theory as the locus of production of a sufficiently secure sense of self; in other words, he is not yet seeing, in the manner of a watermark in a sheet of paper, the function of integration and support performed by this nucleus, by analogy with the roots of a tree vis-à-vis the trunk and branches – i.e. in a structural and not merely a genetic sense. Although Bleger's text admittedly contains statements to the contrary, the psychotic part is seen rather as the residue of the ego's immaturity at birth and of the associated functional organization. Yet Bleger gives an excellent description of how the type of concrete, bodily, presymbolic functioning, for instance, in the concept of the body as buffer, is in dynamic equilibrium with the more differentiated capacities of the ego, and acts in certain critical situations to make up for an ego that remains like a mere *excluded spectator*,[7] and how this regressive movement may constitute the prerequisite for a return to more advanced levels of mentalization.

As to the core of the therapeutic process, Modell (1989) agrees that what matters is for the patient to be able to experience the symbiotic bond in a situation of security. Symbiosis – paradoxically – treats itself. Hence the contradiction with the idea that analytic therapy has an essentially antisymbiotic function is only apparent. The important point is full acceptance of the complex, mutual interdependence of the various ways in which experience is generated in the mind. Treatment will then seek not so much to eliminate the agglutinated nucleus as to re-establish the conditions for adequate mobility of the processes of introjection and projection, without the subject feeling the need to resort to massive projective identifications and untenable distortions of reality.

Just as mental pathology stems, as stated, from the collapse of one of the various 'positions' of the mind in a single direction, therapy itself may lapse into an impasse or become iatrogenic if the emphasis is placed solely on the autistic/symbiotic level (empathy/sharing/unison, etc.), on the hyper-discriminating, antisymbiotic level of the paranoid-schizoid position (highly 'separating' styles of interpretation which idealize knowledge), or on the level that leads to the sense of emptiness that is characteristic of depression. Whereas paranoid-schizoid functioning helps to reduce the agglutinated nucleus, the:

> danger of psychosis posed by the fragmenting and evacuative pro-cesses of the paranoid-schizoid mode are [sic] contained in two ways: (1) 'From above' by the binding capacity of symbolic link-ages, historicity, and subjectivity of the depressive mode; and (2) *'from below' by the sensory continuity, rhythmicity, and boundedness of the autistic-contiguous mode.*
>
> (Ogden 1989: 45, my emphasis)

In this way, analysis also becomes a factor in the regulation of the sensory floor and in overcoming the crisis into which this funda-mental sense of the space and surfaces of a boundary is plunged in various psychopathological situations. These extend from the terror of psychotic collapse (the fear of falling, dissolving or falling to pieces) to certain reparative activities (stereotypies, or self-harming activities with the aim of 'reconstituting' limits – Civitarese 1998, 2003). How-ever, they can also be discerned in less clear-cut phenomena that are nevertheless connected with attempts to construct a second boundary line, or 'to plug leaks'. A long list of such phenomena could be compiled, and their clinical forms are equally diverse, including skin disorders, the maintenance of visual contact, a kind of incessant talking or of sometimes barely discernible manipulation of objects, and even the use for contact purposes of odours or olfactory hallucinations, as well as of obsessive-compulsive defences, of the schizoid condition, and so on.

Bleger offers some interesting specific suggestions on technique. For example, he maintains that the interpretation of bodily postures or movements may prove persecutory because it impinges not on the patient's ego but on his meta-ego, the psychotic part, and must therefore be used cautiously. Interpretations inspired by the concept of an attack on the setting should also be avoided, as these too would merely succeed in disorganizing the meta-ego, which is often practically all the patient has left. In addition, Bleger distinguishes between two types of interpretation, split and unsplit, according to whether they do or do not contain a split between the figure of the analyst and what the patient has deposited in him. Unsplit interpretations, in which the lack of distinction between the depository and the deposited is preserved, merely show the analysand how the analyst behaved in his eyes, or was experienced, but do not explicitly presuppose that this involves the projection on to him of the patient's split-off internal objects; they do not therefore force the patient to take back the projection. In other words, the therapist agrees to play the part assigned to him in the transference. The analysand's ego can proceed by way of a preliminary process of discrimination and increase its capacity to recognize emotions and affects. These interpretations – perhaps the forerunners of those which Bezoari and Ferro (1989) call weak, unsaturated or narrative interventions[8] – are based on the 'minimum-dose principle' and offer the analysand only what he can accept at a given time; they respect the situation of symbiosis and refrain from prematurely overstressing it, in order not to give rise to *confusional anxiety*. However, as usual, it is a question of degree, because the *state of being moved*, Bleger tells us, is probably also based on the sudden but *bearable* reintrojection of split-off and deposited fragments of 'psychotic' selves in the more mature ego.[9]

Ideally, then, the task of therapy could be defined as that of facilitating a movement leading from the suffering due to splits that have occurred in the self, while avoiding the confusion resulting from the 'violence of interpretation', to the situation of tolerable reintegration afforded by the 'state of being moved that cannot be expressed in words'. Ultimately, therefore, an 'aesthetic' experience would appear to lie at the centre of therapeutic change, in the sense of contact with aspects of the self that are not irrational and illogical, but hyper-dense and ambiguous, and if anything carry with them an excess of meaning (Bodei 1999: 184). The regulation of secure symbiosis and respect for the immobilization of the psychotic levels may then be the appropriate instruments for managing the quantum of destabilization necessary for moving on to more integrated levels of the ego.

Fusion

Bleger's theory can supply a conceptual framework for some of the more recent theoretical conceptions of therapeutic action, such as, for example, that of Stern *et al.* (1998). For these authors, essential therapeutic factors are so-called *now moments* – that is, particularly significant moments within an analysis. Described as 'hot', special or authentic, these encounters involve reorganizations of the patient's implicit relational knowledge. Their characteristic feature is that they bear the analyst's highly personal stamp – as it were, his signature – so that they lie outside the normal repertory of technical resources, present a high degree of spontaneity and specificity, and transgress the rules of the normal frame.[10] These moments cannot be replaced by a transference interpretation and their meaning need not necessarily be made explicit. Translated into the language of Bleger, 'now moments' can, I believe, be said to *move* the patient's meta-ego, whereas traditional interpretations are directed principally to the ego, although clear distinctions are not possible in this sphere. They are consequently situated on a non-verbal, procedural, intersubjective level, where the watchwords of action/structure/relationship are contrasted, theoretically speaking, with the traditional concepts of language/repression/knowledge.

An echo of Bleger's emphasis on the setting as the depository of symbiosis can be found in the contributions to a panel on fusion published in the *Rivista di Psicoanalisi* in 1985. The participating authors stressed that the persistence of a stable and solid unconscious phantasy of fusion throughout life is important for mental health (Pallier 1985); that an affective relationship cannot exist unless it is based also on a fantasy of fusion (Soavi 1985); and that the specificity of objects and emotions can be recognized only within a stabilized fusional system (Tagliacozzo 1985). The discriminating factor which protects the subject from pathology in fact arises from the subject's capacity to alternate, with regard to symbiosis, between the two terms of the dichotomy of continuity and discontinuity. The vector of fusion should be represented not by a solid straight line but rather by a broken line, suggesting a sufficiently permeable frontier of the self and of the ego–object interface.

When reconsidered in the light of the contributions of these authors, the setting increasingly takes on the characteristics of the boundary between the bodily and the mental that is also proper to fusion. Neri (1985) was the author who drew attention to the *containing function* of fusion, which may in some cases take the form of a psychosomatic and sensory unity of the patient with the analyst and the environment. This unity – it might be preferable to call it somato-psychic – which appears as a constant of relationship, seems unthinkable in certain excessively disembodied or mentalized models of psychoanalytic therapy. The idealization of knowledge and separateness, on the other hand, leads to an arid technique of distancing, which may arouse guilt and hostility, and to the paradoxical risk for psychoanalysis of undervaluing emotional thought – the non-verbal system of communication which, according to Brazelton and Greenspan (2000), remains the most important, even if it ultimately operates in association with symbols and words.

For this reason, a more realistic conception of the treatment would not ignore the fact that the symbol constantly aims at recomposition, and that any separation can only be in a dialectical relationship with fusion, its necessary premise; while a realistic theory must in addition take account of the inescapable fact of the anchoring of the ego[11] in corporeality. From this point of view, an essential requirement will be fine modulation of the sensory aspects of the encounter (for instance, interventions in which the analyst's tone of voice or an indication of his presence is more important than the content), as well as a degree of sensitivity to the concrete, pragmatic component of words. Attention to the body, as the place where symbiosis is instituted and operates, and to corporeality as the place where, following interaction, emotions that cannot yet be felt as such are recorded in both patient and analyst, is one of the most fascinating facets of Bleger's thought. By listening to physical sensations, the analyst is engaging in reverie in its sensory dimension, the aspect to which Ogden was referring by his use of Tustin's concept of autistic forms.

In conclusion, Bleger's theory of the glischro-caric position, supplemented by some of the more interesting developments in psychoanalytic research, stresses the theoretical and clinical importance of the non-specific or relational factors in the treatment and of the strictly non-process elements of the setting, such as tone, tact, timing, context, support, respect, waiting, the analyst's person and spontaneity (the latter certainly not being pre-technical), 'moments of encounter', the conversational register, 'negative capability' (Bion 1970), narrative formulations of interpretation (Bezoari and Ferro 1992a), discursive strategies of 'mitigation' (Caffi 2001), or the avoidance of excessive attributions of meaning and of interpretative techniques likely to be experienced by the patient as intrusive or lifeless.

The distinction sometimes made between pre-analytic, in the sense of psychotherapeutic and/or supportive, phases of therapy on the one hand and actual analytic phases on the other thus seems to overshadow the 'basic' dimension of the person to which Bleger is referring by the concept of the meta-ego. Yet the talking cure increasingly appears also to be taking on the characteristics of a touching cure; after all, as we know, what actually cures are 'words that touch' (Charles 2001; Quinodoz 2002). There is a paradox here, as if the highest degree of symbolization – words that truly reach the other's heart, which truly *move* the other – thereby ultimately abolishes itself, in re-establishing a primitive, primal, albeit non-physical contact, but is then reborn in a continuous motion from and to the object, from and to the body.

3

Metalepsis, or the rhetoric of transference interpretation

In a certain way, the Pirandello manner of *Six Characters in Search of an Author* or *Tonight We Improvise*, where the same actors are in turn characters and players, is nothing but a vast expansion of metalepsis [. . .] characters escaped from a painting, a book, a press clipping, a photograph, a dream, a memory, a fantasy [. . .] All these games, by the intensity of their effects, demonstrate the importance of the boundary they tax their ingenuity to overstep, in defiance of verisimilitude – a boundary *that is precisely the narrating (or the performance) itself:* a shifting but sacred frontier between two worlds, the world in which one tells, the world of which one tells. Whence the uneasiness Borges so well put his finger on: 'Such inversions suggest that if the characters in a story can be readers or spectators, then we, their readers or specta-tors, can be fictitious.' The most troubling thing about metalepsis indeed lies in this unacceptable and insistent hypothesis, that the extradiegetic is perhaps always diegetic, and that the narrator and his narratees – you and I – perhaps belong to some narrative.

(Genette, *Narrative Discourse. An Essay in Method*, 1972)

'Now [. . .] what the devil am I going to do with you?' No, this is not the despairing cry of a therapist at grips with an untreatable patient, but the rumination of John Fowles (1969) in Chapter 55 of *The French Lieutenant's Woman* when he meets Charles, the protagonist of his novel, on a train: while casting stealthy glances at him, the author wonders how to continue the story. For an analyst, there is something familiar about this scene. As a reminder, one need merely revisit Volume 12 of the Freud *Standard Edition* (1913: 135): 'So say whatever goes through your mind. Act as though, for instance, you were a traveller sitting next to the window of a railway carriage and describing views which you see outside.' Besides the identical setting, the two situations share a narrative element – namely, the transgression of diegetic levels, or, if you will, of the spatio-temporal universes within which the story unfolds (as in Woody Allen's film *The Purple Rose of Cairo*, when Tom Baxter walks off the screen to meet his devoted fan Cecilia). In narratology, such a situation is described by the term *metalepsis*.[1] In the analyst's consulting room, a similar scene to the one thought up by Fowles would exist, strictly speaking, if a patient were to look out of the window and see, or be induced to see, himself in the landscape outside *in the company* of the analyst – not the analyst as one of the many figures who may appear in the material he brings, but precisely as the co-author or reader of the text of the analysis who, at the very instant of his appearance, is also sitting inside the window, actually within the railway carriage. This, perhaps, is what is more or less clearly seen to occur whenever a transference interpretation is given. This, perhaps, is what is more or less clearly seen to occur whenever a transference interpretation is given. Both the Fowles episode and the analytic scene take the form of prototypes of 'self-conscious' narratives, which are characterized principally by the highlighting of the meta-narrative and inevitably 'ideological' nature of the respective spaces of representation.

The central thesis of this chapter is that transference interpretation, which has – at least since Strachey (1934) – been one of the main therapeutic factors in psychoanalysis, is in its typical form a metaleptic operator, or, in other words, the rhetorical device – a specific type of 'narrative schema' or figure of discourse – whereby constant intrusions by the analyst, as an extradiegetic reader (or interpreter or addressee), take place into the 'text' of the analysis, which is seen, as a first approximation, as the patient's autobiographical account. However, since an interpretation too has a narrative character and may be formulated not by the analyst alone, it would be more correct to say that both participants, seen now as co-narrators and co-addressees, by turns systematically introduce themselves, as extra-textual authors (or off-stage dramatists or members of the audience), into a text or on to a stage from which they had previously been absent because they belonged to a different diegetic universe.

In this way, the encounter comes about, in the text of the analysis, between the 'characters' and their authors/readers, who have now, after the dénouement of the unconscious plot, themselves become 'fictitious' (as Borges would say) instead of being real and historical as they had been before. In other words, the boundary between the world of the author or reader and that of the 'text' – between the observer and the observed – is violated. The referential alibi underlying the obvious and spontaneous reading of the events of the analysand's past and present life – the tautology of a reality taken literally – is shown to be flimsy. The way in which rhetorical structures, with their categorial oppositions – each of which constitutes a 'framing' – construct experience is rediscovered.

In this context, then, the term 'rhetorical' is by no means used in the sense of 'artificial', 'ornamental' or 'emphatic', or in that of 'purely persuasive'. Instead, my reference is to a conception of rhetoric as figural intelligence or a theory of sense (Bottiroli 1993) – that is, as an instrument for the interpretation of the discursive strategies underlying the general processes of attribution of meaning (Simons 1990).

The concept of metalepsis, which I use here as a heuristic instrument, focusing on the figural and narrative nature of the text, therefore emphasizes the constructive, anti-essentialist or 'make-believe' (not, of course, in the sense of false or unreal) character of interpretative work in analysis – that is, the fact that it is inevitably bound to specific semiotic and linguistic codes and to their performative effects. The process of identity differentiation can no longer be seen as a fact of nature, but itself appears as the fruit of an activity of co-construction conducted moment by moment between patient and analyst. Upon each metaleptic dislocation, redescription or re-enframing, the subject is simultaneously deconstructed and reconstructed – that is to say, both relativized and reinforced in his degree of awareness of self and the world.

Seen in the light of this surprising figure of speech, transference interpretation appears as a device with the function of systematically and intentionally 'breaching' the setting/frame (these breaches not being fortuitous like those discussed by Roussillon 1995), or rather an essential level of the setting, namely the level associated with the order of discourse. By this I mean repeated violations of, or 'inflictions of force' on, the meanings assigned by the patient himself to the vicissitudes of his life. These perhaps resemble the necessary 'misunderstandings' that Riolo (1999: 25, translated) attributes to the 'conscious application of the kind of thought that is characteristic of dreams'.[2]

These acts of 'breaching', which are in fact the only kind permitted by the rules, and are indeed required by them, are not merely intrinsically transgressive but also virtually transformative. In order to open the way to new modes of being and new realities, established boundaries are dissolved and new delimitations of meaning are assigned. The technical problem of determining the appropriate dosage of this 'violence' and of how to 'dress' one's interpretations so that the patient can accept them is discussed here in clinical terms too. However, some preliminary definitions must first be given.

Which text, and which author?

Let us begin with an initial postulate: that an interpretation is structured like a narrative in itself, so that it actually contributes to the making of the text it deciphers, of which it eventually comes to form an integral part. It is no coincidence that Freud, who was the first to see his own case histories as 'short stories', preferred the term 'construction' to that of interpretation, arguing as follows (1937: 260f.): 'The analyst finishes a piece of construction and communicates it to the subject of the analysis so that it may work upon him; he then constructs a further piece out of the fresh material pouring in upon him, deals with it in the same way and proceeds in this alternating fashion until the end.' The patient's text and the analyst's interpretation/text are ultimately indistinguishable (Schafer 1992).

At least two things may be meant by the word 'text'. From a vertex external to the setting, it is the vignette or case history reported in a scientific paper – this would be the simplest and most radical operational 'reduction', even if counter-intuitive – but it is also the transcript of a session. From inside the analytic situation – and here the text will be considered in a figurative, wider semiotic sense – it denotes the verbal exchanges between the members of the analysand–analyst couple in the consulting room, or, in a word, the actual live performance of a session.

In the first case, that of a clinical vignette, the analyst is to all intents and purposes the empirical, real author, while the patient and the analyst as represented in the text are two characters among others who meet and talk to each other, as in the pages of a novel or in a play. The 'grids' of narratology are relevant and applicable here. In so far as it can be understood – especially if the role of the analyst's person is taken into account – as the product of a 'composition for four hands', the text which goes by the name of a clinical 'illustration' or 'material' is that written by the analyst.[3] It usually takes the form of a dialogue reproduced in either direct or reported speech, but could also present itself as a long monologue by a patient faced with a silent interlocutor. That is what happens in Abraham Yehoshua's (1989) novel *Mr Mani*, in which the reader is not provided with the words of the character at the other end of an imaginary telephone line.

In the case of a 'pure', faithful transcript, not very much would change: the graphic notation, division into paragraphs, inverted commas and other punctuation marks would represent interventions by the author, each a telltale of the constructed or make-believe nature of the text. Even listening to a recording would immediately introduce a second-degree narrative frame and a single empirical author, because it would after all be the outcome of selection and editing of the clinical material.

In the second case, on the other hand, from a vertex internal to the session, the narratological simplification closest to the reality of the situation is to regard analyst and patient as co-authors and co-readers, and hence at one and the same time originators and addressees of the improvised flow of words which they progressively bring to life. Here again, substantially the same theoretical model could be taken as a reference, but this time there would be *two* narrators, *two* 'readers', etc., to consider.

Another postulate, following that of the narrative character of interpretation, which is in no way taken for granted, concerns the *embedded* structure of this particular text, which comes to be inserted into the clinical vignette or the spoken text of the session. In the clinical vignette, analyst and patient, as voices of the text, can become second-degree narrators when their words are reported in inverted commas. All their stories are situated on the same level (horizontal insertions), but in each story – as in the *Thousand and One Nights* – one could go down further narrative steps to a lower level (vertical insertions).

Let us consider the typical case of the bringing of a dream scene. I choose this example because it touches on a key point in my thesis: to be precise, the account of a dream would not in itself involve a change in diegetic level, but it would be absurd – scholars of narratology argue – to deny this event and not to regard it as a 'second' or 'inserted' narration on the basis of an 'ontological', if not strictly formal, slippage (Bal 1985; Ryan 1991; O'Neill 1994; Nelles 1997). As Genette (2004: 115f., translated), writes:

> The act of dreaming is – in principle, the converse not being possible – contained in the life of the dreamer, and [. . .] the account of one of his dreams can quite naturally be inserted into that of his life. Strictly speaking, this insertion ought not to entail any change of diegetic level, since the unfolding of the oneiric events or visions falls, without any modification of the narrative instance, within the lived duration of the character in question, as reported by himself or by an external narrator [. . .]. In fact, when the account of a dream features in an account of life, the reader does not fail to perceive the former as *second* relative to the latter, and hence its 'action' as metadiegetic in relation to the diegesis represented by the character's daytime existence.

Given these premises and adopting the same viewpoint, I hold that transference interpretation can be equated with the analyst's 'dream' about the patient's narration. For the plots revealed by transference interpretation unfold on that *other* stage represented by the unconscious, which obeys the same laws as dreams. Precisely for this reason, a transference interpretation of a patient's dream may be deemed to share the same modal shift (namely, the opening of access to another possible world), and can thus be seen as a narration 'mounted' within the main text, bounded by a frame of its own, located by its very ontological status on a different narrative level.

The 'insertion' is effected in the same way as in certain paradigm texts, such as in the dreams induced and dramatized in Brosse's comedy *Les songes des hommes esveillez*, or in *Hamlet*, when the young prince has the players who have come to the castle act the murder of Gonzaga (in this example, however, both the structure *en abyme* of the scene and the metalepsis remain implicit). The analyst, already present in the text of the analysis, thus does not yet belong to the unconscious scene constructed by his interpretation; he is a character among others, who introduces himself and, like Hamlet, suggests the establishment of a new performance space, the construction of a new, refined theatrical stage. He is in effect saying: 'What if we were to look at things from this point of view too?' What entitles us to use the term metalepsis is the existence of these different narrative planes or frames, as well as, still more, the fact that they are transgressed.

These initial definitions afford hardly a glimpse of the incredible complexity that characterizes even the most elementary narrative act. They are, however, in my view useful for putting in perspective any naive conception of the 'veracity' of the facts reported in scientific contributions, of their presumed naturalness or immediacy. I do not of course wish to imply by this that these accounts, which are presented as documentary (and not literary), do not have more or less stringent links with the reality of the session, or that they should not satisfy the firm criterion of overall textual consistency. Yet clinical material in itself cannot readily be said to possess any direct demonstrative, as opposed to evocative or quasi-poetic, value (Racalbuto 2004; Ogden 2005a). There is, for example, no guarantee that a dialogue transcribed with absolute fidelity, or indeed a recorded dialogue, will succeed in conveying the sense of the lived experience of a session more effectively, with more 'truth', than other seemingly less mimetic rhetorical or narrative forms.

Transgressions

In Greek and Latin antiquity (*metálepsis* and *transumptio* respectively), the trope (a term that in itself already means 'turn' or 'transfer') of metalepsis signified an exchange or transposition of meaning which involved inter alia the 'effects of "equivocal synonymy" [. . .] used in jokes', or 'an effect in the present attributed to a remote cause, where there is no direct connection between the two, but where a number of intermediate links, which are omitted, are required' – 'the replacement of a term by a figure resulting from (implicit) transitions through a number of notions that remain unexpressed, each of which is, relative to the others, synecdoche, metonymy or metaphor, whether alternative or coexistent' (Mortara Garavelli 1988: 140–141, translated). In other words, it is an interlacing or combination of several figures. The complex architecture which distinguishes it is that of extended metonymy, made up of propositions, between terms connected by a relationship of causality or succession – an intermediate element that unites terms which are dissimilar but have a feature in

56

common. Furthermore, inherent in it is an act of 'censorship', which can be undone by interpretation, concerning the missing link in a causal chain, as when we say, in Genette's famous example, that in Book 4 of the *Aeneid* Virgil 'puts Dido to death', without specifying the indirect nature of the act – namely, that we are talking about the author of the poem and not one of the characters appearing in it.

The subsequent extension of the meaning of the term is suggested precisely by the content of this example (as if Virgil himself were 'stepping into' his text), which is absolutely classical in its form, due to Fontanier (1968), the author of a famous early nineteenth-century treatise on rhetoric. In Genette's (1972, 2004) new conceptualization, after all, metalepsis is called upon to denote a writer's abandonment of the role of an 'external narrator'. Metalepsis is thus annexed to the field of narratology, where it denotes transgression of the frames of the story, subversion of ordinary narrative ontology and, typically, the bursting of the narrator into the textual universe in which his characters themselves live.

It is in this last sense that metalepsis, together with the chiasm, has come to occupy a privileged position among post-structuralist theories, as a figure of self-reflectivity and a component of a meta-signification that allows the text to take itself as its subject (Malina 2002; Pier and Schaeffer 2005). As an icon of indeterminacy, of self-referential irony, of violation of the tacit representational contract and of demystification of the very linguistic game that it introduces, metalepsis is thus reborn in the so-called cultural climate of post-modernism as an extension of the restricted definition already present in classical rhetoric.

In the written or spoken text of an analysis, transference interpretation is the narrative device which is structured like metalepsis and which 'constructs' subjectivity on the basis of the category of an already disavowed, repressed or split-off causality that is ultimately revealed. In the most frequent case, the antecedent – the story told by the patient – is taken as the consequent of another story, held to be truer or deeper, which unfolds at unconscious level and concerns the relationship existing in the here-and-now. In this way, the patient and indeed also the analyst constantly (re)discover themselves as characters in a work of fiction – as being, in turn, 'narrated' by the unconscious and by its defining linguistic and cultural codes; and the ego, which is continually displaced from its central position, cannot aspire to any primal principle or ultimate truth (to any archaeo- or teleo-logy).

57

Expressed in terms of Derrida's anti-metaphysics, 'there is no natural frame. *There is* frame, but the frame *does not exist*' (Derrida 1978: 81).

A fact is transmotivated; a cause is replaced by another; and, mostly, an external event is 'internalized'. In this way a proximizing or 'centripetal' semantic transformation is brought about with regard to the analytic relationship: Freud's deconstructive strategy of reintegrating into the picture of consciousness what the frame excludes from it because it is marginal, irrelevant or negative is reiterated in a movement without end. The analyst constantly signals to the patient that he (the analyst) inhabits the material the patient brings even when he is absent from the manifest text. It is as if the analyst were saying: 'What? Didn't you notice that outside the window of the railway carriage, when you thought you were looking at X, Y or Z, you were actually seeing me?!' The golden rule of commutative translation to be applied in transference interpretation then becomes: ' "When you say them you mean me". I am "them" ' (Roth 2001: 536). Where everything appeared to be purely factual, on the other hand, a make-believe, or 'effect of the real' (Barthes 1982), must be presupposed. The reality expressed by the surface of the text is a dream of the treatment, dreamed about the analyst and the analysis – *a dream awaiting interpretation.*

All transference interpretation does is to draw attention, by continuous metaleptic slippage from one frame to another – which already occurs virtually in every case of embedding (Nelles 1997) – to the importance of the frame itself (or the setting), as well as to the fact that we live in more than one world at a time, so that there is no such thing as a single, fixed reality. Metalepses are essentially *violations*, which are tolerable (but by no means innocuous), of the splits on which the subject's identity is built. In psychoanalytic terms, of course, crossing the 'shifting but sacred frontier' between the two worlds, as mentioned by Genette in the quotation reproduced at the beginning of this chapter, is equivalent to the uncanny intuition of the unconscious.

I shall now return to the central question about which this chapter revolves: how is the traumatogenic risk of interpretation to be evaluated, and with what conceptual instruments? What is it that causes the boundary to be crossed from primary violence, as the necessary and radical act of attributing meaning that lies at the origin of the maternal discourse, to secondary violence, which 'makes its way in the wake of its predecessor, of which it represents an excess' and is always harmful to the functioning of the ego (Aulagnier 1975: 12; see also Kluzer 1988; Bonaminio 2003)?

The fortress

As usual, having entered the room and before lying down, Sara raises the backrest of the couch and adjusts it to suit herself, as a part of the singular, systematic *reframing* of the setting that she undertakes at the beginning of each session. For a long time in the early stages of her analysis, now in its second year, she kept her head raised on the cushion, in an untiringly watchful position that appeared, if anything, unnatural.

I tell her almost immediately that for personal reasons I shall be unable to see her next Friday for the third and last session of the week. She remains silent. Meanwhile I feel oppressed by a sense of heaviness and constriction, as if the hands of the clock have stopped moving. I suddenly find myself leafing through some sheets of notes on earlier sessions – not even hers! – scattered on the desk, at first purely, as it were, on account of the need to touch an object, a kind of tension impelling me to grasp something, perhaps contained in those sheets of paper, that might help me to emerge from this mildly restless state. However, I do not get around to scanning my almost indecipherable notes owing to the spontaneous surfacing of the memory of the beginning of another session some time before – in which virtually the same atmosphere reigned! The session before that one had ended with a 'comprehensive' transference interpretation centring on Oedipal rivalry and on the past, applied to the present situation of the analytic relationship. With hindsight, I could say that I had, no doubt rashly, defamiliarized her account, compelling it to accommodate an intruder, a truth – specifically, that of a presumed father-analyst equivalence – for which a 'reception centre' did not yet exist, and which was there-fore perhaps tantamount to an act of violence or a pseudo-truth. At the time I had been quite pleased with this interpretation, although I had almost at once become aware of a black look on Sara's face as she left. In addition, an almost instantaneous sense of discomfort informed me of a probable failure of neutrality (in the sense of con-tainment, reverie and the maintenance of an adequate distance from theory), but, by then . . .

On that occasion, in the next session Sara brought me a dream which opened dramatically, and which I could not fail to see, too, as a comment on what I had said to her at the end of the previous session. I recall it distinctly: 'Everything is in ruins after a nuclear conflict . . . the earth is red and burnt . . . the war is over and there are only prisoners. I'm inside a fortress which has been utterly gutted – a structure covering such a huge area that I can't see any end to it . . . There is no law now; all the survivors are outlaws. I make my way to the centre of the structure and go down some enormously long flights of iron stairs. I keep going down, down, down. I descend from one platform to another, but never seem to get below the surface – as if I had never left it. All of a sudden, I realize that I too am a *prisoner* and that there are lots of other prisoners inside this structure. I recognize a contemporary of mine. He always *hated* me, even if there is also an underlying affection between us. He decides to help me. We set off . . . Everything is dark and I feel giddy. To avoid being seen, I lie down on the ground, among the stones, which are highly coloured in brilliant hues, with *diamond* inclusions. The stones are moving, moving towards me and dragging me away. They look beautiful, but I feel somewhat anxious. Then I woke up.'

Then, after remaining silent for some ten minutes, Sara seems about to say something. Sometimes, she begins in a slightly hesitant voice, she feels that the time of a session is too short for all the things she would like to say, or that those things are too 'heavy': 'Whenever my need to talk exceeds my ability to do so or to express myself, I get tongue-tied. There's so much I'd like to say. But I just stay silent. Maybe I'm afraid of not making myself clear enough. Then again, the problem might just as well be the opposite: suppose I was too clear and laid myself bare. It's quite possible. Anyway, this too is a constant battle – between wanting to "deconstruct" myself as quickly as possible and my inner emotional resistance to doing that.'

I feel somewhat relieved because Sara seems – albeit with difficulty, as I sense from the restrained rhythm of her speech – to have overcome a gloomy, desperate emotional state, whose existence one might not suspect behind her apparently good adaptation to reality. I reflect on the possibility that some of the many things that have passed between us in these last few minutes – my initial announcement, and the reverie/memory of the fortress dream – might have a meaning connected with what she has just told me.

I draw my ideas together. The dream contained the subversion of rules, the outlaws, the labyrinthine structure and the devastated landscape; whereas the few sentences just spoken included an explicit demand for allowance to be made for her capacity and needs, the *excess*, the prison-as-a-refuge-of-silence, as well as the extraordinary comment about the risks of interpretative deconstruction. I now attempt to formulate a theory, which I put to Sara. I wonder, I tell her, whether the announcement of the cancellation of the session, which I was indeed able to impart only at the last minute, came as an unexpected bombshell for her. She might then have felt exposed to intolerable emotions – maybe rage – because she feels she has so little time left (in this session, in this week, or in her life, I am thinking). 'Yes,' she slowly concedes, 'that's something worth considering,' but then falls silent again. Eventually it is I who break the silence, suggesting to her that perhaps she has *already* thought about it in mentioning the *excess*, rather as if she had said: 'Today you went too far with me!' – so much so that she can no longer say or ask anything. Meanwhile I am thinking again about how petrified she became, turning herself into a stone among all the stones in her dream; and today she is equally stony in her silence, which, this time, I too am experiencing as 'radioactive', like a forcible intrusion into the uneventful mutual attunement of our work during this period.

After another pause, Sara's associations turn to some old memories and to her father. Whenever they argued, she would respond sharply; she rebelled, she tells me, as if wishing to contrast her old way of reacting with today's silence and passivity. Yes, I agree, I might indeed seem to her today rather like the authoritarian and remote father of her infancy. But then she starts up, as if surprised to rediscover something she had forgotten: 'Actually,' she recalls, 'you're right: for four years I didn't say a single word to him . . .'

'As if you had been utterly defeated . . . as if the "tank" had come,' I venture almost in an undertone (in our dialect, the 'tank', as a metonym for the father, is the name given by Sara with bitter irony to his huge 4×4 in a dream in which she herself was sitting in a little two-seater Smart with her mother).

'Oh yes, with my father there was one missed appointment after another,' replies Sara, apparently quite unaware of the ambiguity of her words – so I find myself bringing her back into the present by saying: 'Well, as far as missed appointments are concerned, there will certainly be one for us too this week!'

The critical moment in this session – the turning point – comes when my feeling of discomfort compels me to look for something

concrete, to 'do' something, because the silence has become intolerable to me, just as it must have been for the patient over the years. The
impulse to touch the sheets of paper on the desk can be seen as an
attempt to repair the crack in the fusional or sensory component of
the setting resulting from the sudden anticipation of the void of the
cancelled Friday session, which is experienced painfully by the patient
and somehow reverberates in me. It is a moment of disorientation, of
absence of thought – as if I were trying, in the vague tension noticed
at the beginning of the session and then in the abortive search for the
written traces of previous meetings, to re-establish a channel of communication with Sara. And indeed, the memory of the 'post-nuclear'
devastation dream immediately resurfaces, reopening the path to
symbolization and representability.

The sense of abandonment due to the breaching of the frame of
the setting, experienced by the patient and projectively transmitted to
me through her stubborn silence, is at first absorbed by an enactment,
but is soon followed by the recovery of a function of reverie and a
capacity for containment. A visual screen is then reconstructed, but
only after the replication in the analyst of Sara's probable experience
of the interpretation as a 'bombshell'. The dream had recorded its
destabilizing, violent effect, which was perhaps also amplified by the
caesura of the weekend, as well as, however, the recovery of a capacity
for thought and the appearance of a new and unprecedented transparency vis-à-vis some of the patient's defence mechanisms, such as
de-animation and de-differentiation (she turns to 'stone' when faced
with the *diamonds* – the Italian for which, *diamanti*, contains the word
amanti, meaning lovers – so could this be a reference to the primal
scene?).

Analysis of this clinical vignette in terms of narrative levels immediately highlights the complexity of the series of framing operations
characterizing even a brief sequence – and the large number of
instances of breaching. First comes the announcement of the cancelled session. This is followed by the narrative insertion of the
patient's dream as summoned up in my memory (the 'bomb blast'
passes from that remote scene into the current session); and so on.
Albeit with a modicum of explicit interpretation of the transference –
and hence by resorting to the rhetorical device of metalepsis –
while 'changing the frame' I am looking at the same canvas as that
seen by Sara. This may be the only way of not giving 'radioactive'
interpretations – that is, of not replacing both the frame and the

canvas of the picture. Otherwise the patient would again end up 'in captivity', imprisoned – this time for real – in the phalanstery of infinite *de*constructions, annihilated and mortified. Again, 'seeing the same canvas' is necessarily tantamount to a sharing of emotions – and hence to an unpredictable experience. All that can be done is to pave the way for it – to let it happen and to be ready to receive it if it does.

Radioactive or foam–rubber interpretations?

We now move on to the beginning of the next week, when the analysis resumes after the missed Friday session. 'I had a row with a friend of mine,' says Sara. 'I got angry rather than anything else. I can't stand it when I see him being more destructive and defeatist than I am. I need something positive at this time of my life. Maybe he had his own problems. Afterwards he realized that he had offended me, and things settled down again. Yet when I decide not to assert myself, I pay for it by feeling bad, as if such a minor wound had trouble healing. For a mere trifle, although we had been friends for years, I could have ruined everything. Well, that can't happen with him, but it does with women. That's what happens in our family too: "You attack me over such-and-such, so you don't care about me" – and then one feels entitled to destroy everything. All for a moment's disagreement. Then, next day, I found myself looking at a cupboard and thought of my degree certificate; then I recalled something my mother once said to me while she was reading one of my books – that *there were bacteria that destroyed paper*. At that moment it occurred to me that this object might decay. At any rate, I know that there are two destructive agents: air – that is, oxygen – and light. Then I started wondering to myself how I could prevent this decay. I thought the best way of preserving the certificate would be to coat it with plastic, but then the process of plastic coating might itself cause damage. The interesting thing is . . . that I yielded to this frenzy for action and went off to get information, so . . . [laughing] I became an expert on parchment conservation in the space of a few hours! I questioned the first miserable old cow of a *frame-maker, who was not quite all there*: was it better to use two pieces of glass, or silicone, or something else . . .? Then, of course, I didn't do any of these things. As usual, what matters to me is to know something; but as for translating that knowledge into action . . . As soon as I knew, I calmed down. If there's a remedy . . . It was the same obsession as I had when I was small, the same way of thinking . . . *that some object or other might not survive.* Why? Perhaps because it somehow stood for my identity. When I was a child, it was toys. I was obsessed with materials. When I grew up, I thought, I would invent a material for making any kind of object, which would then be indestructible and unscratchable. The sight of a scratch seen against the light really hurt me and disturbed my vision. What is more, all my life I have felt that anything I valued would decay. And I apply this merciless, unpleasant way of seeing to everything – even to myself. Anything subject to time and wear immediately becomes worthless.'

'You didn't expect a misunderstanding like to happen with your *friend* . . . You felt disappointed,' I remark.

'I suppose so,' she answers. 'The thing is, he had his own problems at the time. I was very hard on him, it was over the top, and he was surprised. I'm afraid I insulted him. I cut him to the quick, and then his tone changed completely, to one of mortification, like someone who knows he is in the wrong and needs to apologize. He had been harsh and destructive. I was laughing and joking, and he *threw me off balance.* But then, when I saw how quickly he was able to get back into a dialogue, I felt hurt and irritated inside. *I was offended, like a child who says: "You've hurt me. All right then, I won't look at you any more."* What happened that day – fortunately the "frenzy" I was feeling was quite out of the ordinary – reminded me of my obsession with materials *and my enthusiasm for foam-rubber, which absorbs impacts without deforming,* and how I was once telling a friend about this material, singing its praises and going through all the things you could do with it, as a little girl might imagine them . . . until one day I probably discovered that the only thing that could ` protect my mind from scratches and corrosive agents was the body, and then I *turned my body into an object.*'

'How can the body protect you?' I ask.

'By a very concrete way of looking at things . . . I constructed a body capable of protecting one . . . the idea being that, if it was suitably shaped and reinforced, it could be made of a material able to ward off blows . . . (That's what I think now.) Before *I came in here, I noticed something* – a car parked near the entrance with an *anti-theft device* (called a *Bulldozer*) that covered the entire steering wheel, with a pin that stopped it from being turned. What a cumbersome mechanism – a kind of *excess of defence*, and anyway you could easily defeat it; and all for such a worthless vehicle.'

At that moment I realize that Sara, as she lies on the couch, is facing my bookshelf, and all of a sudden I too 'SEE', so to speak – as if by an abrupt perceptual and emotional reorganization – 'the book her mother was reading'. It is as if it has actually entered the room. Only then do I realize (although I already knew it) that what worries her is the possibility that her analysis might prove to be perishable if her soul is scratched by hate and resentment (the *bacteria*), and that she needs something to enable her to survive, something – an interpretation? – like foam-rubber and . . . a good frame! I tell her that, while light and air can admittedly spoil the books, keeping them in the dark would prevent her from bringing them to life and from feeling emotions, and would deprive her of the pleasure of reading.

'I wouldn't be able to read them,' she answers, 'but . . . *I have never had such a painful, intensely present sense of the transience of things as I have at this very moment.*'

I feel that the irruption of the books (the *perishable objects*) into the consulting room might pave the way for a transference interpretation that will make the metalepsis explicit; the interpretation can be given two minutes, two days or even two months later. It would have been easy, but perhaps again premature, to interpret the meaning of the rage (the *Bulldozer*) and of the silence of *excessive defence* due to the fear of being deprived of an object (the analysis) that is seemingly *worthless*, and so on.

What ultimately seemed clearer to me was a movement I had noticed for some time – a fleeting expression of something like bewilderment on her face and a moment's hesitation – at the end of each session before she leaves the room, treating some books at the end of the shelf to a final caressing glance.

The sense of transience Sara is thereby able to express represents the core of her suffering, a constant turning backwards à la Rilke,[4] the riddle of her 'aching despondency' (Freud 1915b: 305), of her rebellion against her father and her impoverished capacity for love. An opaque affect, as expressed in an awkward silence – but one that, as we saw, is laden with all kinds of other silences! – is transformed into a feeling for which the ego is now inclined to take responsibility. A breach inflicted on meaning (the first unfortunate interpretation, followed by the dream of the nuclear holocaust) reawakens the patient to the event.

The patient's feeling of having been thrown off balance, due to the pain of separation, the transience of things and the fear that my (her) books – that is, my (her) consulting room, or setting – might be spoilt, is re-experienced by the analyst. Only after the temporary vacillation of being not quite all there and the recovery of his inner working attitude – as well as the identity of a decent 'frame-maker'! – is he able to frame a shot from a different viewpoint, having first somehow made sure that he is on the same film set as the patient.

In this clinical fragment, in which the theme of the frame is both dramatized and unconsciously theorized by Sara, I have attempted to show what goes, or ought to go, before an interpretation – namely, an emotion or intuition: *something that surprises*. The unconscious level of the communication in effect leaps out of the frame, and can be recounted only later, perhaps at first using just a few foam-rubber-type materials by which the subject is dislocated without being deformed. If appropriate, this can then be followed by actual transference interpretations (as we all know, even radiation can be a powerful form of medical treatment). Clearly, though, in referring to the *friend* and the *books* – using an open, elliptical, 'unsaturated' approach – the analyst is inspired on both occasions by his own experience of the short-circuiting of narrative levels, or the collapse of the various temporalities; in a fictional narrative this would be equivalent to the simplest, basic case of metalepsis.

What also seems significant to me at the two key moments (the notes and the book) is the sensory spark kindled in the darkness of the scene – as if, one might speculate, every authentic movement towards symbolization had to commence with the materiality of the setting, the body or the meta-ego (Bleger 1967a). In both cases, so to speak, a sensory perception (first tactile and then visual) was needed to set the process of thought in motion again.

In my view, this effect of surprise, or sensation of 'truth' (Ogden 2003b), can help us to avoid the iatrogenic risks of interpretation and to strike a balance between subversion and containment as subsequently mediated by interpretative metalepsis. By this I mean a manifest sensory or emotional event, which, for the purposes of interpretation, assumes the significance of a preconception. This might be an event, a detail, of 'uncommon clarity', which is 'ultra-vivid' and *over-signified* (Rella 1999: 44, translated), arising like a hologram out of the virtual reality of the setting, along the same lines as the intensely clear memories (*überdeutlich* – Freud 1937) that sometimes surface unexpectedly and stand out against a more extensive, fuzzy background.

Other instruments illustrated in the clinical vignette that help to reduce the collateral effects of interpretation are, on the one hand, a rigorous theory of the analytic field and, on the other, a flexible model of interpretation that represents its various degrees of complexity and transparency. Roth's classification (2001) could be extended to so-called weak, narrative, unsaturated interpretations (Bezoari and Ferro 1992a), which I would define as those in which the metalepsis of the analyst and/or of the patient as extradiegetic authors/readers in the patient's or the analyst's intradiegetic story is not made explicit. The narrative or unsaturated interpretation wears a Franciscan habit, shuns arrogance, and administers the necessary 'violence' in the appropriate dose; it presents itself 'without a visiting card' and stays close to the patient's 'unencoded' text. The analyst considers the material brought by the patient as a whole and emphasizes the predominant emotion contained in it, as if a Rorschach inkblot evoked a whole response (W) and a response with colouration (C) (Ferro 1999a: 128). However, if these interpretations too are to be assignable to the area of the transference, the essential requirement is always to regard the facts of the session as possible events of the analytic field.

Hence the degree of saturation of transference interpretations should be inversely proportional to the severity of the patient's pathology. Transference interpretations proper, which may be preceded for a longer or shorter period – sometimes for years on end – by 'barman'-type or 'stupid enough' comments, as Bolognini (2005) might call them, are more suitable for patients with a fairly sound psychic structure, with whom one can work from the beginning with 'undigested facts', and who are better able to tolerate reframing-type interpretations or violations of the frames of the discourse.

Reframing

The potential relevance of semiotic models to Freudian theory needs no further demonstration (Spence 1982; Schafer 1992; Ferro 1999a). The proliferation of narratological literature on narrative frames, from its first post-structuralist outgrowths to Critical Theory, has been paralleled in psychoanalysis by discussion of the role of the setting (*frame, encuadre* or *cadre*), which has come into sharper and sharper focus, especially in the work of authors such as Winnicott (1956a) and Bleger (1967a), as well as of Milner (1952), Langs (1978) and Modell (1989). Roussillon (1995) concentrates on the subject of fortuitous breaches of the setting, which sometimes prove valuable to the analytic process, but which cannot be recommended as an active technique. With regard to his demand for an analysis of the *picture* and of its secret function as the guardian of splits or disavowals, I shall attempt here an initial conceptualization in terms of narratology, postulating that transference interpretation can be seen as a way of producing these breaches in the setting, which, although they often prove with hindsight to have a 'mobilizing' effect, are nevertheless impractical because they are both ethically indefensible and unpredictable in their impact.

Every frame – or margin, border or *parergon* – imposes an order on the story and defines a world within which characters move and plots are structured. The purpose of the performance is to help one of the two actors/protagonists to arrive at a better definition of himself and to construct his own identity – that is, to gain a broader consciousness of self. Identity, by definition, is made up of boundaries, of frontiers. In psychoanalytic treatment the main instrument for facilitating this maturation and activating the micro-transformations that are its substance is transference interpretation, the cornerstone and shibboleth of Freudian analysis. However, if certain notions from the present-day semiotics of literature are applied to the oral or written text of an analysis, it is readily seen that transference interpretation is nothing but a rhetorical construction, whose structure may be akin to that of a micro-story which the analyst addresses to the patient while exhorting him to accept a transgressive change from particular levels of reality to others. Its aim is to facilitate growth of his capacity for thinking thoughts; this can also be expressed in terms of a better integration of his multiple selves.

Let us consider for a moment Louis Malle's film *Vanya on 42nd Street*, which includes a sequence showing a group of actors on their way to a theatre for rehearsals. They go in, and are seen to chatter to each other in what seems for all the world to be a break before starting work, and it is only after a while that one notices that *they are already performing* Chekhov. By means of this artifice the director, while avoiding any discontinuity that might betray the transition to a different plane of representation, achieves a potent dramatic effect. A patient and an analyst are in a position not unlike that of the audience watching Malle's film and its actors.

Transference interpretation can be seen as corresponding to the portrayal of the ambiguous state of transition from one narrative reality to another (Chekhov instead of Malle!). As perceived by the 'audience', this transition is reflected in the moment of disquiet that Freud in his genius summed up in the concept of *Unheimlichkeit*, or the 'uncanny' – in the emotional maelstrom represented graphically in the pivotal point of a picture which, as in Escher's *Print Gallery*, extends beyond the frame, thus causing the image to reflect on itself (Petrella 1993). More classical painters achieve the same effect in less spectacular fashion and with greater realism, and hence with a very different and more convincing aesthetic. An example is the locust placed by Lorenzo Lotto at the bottom of the frame of his *The Penitent Saint Jerome* (now in Bucharest): it is put there precisely as a declaration, by virtue of the difference in scale and perspective, of 'the permeability of two worlds, of the possibility of moving from a physical reality to another that is only virtual' (Lucco 1998: 104, translated).

Interpretation, then, falls between the alien and the familiar. To be effective, it must arise out of areas of overlap between the respective frames of the patient and the analyst. There must in addition be a vertical dimension, which is supplied by the affective content of the interpretation (which also reflects what is happening, or being transformed, in the analyst *before* its formulation), and which thus succeeds in touching the deepest institutional, or 'Blegerian', strata of identity.

The area of overlap is guaranteed by the emotional sharing facilitated by the sequences of enactments that make up the patient–analyst interaction. The experience of being in unison reaffirms the frame and strengthens the floor of the ego. A successful interpretation is thus a paradoxical account that combines these two divergent functions – of subverting the frame and at the same time of confirming its role as a signal of difference, of a boundary and of separateness.

Like the digital processing of a photograph, whereby the various layers can be worked on subtly, separately and consecutively, an interpretation can include a succession of planes, ultimately to be superimposed so as to form a single figure. It is important for the reframing to preserve common areas if it is not to have an excessively destabilizing effect and if it is to bring about a bearable transition from a poorer to a more complex form, without precluding the slight meaning shock that we have in mind when we say that someone is 'moved'.

The patient's responses – cf. 'listening to listening' (Faimberg

1996), the 'narrative derivatives' of waking dream thought (Ferro 1996) or the 'indication of reintrojection' (Bleger 1967b) – which may take the form either of 'receipts for a delivery' or of 'fire alarms', disposed naturally along an extended diachronic scale, will afford clues to the degree of defamiliarization, insecurity and disorientation resulting from an interpretation, or alternatively to the sense of discovery and reintegration thereby achieved. In particular, listening to the narrative derivatives of waking dream thought is one of the instruments for bridging the gap, to which attention was drawn by Bader (1998), between constructivist epistemologies and clinical operationality, between the space accorded to the analyst's subjectivity and attentive monitoring of the responses of the field, of the invalidations or validations of his interpretations. This will enable him to get his bearings among the numerous possible interpretations, while discarding the implausible ones, and not to overlook the patient-specific markers that might constitute signs of validation which can be relied on for understanding and for the hypotheses formulated from time to time by the analyst.

It is essential for interpretations not to be the product of an intellectualistic, mechanical, routine operation reminiscent of those clumsy online machine translations (which may on occasion be useful in providing an initial syntactic outline, but are rudimentary and incoherent), and not to resemble those described by Bolognini (2002: 88, translated, my emphasis) as 'objective, premature, verbose, *enframing* and conclusive': they must always be preceded by an 'effect of presence' of the other scene – namely, the unconscious one – which arises necessarily without being sought and without competition, in the relevant context and situation, like a kind of involuntary memory.

That is what happens when, for instance, a seemingly anodyne detail takes on an extraordinary sensory intensity – when it impresses its stamp because the perception concerned is so vivid as to be almost hallucinatory – thus guaranteeing proper analytic functioning and the emotional truth of what is formulated and communicated to the analysand. Such events can be neither planned nor anticipated. Most of the time, the analyst should stay with the patient's text and respect its surface, allowing himself to be thrilled by the stories interwoven with the analytic conversation and taking care not to force the frame. Experienced as statements that merely decode and are devoid of affect, or, when based on clinical exemplification, as 'radioactive', such interpretations would ultimately substitute the 'terrorist incursions' or 'battlefield offensives' ('shock and awe') of guilt-inducing suppositions for the slight shock and amazed awe stated in the theories of Reik (1933) and Di Chiara (1990) respectively to be components of good analytic work.

4

Immersion versus interactivity and analytic field[1]

The discourse of analysis has a chiasmal structure. The layout of a 'field of fantasies' (Chianese 2006: 21), intended as a space of representation or a fictional device (F), allows the experience of psychic reality (R) and what to common sense seems unreal, as opposed to the concreteness of the material world (F → R). Second, this consciousness of the reality of the inner world becomes so clear that it ends up by revealing the illusory nature (F') of ordinary reality (R → F'). In Freudian and post-Freudian theory, the acknowledgement of the fictional aspect of the analytic situation, its as-if element, has gradually acquired increasing ground, thus allowing the theoretical–technical devices of analysis to become more adequate in highlighting the effectualness of the unconscious.

The theory of the analytic field (Baranger and Baranger 1961–62; Ferro 1992; Bezoari and Ferro 1992b; Gaburri 1997; Baranger 2005) is the extreme product of the radicalization of the artificial character of the analytic scene and, at the same time, presents itself as a strong model of the unconscious social nature of the facts that are represented in it. In this work, using virtual reality (VR) as a metaphor, I show how field theory (FT) seeks to strike a balance between these two aspects, that is to say, the usefulness for the actors and authors of the analytic dialogue to lose themselves in the fiction shaped by the setting – which means intimacy, closeness, spontaneity, emotional intensity, authenticity – and the necessity of coming out of all this in order to access the plurality of the possible worlds in which they simultaneously live.

Fictionality of the analytic frame

In 'Recommendations to Physicians Practising Psycho-analysis', Freud (1912) compares analysis to the receiving and transmitting system of the telephone. This is perhaps the most modern and technological image of all the ones scattered in his writings, which, like golden threads, are woven into the warp of concepts. However, this new metaphor, like others, again presupposes the image of a passive and detached observer. We will need the 'fire at the theatre' of the erotic transference and the discovery of countertransference for challenging this perspective and reconfiguring the roles of both patient and analyst.

At any theoretical turn, psychoanalysis reinforces its specific phenomenological reduction and 'realizes' the psychic. It attributes increasing importance to psychic reality and reduces the weighing of factual reality. Thus, on the analytic scene, the here-and-now and the relationship come into the foreground. The conflict between interactivity (IN) and immersion (IM) is intensified. So is the conflict between the 'external' or meta-narrative vision of the transference interpretation – which, modifying the narrative text through systematic interpolations, leads the patient to discover the rules of the grammar of the unconscious – and the emotional involvement, from 'within', of the analyst who loses himself in the 'novel' of reality and cancels in this way the virtual space of the setting: things, by then, only signify themselves. Interactivity and immersion are not, by contrast, in conflict when the analyst allows himself to become absorbed with the patient in the narratives of the session but remains aware of the fiction and adheres to the manifest text of his discourse without obscuring its unconscious frame. He simply throws on it a weak light by means of unsaturated interventions.

At the beginning of the new discipline, in order to validate his first etiological theory of neuroses, the one of the real trauma, Freud finds the evidence even in the fantasmagory of the dream. However, the dramatic crisis, both on a personal and on a scientific level, concerning the credibility of his 'neurotica' leads him to doubt this model. Freud runs for cover and, as a counter-move, develops, in the notes that he added in 1918 to Chapters 5 and 8 of the Wolf Man (Freud 1918), the concept of '*Nachträglichkeit*'. By supplementing a notion that he had already introduced in 1895, in his third version of the theory of traumatic seduction (Blass and Simon 1994), which he later abandoned, he arrives at his new understanding of a substantial undecidability between reality and phantasy, that is, at a radical crisis in the myth of the subject and of representation.

Thus, by subverting the reassuring, but false or partial 'whodunit' scheme, Freud proposes an antilinear mechanism of psychic causality and a markedly dynamic model of memory. Passing through the Kleinian model of the inner world as a theatre where the meaning pervading the external objects is generated – a hybrid between early Freudian realism, transposed by now to a view of unconscious phantasies as reified elements of a new objective reality, and Freud's subsequent scepticism – we then arrive at an elaboration of the intrinsically deconstructive, interactive and immersive concept of play (Wolfreys 1998). The play, a space for exchanges defined by rules which constantly question their own identity, a space exacting an active participation, is not only a theoretical and technical device essential in child therapy; with Winnicott, it has reached the status of new paradigm of analysis. So are achieved a deliberate suspension of habitual incredulity and a bracketing of reality which, if completely natural when we are faced with fictional situations, have now come to represent two of the main postulates of Freudian technique.

Technologies

The FT develops this trend rigorously, thus aiming at satisfying a poetics and an aesthetics of emotional involvement (how to let one-self be captured by the text and why) as well as a poetics and an aesthetics of disenchantment (how to make one intuit that the text is a fiction and in view of which results). Therefore, I propose on a theoretical level a possible definition of the analytic field as a medium, or means of communication, in which the analyst tries to achieve an optimal interplay between immersion and interactivity, between semiotic transparency and self-referential demystification. I will then try to 'verify' this with a clinical example.

With this aim in mind, and ideally in line with the Freudian image of the telephone, I turn to a new technology, VR, that is to say, to a new metaphor. Moving from Chantraine (1999) who points out the common derivation of *'techne'* and 'text' from the same root, *'teks'*, I suggest that any new technology also implies elements for a new hermeneutics or 'discourse on the text'. I also agree with Ryan

(2001) when she proposes VR as a metaphor of the functioning of the literary text and as a general theory of communication and representation. I extend to the analytic field the use that she makes of the correlated concepts of 'immersion' and 'interactivity'. In the information sciences, 'interactivity' means the possibility offered to the user of modifying artificial systems, for instance, digital texts. 'Immersion', describes by contrast the possibility of 'entering' a computer-simulated VR environment and of interacting 'physically' with the objects within it, of receiving their responses in real time, thanks to an interface adapted to the characteristics of the human body.

VR represents the most illusory technological instrument ever invented, the one that gets the closest approach to the model and to the experience of dream, therefore the most apt for explaining the concept of immersive interaction (immersion + interactivity) in a virtual environment. Interaction does not happen, any longer, with icons or symbols, but completely within the simulated scenarios. It aims to be as natural as possible and enables the user to take points of view otherwise inaccessible. However, before proceeding to a discussion on VR I would like to make some comments on another modern technology, the hypertext. This, in the play of differences and similitudes, is particularly useful for highlighting some of the essential characteristics of VR.

Hypertext

Hypertext (Landow 1992; Briatte 1997) is based on an electronic interactive support. It displays an index from which the reader can choose several routes for visualizing a block of text, knot or lexia (Barthes 1970). A lexia can contain sentences, images, sounds and, above all, links, which are the hypertextual equivalents of reference symbols, to other pages. The hypertext is different from the printed text because of its non-linearity, for the variety of paths which could be activated and, consequently, of stories that can be 'written' while reading. The metonymic relations between the reading units establish bonds of cause–effect. The reader's creativity is emphasized. The rhetorical structure of the hypertext captures his attention, and seduces and guides him. Even though very numerous, the possible itineraries are not infinite, because it is in any case necessary to go through the links containing the events already established by the author. The writer stays in control of the original lexias and of a given number of links, even though he does not supervise the order of succession. The reader's freedom is relative, not absolute. The narrative sequences constructed are essentially of a fragmented, elliptic and repetitive character. If some will appear more coherent than others, the rule is digression. However, the fact that the same elements reoccur in the different narrative plots underlines their significance. Over-luminous lines are drawn which are continuously broken and recomposed within a wider connectivity.

The hypertext continuously expands in different branches, thus heightening the reader's possibilities of choice. Traces, clues, junctions, movement, opening, network, journey, surfing are the terms forming its metalexic. The hypertext is polyphonic, multiple, open, dialogic, discontinuous, unstable, decentred and anti–hierarchical. It is conceived as a network of connections accessible to an interplay of different, and even contrasting, readings. The sense is not located in the text, but, within certain limits, is each time reinvented. There is no absolute centre of authority prevailing on the others and imposing a single perspective. Or rather, given that it is impossible to be completely unideological, there is a centre which constantly moves, thus outlining various perspectives in succession. The reading gets close to the writing, the interpretation to the construction. Eco summarizes this new perspective in one of his most successful books: *Lector in Fabula* [*The Role of the Reader*] (Eco 1979).

The concept of hypertext has value, more than in itself, as a concrete metaphor, and as such vividly represents the degree of interactivity and interpretative cooperation that modern literature theories recognize by now to the reader of any text. It illustrates the basic situation of literary – and even non–literary (!) – signification, and marks the intertextual nature of any text. It is hyperbolic demonstration of the essentially subjective and idiosyncratic nature of the reading/ interpretation process. But it also has value in revealing that, however diverse the constructed stories are, some predetermined narrative links cannot be eluded. We encounter here the classic narratological distinction between '*discours*' and '*récit*', between discourse and story, between the events that are inherent to the plot and the various narrative modes or genres in which they can be told.

In analysis, we can translate this critical instance into the concept of active participation of the analyst to the definition of clinical data and into an anti–essentialist and deconsecrated vision of interpretation.

The interpretation becomes a form of rhetorical argumentation in a process which never has any real final point and which does not allow the reaching of any definite enlightenment or closure. In the maze of narrative, however, some single stories prevail over others because they develop in a more coherent way, thus appearing more significant, or more 'truthful'.

A dream or a dialogue fragment is an open text that when interpreted is recreated by the various reader–writers. The analysand discourse is in its very essence self-deconstructive and aleatory, because it weaves a cloth of signifiers in which designs of meaning not foreseen by the intentionality of the subject are revealed. Along with the analysand discourse goes the so-called evenly suspended attention of the analyst, a sort of 'surfing' on the emotional and imaginative waves of free association. When the analyst intervenes, moving from an emotion, he creates a link, a meaningful connection which organizes the elements of the field in a new, provisional Gestalt. He moves, in a continuous oscillation of the listening vertices, from the paranoid-schizoid (PS) to the depressive (D) position and brings into focus the point in which a thread from the patient discourse ties in with one drawn from his own inner dialogue. Every time that this choice occurs, the operation implies a 'mourning for what is not' and for other possible stories (Ferro 1999b: 745). The narrative transformations of the field are thus the fruit of the relentless work of figurability to which the analytic couple is committed.

The links correspond to associative articulations. As 'selected facts', to use Bion's language, they become for the analysand new texts from which he can select and derive his own interpretations. Fragmented, unresolved plots become more structured constructions, narrative units which can be repeated and inserted in other more articulate interpretative paths. The reader, by now disenchanted, recognizes the artificiality of the connections that organize the text and the non-immediacy of the representations of reality formed by the mind. The activation of associative links is strictly bound to the transference scripts that convey the past[2] and imprint their seal on the quality of the transformations of the proto-emotional and sensory elements of the patient, following the vector $\beta \rightarrow \alpha$, on the events of the individual story and on those of the analytic field. It is not at all, therefore, an arbitrary interpretive drift, as I will try to show in the clinical example. As Barale writes:

'Narration' does not consist in an 'after' in relation to an experience and to the truthfulness of an experience that one has ceased to seek: it is directly, intrinsically and radically constitutive of the experience itself (and of its truthfulness) [. . .] it is not about assuming a renunciatory or naively aestheticizing position, which attempts to replace 'narrations' for reality, for the 'truth' or for 'memory' [. . .] it is on the contrary a position which takes us into direct contact with the actual (narrative) unfolding of the mental experience.

(Barale 1999: 157)

However, it is obvious that the analyst's reveries, which can give suggestions for narrative interpretations, are fundamentally part of the field, because it is argued that they can even be determined by it, and that they can be considered, partially at least, as 'obliged', just like the patient's associations. Therefore, as they are both engaged in the narration of the relational problem of the here-and-now, they strongly anchor the text of the analysis to the realities of the historical, intrapsychic and relational context.

However, compared to the printed text and to VR, the hypertext represents a form of transition. It is situated somewhere between the classic interpreting–deciphering approach and the interpretation-as-co-construction approach, which is centred on the encounter, on the 'who' is speaking, and on modes of signification more than on meanings. Hypertext is multi-sensory and hyper-interactive, that is to say, meta-narratival or self-reflective, but its immersive function is weak and can still be assimilated, in analysis, to all that awakes the patient from the dream of the cure. One could say that it corresponds to a strongly intersubjective but still saturated conception of the interpretation. The transparent, but hard and solid glass of the computer screen separates the two worlds. The medium is still visible.

Virtual reality (VR)

Ferro (1992) has introduced the notion of 'affective hologram', an extension of the less evocative concept of 'functional aggregate', in order to describe the three-dimensional quality of the 'characters' which emerge in the analytic dialogue. If two dimensions of these 'characters in search of an author', the historical and the intrapsychic, are obvious, the third refers to the possibility of seeing them as unconscious representations of the couple in the analytic field and as indicators of the emotional colouring of the dyadic relationship in the here-and-now. In fact a hologram can be observed from several perspectives, thus lending itself as a metaphor for the multiplicity of possible points of view when considering the objects/events of the field. Nevertheless, however much they can be rotated and visualized from all their sides, these 3-D images, represented on a flat screen or projected as holograms, will remain static. The interactivity is limited. The relation will still be the one occurring between an observer and an observed object.

In a VR environment, by contrast, the holographic images become dynamic, change shape, and integrate the fourth dimension of temporality. We enter a new experiential context. The essential characteristic of VR is to reconcile interactivity and immersion. There is no longer the barrier of liquid crystal screen, as for the hypertext, or – thinking of an even lower level of immersivity – the page of a book or a cinema screen acting as interface with a verbal or iconic text. In VR the observer is relating *with all his senses* to an environment which he contributes to shape *in real time* through his own actions. His point of view is completely included in VR, and immersion produces the impression of a direct encounter with reality and an effect of *presence* in the scene of the represented events even when these are complete fantasy. The underlying technology is invisible, because the communication is no longer mediated by instructions, codes and signs.

VR experience is the closest experience to a dream, but this is a dream that can be had while being awake and that can be shared! By contrast, the night-time dream is experienced in a completely passive way – it cannot be interrupted by an act of will, is highly immersive but not interactive. Hence the typical sensation of vividness of the dream experience, which can be more pervasive and potent than in the waking state (Diodato 2005). I am now going to examine some of the characteristics of a VR system: transparency, mapping and accessibility.

Transparency

In VR the body, in its wholeness, becomes a system of channels of communication with the environment. The user has the sensation of moving in a concrete scenario and of relating to its objects as naturally as he would in the real world, in which he could touch, feel and manipulate them. This process of embodiment, this rooting of the experience in the body, which in VR is made possible by the development of specific technological devices, is realized by the analyst through his own 'technologies', through the passage from the two-dimensional transference–countertransference layer to the three-dimensional level and hyper-inclusive structure of the field.

The FT facilitates immersivity because the analyst uses a language which is simple, natural, everyday, and respects the text proposed by the patient, even if only in order to grasp the emotions and the unconscious truth contained in it. He gives priority to the interpretations *in* the transference, that is unsaturated interpretations. He avoids too many interpretative caesuras, which are the equivalent of the abstract symbols of a computer keyboard or of the graphic characters in a text page. The analyst does not hasten to decode the hidden text, thus letting the primary and secondary characters of the patient's discourse develop. As in the Winnicottian squiggle game, he limits himself to adding a pencil mark to the existing drawing, which will help to outline a figure to emerge or be constructed.

Even within the necessary working asymmetry warranted by the setting, the analyst tends to include himself entirely in the field and assesses his part of responsibility in relation to the events occurring in it. These can be thoughts, memories, physical sensations or enactments. He will also assess his responsibility for any other 'climatic' or environmental factor: even the material objects of the setting, be they stable or ephemeral, play a part in the text of the analysis. They are signs, if we apply to the stage of analysis the concept of 'semiotization of the object' of theatre theory (Elam 1980). Handke has thus summarized this concept: 'A chair on the scene is a theatrical chair' (1970: 57). In brief, the more invisible and silent the medium (that is, the setting, the metapsychology and the technique) structuring the virtual scene of analysis, the more the experience is immersive, polymodal and polysensory.

Mapping

Mapping denotes the system which registers the movement of the user within a virtual reality environment, by identifying the position and orientation of the hand and the head in relation to the visualized object. On the basis of the data thus obtained, the characteristics of the objects are modified in real time (Ryan 2001). The construction of the scene depends on the subject's point of view at a given moment. Mapping allows for a *limited predictability* in relation to the consequences of the actions that it continuously traces. In theory, the meanings in relation to the effects that the same VR gesture would produce in the real world could be arbitrary, but in general they tend to be natural. An example, far from the VR world, but obeying the same principle: if I move a file into the AppleMac's waste-paper basket icon, I hear a creeping sound similar to the one that I would produce by throwing some paper into a real waste-paper basket. Mapping systems are matrices of possible correlations; they aim to achieve the maximum level of medium transparency and immersive interaction, but not necessarily to reproduce reality in a faithful way: the scenarios can also be imaginary. This result is achieved by adapting as much as possible the controls to the human body, whose natural perceptive systems are optimized to interact with the real world. Obviously, mapping systems are never neutral. They always mirror the ideology of their makers.

The analyst must also use mapping systems, in his case of a conceptual nature, in order to highlight and construct the connections between events and transformations of the field. For instance, one can consider as immersive a theoretical model which views the analytic session as a series of enactments, if it is true that it is not possible not to communicate and that each communication, even a verbal one, is an act. It is impossible to escape this stream of 'actions' which always entails a quote of unconscious communication. It is a river that cannot be stopped. One cannot withdraw on the shore and 'interpret'. Or rather, one can and must interpret, but with the awareness of being inevitably immersed, or even lost, in the relationship and in the processes of negotiation of meanings. Understanding always arrives, somehow retrospectively. An excess of sense is constantly produced. One is forever running after the sense, but never grasping it, as no sooner does one think it is caught, than it has already transformed itself. The mere 'performance' of an interpretation – as signifiers correspond to body movements (Barthes 1977) – connotes it immediately with new effects of meaning.

Generally speaking, the analyst's theories represent his mapping system. However, in the same way that the satellite or aerial picture of a territory differs from the view of the same area when being there,

81

what matters, in relation to the pursued aims, is the kind of scale employed. The more detailed the model and the more able it is to grasp the most subtle nuances of unconscious communication, the more intimate and immersive will be the experience of the analytic relationship. The listening to the unconscious derivatives in the patient's discourse and the analyst's attention toward his own reveries represent two instruments, among others, which help to construct an accurate cartography. It will be a tool that allows orientation on the ground, that will help to visualize the no-go areas and to reach the patient where he is, to look at things from the same angle, and to live out the emotional consonances which confer rhythm and harmony to the encounter. Of course, the patient has his own theories and his own strategies for the creation of meaning. The work of the analysis can then be seen as a way of negotiating a mutual consent through repeated experiences of unison.

Accessibility

The eventuality of getting lost in a computer-simulated world is for the moment purely theoretical, because the state of VR devices remains rudimentary. So the solution to the problem of accessibility is intrinsic to the very limits of the supporting technology. In order to solve the same problem transposed to the analytic situation – that is, how to resurface from the fiction – one must turn to the technical tool of interpretation.

Just as the world of dreams is only accessible in the waking state, when the mind detaches itself from the colourful and hallucinated matter of dreams, and when the revisions and erasures of memory begin, so is the dream of the session. The interpretation, even if it remains in the analyst's mind, is the device dedicated to the de-immersion, because it is anti-illusionary, metatextual and frame-breaking. Therefore, it is interactive par excellence, as it reveals the fiction, but it is not immersive. It is the agent of metaleptic transgression[3] of diegetic universes, that is, of the spatial–temporal scenarios evoked by the co-produced textuality of analyst and patient. Finally, it is the vehicle of continuous transpositions from the world of the therapeutic relationship to the intrapsychic one, and from the past to the present, and vice versa.

Generally speaking, the more saturated the interpretation, the more visible the medium. A saturated interpretation switches on the house lights in the auditorium. It suspends the virtual reality of the stage of analysis, allowing, at the same time, to maintain a contact with the other possible worlds. At a further level the interpretation shows that the world is a textual world, that everything, even perception, is mediated by signs. As it wakes up the patient from the trompe l'oeil dream of the factual, be it current or historical, it ultimately presents reality itself as an 'effect of the real'. The more realistic the experience of the fictional world of transference, which has, however, a paradoxical reality of its own, the more intense on the emotional level will be the experience of the perspective decentring of the ego and of demystification of the real. Thus, the suspension or attenuation of the text dimension, of the signs and technologies – literally, of the dis- courses on text 'construction' – permitted by the immersive dimen- sion, inaugurates a return to the world of semiosis, of linguistic codes and of the symbolic order.

It is therefore always conceivable that the ideal possibility can occur, where experiences of unison and of emotional sharing render immersive even the transference interpretation. By then it would be possible to renounce the transparency of the medium. By using the new narrative genre of the playing of the unconscious, the patient is ready to insert a second text into the text of reality.

In Arachne's web

It is not the first time that Alessia, a humanities student, who has been in analysis for two years at four sessions per week, tells me of dreams featuring spiders which she finds disquieting and disgusting. Each time she poses the same question: could it not be that they represent the mother, as someone has told her? My impression, in these first minutes of the session, is that everything is happening within familiar tracks, along a predetermined path. It is as if the encounter is – how can I put it? – already *frozen* in a plan, prefigured in advance. I remain silent. But she insists: 'What can it mean? Is that spider myself? Is it . . . you[4]?!' Slightly under pressure I answer that, yes, it is some- thing to do with the neglected corners of the house. This is where cobwebs are found. A spontaneous look at the wall facing the couch had brought to mind what another patient of mine had said, a few days earlier, about the cleaning lady not having removed a little cobweb − alas, still visible − stretching between the bookshelf and the wall. Alessia continues with an intervention which seems to be a turn towards intellectualization: 'And . . . what is Arachne's story? Who had transformed her into a spider? A goddess? A god? And why?' The tone of the voice is 'boiling ice': an intense, concentrated coldness which is at same time exasperated by the tension of a painful feeling of expectation. It does not seem to allow for any of the elusive rituals to which I could resort: silence, for instance. At this point I am aware that I am finding it difficult to preserve a private space of mine. I reflect. Perhaps Alessia only needs to hear my voice. I choose the solution of frankness. *I say that I don't remember.* A few minutes of silence follow. The climate becomes heavier. Only then do I feel, at first indistinctly and then more clearly, that I have lost myself. Things are never so simple. I realize that I was really thinking of the myth of Arachne and wondering in which book I could read the story again. I am now persuaded that by doing so I have gone far from Alessia and perhaps from the most authentic sense of her question − a request rendered even more pressurizing and almost agonizing by its controlled quality. By then, I manage to recover some possible traces for getting back on the right track. At least so it seems to me. Meanwhile I mentally go through the sequence that we have just put into the scene.

Suddenly I no longer see the session as inauthentic, artificial, fore-seen and 'prewoven'. Alessia's seductive strategy, which could have been carefully prepared, is caught off guard by her own language, circumvented by the mechanism of the setting and displaced by the unconscious, precisely when she forces me to admit that, yes, at the weekend I had neglected her (this is a first possible 'story', but others could be possible), I had not thought of her or *remembered* her (and, surprisingly enough this is how I myself come to read my own utter-ance, apparently so interlocutory and spontaneous!). Besides, I think, something of the sort must also have happened with a cancelled ses-sion, on the previous week, on a Friday. However, if there has been a mistake, I still consider that I can make something out of this. So I also, like her, make a rapid incursion into theory. (After all aren't mis-understandings and a certain dissemination of meaning part of the interpretation method? It is not only the slip of the tongue that 'slips'. Sometimes analysts also reason in a dichotomous way. They seem to think that the mind is the perfect mirror of Nature. It is poets, who practise the game of ambiguity, and those philosopher-poets, who recognize themselves in deconstruction, who seem to know a thing or two more.)

Meanwhile, in a fraction of a second, from my personal 'pantheon', Derrida blesses me, while Eco (1997: 31) agrees with the Italian philosopher of the 'weak thought' (Vattimo 1985): 'Yes, being is a little moth-eaten and friable', but he frowns . . . In a corner an old analyst, gloomy, mutters something . . . Another one, perhaps fond of sailing, combative, answers back with a maritime metaphor . . . Ogden (1997), that real Franciscan ('*omnia munda mundis*'), even theorizes, following Winnicott, the usefulness of some drifting and of *uncomprehension* . . . I am taken by a vertiginous stream of thought and I withdraw just in time to avoid the horrid abyss of the apology of misreading!

What really matters, I tell myself, is that comprehension, which is by definition partial, temporary and relative, is activated by a wince, by a shake of meaning, by a light shock. And I think that after all analysis is an art of surprises and of Joycean epiphanies. It was misunderstanding that made me realize how much violence a simple separation can imply, and showed me how the reactualization of abandonment experiences asks Arachne's help with her weaving of the web. By now, the spider can indeed be considered a symbol of maternal negligence, of a 'dead mother' (Green 1983),[5] or frozen by depression and therefore dangerous. (From the corner of my eye I glimpse vague intertextual links: Abraham, 1923 . . . Adams, 1990. However, I try not to follow the impulse of finding refuge in books.) Surely, I say to myself, something has already emerged, and perhaps much more is to come from that apparently ordinary and banal 'I don't remember'.

At this point, although I have found a sort of red thread back to the session, I feel that I have lost contact with Alessia and I wonder where to find her, in which part of the field, with which words. In the meantime, I keep an eye on the little spider, still there, stationary. So, I choose to share with the patient this reflection, that is, the meaning that this sentence of mine may have had for her, in the context of the session. I tell her that her silence after my answer at the beginning of the session makes me think that she considers it confirmation of the fact that I am not interested enough in her, that I neglect her; and that this feeling becomes painful when we have not seen each other for a while.

Alessia answers that it is exactly that. As soon as she detects the least detachment, both in analysis and elsewhere, something is triggered in her. There is no escape. She can't help behaving like a 'spider' and weaving one of her plots, one of her 'texts'![6] She starts by being complacent, only to be invaded immediately afterwards by rage and a thirst for revenge. And she adds, it is not so much a question of a spider, as people are sometimes surprised to discover how poisonous her 'scorpion' bites can be!

A real coup de théâtre! Another character has appeared on the scene. Not a reassuring one, I tell myself, somewhat discouraged. Then I focus on this thought: 'Not a reassuring one'. What is 'not reassuring'?!? Alessia's occasionally mellifluous tone? Or rather her bursts of rage? An inhospitable mind, who cannot remember the myth of Arachne? A 'dead mother'? And what has triggered the story, or rather the multiple stories of this session? Is it Alessia? Or is it my lack of suspiciousness or the hardly analytical ingenuity of my answer, which can also be seen as a kind of self-disclosure at zero degree? Instead of rendering the climate of the session less poisonous, my answer could have made it heavier. Nevertheless, it could have created a space for the expression of something deeper and menacing.

Meanwhile, a new association surprises me. Through some unknown paths, the threatening image of the scorpion's tail is superimposed, in my mind, by the image of the needle for the lumbar injection that Alessia had undergone for an inexplicable occurrence of a high temperature with signs of meningitis, which she had mentioned to me in earlier sessions. An admission to hospital for a few days had followed, and even there the doctor who had seen her had not been spared the usual challenge. It had immediately appeared obvious to us both that the high temperature and the 'risk of meningitis' could represent her usual affective and relational short circuit, which, in analysis, had its correspondence in the more or less conscious fantasy of seducing the analyst. With this in mind, I say to her that this scorpion with a poisoned tail reminds me of that event. I return to her, through this, relying on my preconscious and on the work done around this episode, and using our idiosyncratic lexicon, that the 'meningeal pain' of abandonment, the one she experiences when people do not seem to take care of her, leads to the 'uncontainable' poison of the rage. She defends herself from such rage by enacting the violence suffered through Arachne's strategies. In this way I underline the risks of meningitis she is taking in the here-and-now of the transference, and in her current and past life, with this dangerous game, consisting in becoming, just like Arachne, the victim of yet another abandonment.

However, I must have inadvertently and unintentionally used a pedagogical tone, as Alessia protests: 'But with that Doctor Carter[7] I was honest and correct. *He is no longer telephoning me!* The problem is more with the philology lecturer [*imago* of the father, who abandoned her when she was eight years old to set up a new family, and who is by now a figure totally absent from her life; but also a representation of the risks of psychoanalytical "philology"]. *He is an icy man!*' By now I am on the defensive, 'iced' by her response and taking upon myself, as possible transference personifications, the role of the doctor who is not ringing her any longer and the one of the cold lecturer. Feeling that I am taking a big risk, I say, 'If one has a temperature of 41 degrees C, 37 can seem like ice.' I am trying to convey, in an indirect way, how her intense needs of contact make her feel exposed to even the least distractions on others' part and to any separation, including the 'physiological' ones, of the analysis. She laughs and says: 'Yes, it's true, I am always reproaching you for absurd things . . . like . . . that you are always going on holidays and things like that.' Her tone is now relaxed, no sign of the tension which had characterized the rest of the session. She asks, 'And what needs to be done with that kind of temperature?'

'Oh, well . . . sometimes, in extreme cases, a cold bath.'

I feel that I have talked before having thought and that, at any rate, I have given a technical answer, the answer of a 'reassuring' doctor. Perhaps this is because of the need to cool down the erotic transference, but also because I was reminded of an episode I had been told of a child taken ill while on holiday abroad, *far away* from his parents, who had been saved by this method. She says, 'I understood!' For my part, by contrast, I am left with the impression of having 'enacted' something from a script which is unclear to me and of having played it by ear. I feel that I have still not understood very much. With a certain apprehension, I think of the next session and of what it will hold for me.

Later, I discover that Arachne – because the result of this session, its 'truth' beyond the gloss of dialogue, is *that this time I cannot forget her: she has managed to saturate the space of separation* – used to weave splendid tapestries. In a weaving contest with Athena she represented the outrageous loves between the gods and the humans, and their misdeeds ('*caelestia crimina*', Ovid 1995, vi, 131). By this she incurred the hostility of Athena. So, we are faced with an image of transgression, expressing the theme of incest and of violation of generational boundaries.

In the following session Alessia arrives, breathless, in an anxious state. 'This time you really must advise me!' She tells me that the famous lecturer has unexpectedly touched her hand, in a way that has never happened before, and she is troubled by this. What is she telling me? Did I give her a hand? Or did I fall into the spider's web? Or both? Has she been perturbed by a mistake of mine? Or is it, on the contrary, that she is afraid of intimacy and is defending herself from it?

While Alessia is telling me this episode, I find myself rearranging the cushion that I normally keep on the armchair. Then, finding it uncomfortable, and not knowing where to put it, I take it to my chest and, with an automatic gesture, I put my arms around it. Just a few seconds and . . . I remember how so many times Alessia has told me that she uses the cushion like that, at home, when thinking of the analyst. A representation of absence, I tell myself, something between erotic play and Linus's blanket. What could this gesture of mine communicate in the analysis? What is its significance in relation to what has just happened? Is it the evidence of some subtle violation of the setting? Evidence of the difficult search for a balance between involvement, which can be excessive, and distance, which can become neglect? Or is it an attempt at neither mortifying nor gratifying transference love (Bolognini 1994)?

But Alessia is there, waiting for an answer. She does not know how to behave. Once again, I must resist the impulse to tell her, as she is asking me, what would be right for her. If I did so, I would make her feel guilty. I keep thinking of the hand and of all the possible meanings that it may have. I feel confused and disoriented. Inadvertently, I try to put over my glasses a second pair with an identical frame, the ones for long sight which I keep on my desk! I smile at myself . . . I am surprised . . . I do not remember such a thing happening to me before. What better representation of a need of understanding could I have found! And yet this clumsy gesture helps me to maintain a situation of neutrality, an attitude of waiting, rather than trying to see clearly at all costs. I manage at least to avoid the greater risk of becoming the agent of the superego projections of the patient. I avoid taking a cold and distant attitude. But I also renounce aiming for a closeness which I do not feel is sustainable for Alessia.

I end this clinical section, in which I have tried above all to show the play of interactivity and immersion *in the analyst* in relation to the theoretical model of reference, with the image of the two pairs of glasses. It represents the sense of myopia and uncertainty, but also –

and I do not think I am just trying to reassure myself – something not far from Bion's negative capability, or even the need for a more acute vision that can only be obtained with the microscope's highly sophisticated system of lenses. In any case, I feel that these sessions have changed us and brought us towards greater immediacy and affective intensity. They have left a profound mark on us, a multi-coloured array of threads – of emotions and thoughts – which are waiting to be woven into new stories.

Possible wor(l)ds

The spiders, the scorpion, the cleaning lady, Arachne, the gods, the goddess, the neglected corners of the room, the abandonment, the glasses, the fury, the infectious diseases ward, Eco, the needle, the cushion, the fog, the theories, the authors, Dr Carter, the temperature, the risk of meningitis – these are only some of the countless fantas-magorical characters populating the virtual reality of the analytic field. It is this radical assuming of an antirealist perspective – that is, a fictional perspective, in the sense that everything, in so far at least as there is any sense in keeping a setting, is pervaded virtually by the shadow of transference – that allows to know more in depth, with more affects and more eyes, what these characters have to say about Alessia's inner world and her personal story. Such stringent assumption allows us to see these characters as diffractions of the transference and to treat them, in order to get a closer vision 'with' the patient, as 'restrictions of the field' or *focus points internal to the text of analysis* (Blin 1989). Each character can offer some indication of how a given intervention has been received and help to select the level of the relationship to which the next one can be addressed.

Interventions could in fact be ordered by assigning them to one of the two opposite categories – the immersion category (IM), as in my initial 'I do not remember' and my suggestion of a 'cold bath', and the interactivity category (IN), as in the interpretation of my 'I do not remember' and the equivalence of 'needle-scorpion' – or to the inter-mediate category of immersive interactivity (IN+IM), as in the 'neg-lected corners of the house' and the 'high temperature at 41 degrees'. Ultimately, the various categories differentiate themselves according to whether the fiction is in the background, in the foreground or denied. Various categories can be active simultaneously. For instance,

I offer the saturated interpretation on the effects produced by my 'I do not remember' because I think that Alessia may experience it as immersive and not as an unpleasant cognitive turn.

The meaning of the session is gradually outlined as the micro-stories are arranged in greater units. In the end it can be seen that the same plot is repeated in a series of different worlds, different ways and different words. The central phantasy is incest, the violent sexual inter-courses of Zeus with humans, represented by Arachne in her tapestry, which becomes *the point of maximal fiction* in the text of the analysis. The maximal fiction coincides with the truthfulness of the ancient stories of 'crimes by the gods'. But this narrative framework is only the last of a series of vertiginous duplications *en abyme*: the same story is repeated somehow in Alessia's biography, in the vicissitudes of her current life, in the transference, in the myth of Arachne's competition with Athena (*mythos* = thread!), and lastly, indeed, in the subject chosen by Arachne for her woven text (Civitarese 2006a, 2007a).

Now, what is important is whether the analysis can constitute itself as a representational space of this story, that is, to fall ill with Alessia's disease. But also, whether it can cure it. In this vignette I have tried to show how all this happens; how the contact with the truth of the patient's inner world is constantly lost and refound – a truth that can only be subjective and can only be based on emotions and on the shared experience. It is the analyst's 'second look', that is, the use of his countertransference experience, the attention to his own reveries and the listening to the unconscious communication of patients – how do they receive an interpretation and how they experience ('picto-graph') the relational instant – that regulates the degree of interactiv-ity or immersion of the interventions and guides the diagnosis and the cure of the field's illnesses (Ferro 2006).

Indeed, the emergence of the Linus's blanket character, concealed by the cushion as an image of reciprocal seduction, as well as the emergence of the far-away-from-home-and-ill-child character, hid-den in turn by the feverish excitement of the erotic transference, speaks of the more archaic drama of the absence of the mother and then, in the cure, the absence of the analyst. Thanks to this reverie, the unexpressed backstage of my response, a contact with the glacial, depressive climate of the internal world of the patient, which needs to be warmed up by the fever, is realized. In the analysis, this pattern had been represented several times. It was sufficiently known. But how true that each session is as if it was the first! From this point of view, my initial 'I do not remember' and the two pairs of glasses can also be seen as symptomatic of a good internalization, as one of the analytic field's technologies, of Bion's theory of negative capability.

In order to construct its fictional truths, seen as the fruit of a dramatization which takes place within the frame of the setting, an analysis requires its actor-authors, or reader-writers, to lose themselves in the story and then to re-emerge from it. After each oscillation the analyst tends to return to the equilibrium point of the inner setting/or of the immersive interactivity. He tends to interrupt the immersion with the interpretative ruptures, constantly keeping contact with the other levels of the real through a disciplined use of his reveries, that is, of the dreaming state of abandonment to the preconscious allowed by the immersive device of evenly floating attention. The field itself indicates, through the various characters of the sessions, when it is necessary to become immersed and when it is necessary to come back to the surface. It indicates the amount of oxygen needed to explore the 'seabed' of the relationship in a way which is safe, but also effective, that is affective. In fact immersion is valuable because it enables, in the here-and-now, the activation of transference patterns involved in the emotional conflict, and because there is no change without a passionate attachment.

Moments of re-emergence in the clinical vignette include: the cushion leading to Linus's blanket; the two pairs of glasses, which preclude any premature crystallization of the sense; the 'heroes' of psychoanalysis, because they mean 'closeness' and because theory is the 'third pole of reference for the construction of the virtual space of the analysis' (Chianese 2006: 21); Alessia's silence; the *retroactive* reflection on the experiences and the acting within and outside the session: for instance, how to re-read Ovid. These are moments of shock which make one go beyond the theorizing of the erotic transference as resistance (a concept that, if reified, can constitute itself as a β-screen or a bastion in the field). They allow us to see the defensiveness of my somewhat pedagogical comment of the 'needle = scorpion' and to consider the answer relating to the poison of the scorpion not only as a negative reaction to the interpretation but also as the emotion of rage that can eventually be expressed. A greater degree of intimacy in the relationship would have by then permitted some split-off aspects to make their appearance. These are dangerous aspects, but already less dangerous; closer, in other words, to being perceivable and thinkable.

The clinical vignette exemplifies some of the properties of the analytic field which, as hypothesized in this work, configure it as a medium in which an ideal equilibrium between interactivity and immersion is sought. I will try to summarize my points: the naturalness of interaction and the invisibility of the theory and technique (*transparency of the medium*); a qualitative, and not quantitative, vision of the analyst's participation – one which preserves a space for privacy and silence; an awareness of the conventional character of theories, and a theory of psychic transformations (*mapping*); the hyper-inclusiveness of the field and an extended conception of enactment; the narrative structure (*tensivity*) and its continuous pace; the auto-reflexivity of the analytic setting (Arachne representing in the tapestry the violence she is suffering in her contest with Athena by weaving with precious threads archaic stories – '*et vetus in tela deducerit argumentum*', Ovid 1995, vi. 69); the conceiving of the transference interpretation as interactivity, that is as non-immersive interaction, at least at a first degree, and the privileging of its unsaturated, narrative forms; the deferring of the sense, and the way comprehension is reached through recursive patterns; the focusing on the here–and–now of the session, on the unconscious narrative derivatives of the patient's discourse, and on the analyst's reverie and countertransference as indicators of the couple's affective functioning, and possible indicators of the degree of comprehension of the patient's inner world (Ferro 2002b); the emotional and intellectual ability to tolerate the paradoxes of the analytic situation, to accept the ambiguity[8] of one's own and the other's identity, to write the text of an adventure while simultaneously living it out with passion; the presence *in* the consulting room, in the processes of negotiation of meaning, of the intertextuality of theories and of the different communities to which we belong as the indispensable anchorage to a consensuality which goes beyond the therapeutic couple and limits the intepretive drift; the asymmetry of roles reflected in the fact that the analyst's deliberate suspension of incredulity, necessary to the immersion, is never absolute nor definitive.

If there are moments in which the inner setting reaches the zero point and he himself 'hallucinates' the real, the analyst has learnt, just like one of those 'amphibious creatures who are plunged simultaneously in the past and in the reality of the present' which are human beings for Proust (1993 [1913–1927]: 610), to use that amphibian state of mind that we call 'reverie'. The analyst, too, can be behind the window and in the street, in a daydream, trying to capture, as in the fascinating paintings of Paul Delvaux, the unreal and the natural world.

Escape from *The Matrix*

The field model redraws the analytic situation as an artificial, immersive world. The rigorous inclusiveness of the field is the same as the oneiric world. Analyst and patient alike stipulate a virtual world whose ontological status is different from the factual, external world, but is homogeneous to the oneiric, to the unconscious, and to psychic reality. Any event is seen above all as rooted, by virtue of the transference, in the here-and-now of the session, generated by an intersubjective matrix (Ogden 1991). In the verbal and non-verbal exchanges of the analytic field there are no 'neutral', purely denotative objects, but only elements of a differential system of signs, that is, a text.

History in itself is a place of the field, a narrative gender of it (Ferro 2002b). Historical reconstruction in itself has no therapeutic significance, but only as a reflection of an increased ability of the mind to symbolize, that is, to give shape to the experience. It is a 'by-product' (Meltzer 1984). It is only secondarily that the development of the α-function resignifies even the History, here meant as the biography of the patient. But the reciprocal is not true. Historical reconstruction is not indispensable for expanding a subject's ability to think his own emotions.

No text, however, can afford to be completely self-referential. It is, instead, part of a net, connected to other texts, histories, events which belong to several worlds, real or imaginary. Therefore, the historical and material world remains – in a process of circularity which can be visualized as the two faces of a Möbius ribbon, continually shifting into each other – the basis of comprehension, that is, the 'encyclopaedia' of the fictional world.

> No fictional world could be totally autonomous, since it would be impossible for it to outline a maximal and consistent state of affairs by stipulating ex nihilo the whole of its individuals and of their properties [. . .] A fictional text abundantly overlaps the world of the reader's encyclopaedia.
>
> (Eco 1979: 221)

However, in clinical practice certain data can happen to be read not as signs, both real and constructed or 'fictional', but only as referential, thus mute for the transference relationship, insignificant, in a certain way inert. If taken literally, these emissaries from the physical world, and of 'what has really happened', induce a paralyzing effect of reality. This is the immersive situation in which the playful space of the setting is erased. Reality is experienced as the dream without a reawakening of the humanity imprisoned in the virtual world of *The Matrix* (Wachowski and Wachowski 1999), which is a perfect allegory of a machinal or 'alexythymic' mental functioning.

In order to escape from the Matrix one needs interpretation. Whether or not explained, interactive or immersive, saturated or unsaturated, intepretation allows all the knowledge, the maps and the histories conceived in the consulting room to be exportable into the real and historical world or into the inner world of the patient. Vice versa, the elements of the field can be intelligible on the basis of experiences, facts and structures external to it. The interpretation is the operator of exchanges or the metaleptic device which makes possible the passage from some given diegetic levels or narrative worlds to others counter-distinguished by a different ontological status.

The cure aims in fact to help the patient, loaded with hyperluminous memories and traumatic and frozen events, to play or to dream (Ogden 2003a) or, better, *to dream while being aware of dreaming*, given that the dream experience, in itself, belongs more to the register of the hallucinatory. What matters is that the patient manages to discover those virtual worlds in which, as for each one of us, his multiple selves cohabit.

Interpretation can act as a shuttle, because it is anti–illusionist. It breaks the transparency. It abandons mimesis. It reveals the technical devices of the mise-en-scène. It keeps at a distance. It practises discontinuity. Paradoxically, it also has another function: if the timing is right, it produces an effect of immediacy, reality and intensity. But when it is not a success, because it is 'violent', or inefficient because it stops the play, thus coming across as intellectualized, it can adversely affect the field.

FT aims at preventing the illnesses of the field by seeking to strike a balance between the immersive techniques (an open attitude, playfulness, curiosity, involvement, attunement: a poetics like the Actors Studio, which is based on Stanislavski's method of deep personal identification and lifelike, realistic performance) and the interactive techniques which risk of interrupting too abruptly the fiction (a poetics of Brechtian estrangement). In fact, if interactivity prevails, too much emotional distance is created. If by contrast it is total, non-interactive immersion in the real that lasts for too long, as in the β-world of *The Matrix* (Cartwright 2005), the virtuality of the field is lost. Signifier and referent then short-circuit on the concrete and the historical.

The technical indication that can be inferred from these notes is for the analyst continuously to reconstruct an inner setting (Alizade 2002), 'an amphibian state of the mind', which helps him not to lose sight of the significance of what happens in the here–and–now and not to awake the analysand prematurely from the dream of the session. Ultimately, it can be the transformations in the analyst that constitute the factors of the cure, while the latter can, in certain cases, be carried out apparently and mostly on the level of a 'normal' conversation.

5

Nachträglichkeit

Discussing the issue of the *après-coup* at a recent meeting
with some English-speaking analysts, I was struck by
how difficult we found it not just, I would say, to
understand each other, but even to know what we were
talking about.

(Le Guen 1982, translated)

Retranscribing memory

The concept of *Nachträglichkeit* appears for the first time in Freud's
letter to Fliess of 6 December 1896: 'As you know, I am working on
the assumption that our psychic mechanism has come into being by
a process of stratification: the material present in the form of memory
traces being subjected from time to time to a *rearrangement* in accordance with fresh circumstances – to a *retranscription*' (Masson 1985: 207).
At this time Freud was grappling with the formidable problem of
memory and its fallibility, and was just embarking on the process of
revision that was to culminate in the painful experience of abandonment of the infantile seduction theory. The 'official' date of this crisis
is, however, later: it is that of the other famous letter to his Berlin
friend and correspondent – namely, 21 September 1897. He wrote:
'And now I want to confide in you immediately the great secret that
has been slowly dawning on me in the last few months. I no longer
believe in my *neurotica*' (Masson 1985: 264).

Freud's theory of the aetiopathogenesis of neuroses presents itself
from the outset as a theory of memory. In what was to become a
famous formula, he postulated that hysterics were suffering from
memories, or rather from the repression of memories concerning

96

sexual traumas. Years later, in 'Constructions in Analysis' (1937), he added that the same applied to psychotics. Yet, until October 1895 at least, these traumas were seen as real events. It was only with the 'third' seduction theory that the revolutionary shift from an epistemology of representation to one of construction occurred (Blass and Simon 1994). The fundamental new idea was that memory possessed a dynamic structure: memory traces could take on a different meaning and on occasion become pathogenic as a result of subsequent events. This would explain the dramatic discrepancy between the memories of infantile sexual traumas so frequently reported by patients in analysis, which, however, often ultimately proved false, and accounts of actual facts. After this turning point in his theory, Freud was to interpret seduction scenes as fantasy reconstructions having the aim of masking infantile autoerotic activities.

Yet the extraordinary intuition that led Freud to formulate the concept of *Nachträglichkeit* came to be marginalized in the subsequent development of his own theories. In the case of Freud himself, this is because, whereas on the one hand he was introducing a bold and original theory of memory, on the other he seems to have continued to adhere to the dictates of an empiricistic psychology in seeing memories as 'simulacra' of perceptions – that is, as the recording and preservation of fixed memory traces or engrams in specific areas of the brain.

However, the sophisticated dialectic between past and present established by *Nachträglichkeit* is blurred in post-Freudian theoretical developments, in which the concept is only intermittently granted the right of abode. First, the sense of the subject's history is reduced in its significance in favour of the here-and-now and of the present relationship, while, second, it is subjugated to the hypotheses of a developmental psychology that assigns value to it only from the perspective of a rigid genetic determinism (Baranger *et al.* 1983). In other cases the concept seems manifestly to have been misunderstood, as in Strachey's English rendering of *Nachträglichkeit* as 'deferred action' in the *Standard Edition* of Freud's works. Critics hold that this terminological choice achieves the negative result of reducing a complex principle of mental functioning and causality to an economic theory of abreaction. In this overall landscape a relatively isolated position is occupied by Lacan (1966), as the only author to discern the full importance of Freud's concept, which he summed up in the term '*effets d'après-coup*'.

Laplanche and Pontalis must take the credit for a particularly clear illustration of the concept of *Nachträglichkeit*, albeit one that is not entirely lacking in ambiguity. The authors of the celebrated volume entitled *The Language of Psycho-Analysis* begin by drawing attention to the concept's relationship with the Jungian notion of 'retrospective phantasies (*Zurückphantasieren*)'. They therefore go on to summarize some of its characteristics as follows: the rearrangement or retranscription of memories concerns what it has not been possible to assimilate or integrate in memory (i.e. by definition, trauma); this mnemic activity is occasioned by life situations subsequent to those recorded in a given memory, such as individual maturational processes and in particular – owing to its diphasic nature – sexual development; and the transformative activity of memory assigns to past events, in the widest sense, new *meanings*, unprecedented *effectiveness*, or a *pathogenic potential*.

Freud's conception, then, is far more complex than that of Jung, which seeks primarily to identify the defensive character of retro-active imaginary constructions – that is, how the individual can evade the potentially overwhelming 'demands of reality' by abandoning himself to illusory channels of escape. Freud's model, on the other hand, is thoroughly modern in its radically constructivist view of knowledge, which anticipates by nearly a century the present-day theses of, among others, the exponents of the so-called epistemology of complexity, certain aspects of Edelman's theory of the mind, and some key points of Derrida's critical philosophy. In psychoanalysis, this model has secured for itself a permanent domicile in the ideas of the intersubjectivist schools.

Memory as a higher level organizing principle of consciousness or activity of recategorization

The theory of mental functioning due to Gerald Edelman – winner of a Nobel Prize for medicine and founder (in 1981) and director of San Diego's Neurosciences Institute (NSI) – which is known as 'neural Darwinism' or the theory of neural group selection (TNGS), is considered by Antonio Damasio (1999) to be the most exhaustive attempt ever published to address the subject of consciousness. This highly complex theory cannot be summarized in a few lines. I shall therefore confine myself to drawing attention to some fundamental points, in particular as regards memory.

Edelman sees the mind as a process resulting from the activity of cerebral systems organized on various levels – molecular, cellular, organismic and transorganismic. For the individual, the mind has an adaptive function. Its appearance, which can be regarded as coinciding with the acquisition of intentionality (awareness always has an object), has been rendered possible by events describable in terms of an updated Darwinian theory, on the level of the morphology of the central nervous system. These events can be thought of as the emergence of a field of possibilities based on the interaction of constitutional and environmental factors: systems of connection between neural maps are structured, and the most favourable solutions are subsequently selected. Memory is the higher level organizing principle or keystone of consciousness, permitting as it does the formation of concepts, or 'maps of perceptual maps', and the development of a consistent model of past, present and future. Consciousness is a 'remembered present', the fruit of a dynamic perception between memory and current perception (Edelman 2004: 55). In a system of this kind, memory can function as the relay that correlates perceptual activity with the value system expressed by the hedonic centres, and is at the same time endowed with both species-specific characteristics and others determined by individual history. These value systems have a peculiar feature: 'by projecting diffusely, each affects large populations of neurons simultaneously by releasing its neurotransmitter in the fashion of a leaky garden hose. By doing so, these systems affect the probability that neurons in the neighbourhood of value-system axons will fire after receiving glutamatergic input' (Edelman 2004: 25). Furthermore, they 'could provide a basis for the selective inhibition of pathways related to particular memories' (p. 95), and hence also to repression.

Memory, then, takes the form of a system that integrates various neural subsystems. Its neurophysiological mechanisms are so complex and its network of connections so extensive that it is itself inevitably subject to continuous variation and recasting. Edelman compares it to a glacier. Input signals (climatic conditions) give rise to dimensional variations; the neural pathways are the rivulets of water flowing downstream; and the output signals are the pool at the bottom in which the rivulets come together. Subsequent cycles of melting and refreezing (i.e. variations in synaptic strength) may result in the formation of different channels, which can also merge. This does not necessarily mean that the output signal (the pool) is very different from what it was before. The degeneration of the neural pathways (the rivulets) – that is, the capacity of different structures to perform the same function or to achieve the same result – accounts for the necessarily associative rather than representational character of memory.

Hence memory, rather than being reducible to one of its components, 'is a system property reflecting the effects of context and the associations of the various degenerate circuits capable of yielding a similar output. Thus, each event of memory is dynamic and context-sensitive – it yields a repetition of a mental or physical act that is similar but not identical to previous acts' (Edelman 2004: 52). An individual's adaptation to the facts of external and internal reality is based on a continuous process of 'focusing'. Memory, which is so closely correlated with the self, is the location of this process of incessant matching of present and past perceptual categorizations. It therefore presents an extremely dynamic structure – not as a mere warehouse for the storage of data, but as a laboratory in which the most suitable solutions are constantly being sought, albeit subject to certain constraints, within a field of variable extension which is, however, not infinite in its possibilities. 'Re-entry' phenomena – that is, the parallel connections between independent neural maps that permit perceptual categorization, or, in a sense, a transfer of data that saves on perceptions and allows the formation of concepts – undergo a further, experience-based, selection within the memory system: 'Because of synaptic change, responses to present inputs are also linked to previous patterns of responses' (Edelman 1992: 90). In this way, the subject's sensorimotor activity constantly selects, and thereby reinforces, some neuronal circuits at the expense of others.

Unlike the situation in a computer-type model of the mind, which would be endowed with replicative memory, in Edelman's theory changes on the various levels of organization take place by way of epigenetic mechanisms (which are dependent not directly on genes, but on factors external to these or on cytoplasmic factors that regulate their expression); they are not pre-specified but depend on configurations of neural activities ('Neurons that fire together wire together' – Edelman 2004: 29). They occur within a selective system, depend on context – that is, on the subject's history – and, involving as they do modifications of structure by way of variations in synaptic strength, activate an intrinsic autopoietic function. Imbasciati (2005: 75, translated) describes this function as an 'active process of self-growth of mental functions: the mind as the progressive construction of ever more complex symbols; *symbolopoiesis*, in the sense that the acquisition of one symbol makes possible the genesis, or *poiesis*, of a further symbol and determines its quality.' A memory trace is a *function*, a thought that determines the mode of formulation of another thought, and not a mere inert content deposited in an archive; it is the device by which the world is read.

According to the theory of 'neural Darwinism', the brain resembles the immune system in taking the form of a somatic facility for selective recognition, a device that organizes itself and can undertake the categorial definition of objects concerning which it lacks a priori instructions, in a world without labels. It is a system which, subject to certain constraints, presents structural variability and an extensive repertoire of possible responses to external and internal disturbances, these responses being selected a posteriori on the basis of actual comparison with the environment. Memory is the system constant that guarantees the continuity of the self in the chaotic and ever variable flow of stimuli. Moreover, it is organized not as a set of fixed memory traces – which would presuppose an impossible invariability of context – but only as the device that carries out the continuous search for and selection of perceptions on the basis of criteria of similarity, thus undertaking a recataloguing activity based on the capacity to categorize. There is no such thing as two identical memories. Even in the case of names, numbers and the like, the context always varies. In each case it is a matter of categorial rather than properly specific references. The adaptive value of memory lies precisely in the fact that it increases the number of categorial responses that can enrich learning.

Edelman bases the more speculative hypotheses in his theory on the sometimes surprising findings of neurobiology. He himself contributed to the discovery of the morphoregulatory cells that organize the formation of neural networks. Before birth, it is the position occupied by cells at a given time – this therefore being a context-dependent parameter – that determines their fate on the basis of variations in adhesiveness. Neural Darwinism merits the attention of psychoanalysts for a number of reasons. Edelman criticizes behaviourism, which he regards as a new edition of Cartesian dualism, and cognitivism[1] as 'scientific aberrations'; he holds that physics (or rather physicalist reductionism) is inappropriate for the study of biological systems, which have had a historical evolution; he attributes a key role to context and history in the subject's mental organization; he renders the antithesis of nature and culture obsolete with the concept of *epigenesis*[2]; and, lastly, he maintains that a theory of knowledge, of the observer, of meaning and of intentionality is an essential part of a model of brain function. Again, it is on the basis of these premises that he redefines memory and mental causality – which are, as we know, among the primary objects of psychoanalytic reflection.

Repetition as a fundamental biological function

Indeed, it was a famous psychoanalyst, Arnold Modell, who took the view that Edelman's theory of memory was revolutionary precisely because it provided a neurophysiological basis for Freud's concept of *Nachträglichkeit*. Memory, he noted, is no longer seen as a recording that is isomorphic as between the event and the memory trace. What is stored in 'memory is not a replica of the event, but rather the *potential* to generalize or refind the category or class of which the event is a member' (1990: 64). This thesis can constitute the starting point for the critical reformulation of a key psychoanalytic concept such as the compulsion to repeat, which is in turn bound up with trauma theory.

In Freud's theory the compulsion to repeat, a phenomenon that manifestly conflicts with the pleasure principle, is traced back to another biological force of a highly speculative nature, the death drive. Modell holds that the neurosciences do not offer any evidence in support of the existence of the death drive, whereas certain data suggest an alternative interpretation, which is also biological in character. The compulsion to repeat could be explained by the need constantly to rediscover a perceptual identity between past and present in terms of both conceptual and affective categories. The search for these perceptual identities clearly has adaptive significance and constitutes the very foundation of the sense of time[3] and of the continuity of the self. Just as, in the immune system, an encounter between a given antigen and the relevant antibody is resolved by development of the potential to confront any similar event occurring in the future faster and more effectively, so the rediscovery of perceptual categories that have been used before and their reincorporation in ever-changeable contexts would 'prevail' over the search for pleasure in so far as it would permit active exploration and mastery of the environment.

For this reason, a description in relational terms of the search for object constancy, of the tension directed towards the finding of elements of identicality and of the manner in which reality testing is structured seems to be a more appropriate explanatory model than traditional drive-based notions. In this context, *Nachträglichkeit* as a theory of the origin and fate of traumatic manifestations would represent a limited, circumscribed application of a general principle of mental functioning. Repetition would no longer be in thrall to a blind, destructive demoniac force along the lines of the death drive, but would coincide with the activity of an ego engaged in the unceasing (re)organization of time. It would then be a fundamental biological function, a kind of flywheel of psychic activity, and the very heart of the work of memory and of learning phenomena.

Retroactive temporality and psychic causality

Formulated by Freud to address the problem of the aetiopathogenesis of the neuroses, the concept of *Nachträglichkeit* – mentioned by Edelman (1992) in his best known text, *Bright Air, Brilliant Fire: On the Matter of the Mind* – is the theoretical foundation of an extremely complex principle of psychic functioning which is remote from commonsense conceptions. In the view of some authors, the possibility of temporal slippages, whereby a past event acquires new effectiveness by virtue of occurrences subsequent to it, introduces a new idea of causality definable as *bidirectional*, and hence different from the Newtonian causality of physics. This has opened the way to aetiological theories that postulate a radical discontinuity between psychoanalysis and developmental psychologies. In addition, criticism has been levelled at 'strong' historico-genetic models of psychic causality such as that of the Kleinians, which are deemed to run the risk of imprisoning the subject in a closed temporal horizon – as Thomä *et al.* (1991) comment ironically, in a kind of neo-Calvinist doctrine of predestination.

In fact, as indicated earlier, the distinction between cyclic/circular time as subjective/psychic time, on the one hand, and linear/physical time, on the other, remains controversial. This is clear, for example, from the polemical tone assumed by Thomä *et al.* (1991) in accusing Laplanche and Pontalis, Lacan, Wetzler and Baranger of having, in their understanding of *Nachträglichkeit*, endorsed what they see as the illogical conception of a 'retrocausality'. The judgement is in some cases too severe, considering that, for instance, Laplanche and Pontalis seem to characterize retroactivity only as a retroactive *illusion* – and that in the definition of *Nachträglichkeit* they refer only to *memory traces* as the elements that are assigned new meanings or as the vectors of a new effectiveness; these authors certainly do not claim that the past *as it actually was* can be modified. Some ambiguity might be discernible in another of their introductory statements, to the effect that the concept of *Nachträglichkeit* excludes 'the summary interpretation which reduces the psycho-analytic view of the subject's history to a linear determinism envisaging nothing but the action of the past upon the present' (1967: 111f.). In the absence of further clarification, this assertion potentially lends itself to conflicting interpretations, including that of a presumed reversal of Newtonian time.

The logical scandal represented by these ideas can perhaps be resolved only by recourse to systems theory. The paradox of different, alternative conceptions of temporality and causality results from the fundamental antinomy governing the relationship between knowledge and reality – that is, from the simultaneous existence of, on the one hand, a subjective construction bound up with the individual history and with idiosyncratic elements and, on the other, the possibility of sharing a set of natural constraints with an external observer and hence of arriving at consensual judgements.

What happens as seen from a hypothetical external perspective is that it is *the memory*, in the widest sense of the word, of a prior event that is remodelled or assigned a new meaning on the basis of subsequent experiences and takes on a new effectuality from the moment when this occurs. Rather than on the past, the present acts causally on the *(present) recording of the past*, which is indeed modified within certain limits and is incessantly recontextualized. *The past also changes*, in so far as new meanings come to be assigned to it, but only on the metaphorical level and as regards the subjective 'illusion', because, after all, the process of rewriting and resignifying memory traces takes place in the here and now. In other words, we do not possess a time machine. In order for full advantage to be taken of the concept of *Nachträglichkeit*, there is no need to postulate any kind of retrocausality or reversal of the arrow of time, since all the interactions described by the relevant theory take place between the contents present simultaneously in the psychic system of conservation of memory traces.

From a point of view internal to the system/observer, on the other hand, the word 'illusion' is misleading because it minimizes the radically constructive character of cognitive processes in relation to both present and past reality. These processes are situated outside the realm of any logic of one-to-one correspondence, of a perfect mirror-like match between words and things. At the same time, they draw attention to what can be described as the fallibility of the subject's perception and memory, a concept that also includes its opposite – namely, the presumption of an ideal locus of observation and explanation, of a 'divine' vision of the world, or of what Derrida would call a metaphysics of presence and of the 'originary'. It may be supposed that, on the contrary, the present, and indeed also the past, is constructed continuously, and that there is no such thing as a past that is true in itself, outside the possibility of interpretation, that is *out of context or of the text ('hors-texte')*. In other words, the frame is an essential part of the picture and not a mere ornament; the past changes and, in its various versions, influences the present and the future in ever-varying ways. Hence the assertion that it would be illogical to conceive of a non-linear causality would be tantamount to espousing a representational epistemology in which what changes is the memory (the representation) of an external *objective* reality, as opposed to a constructivist epistemology, in which the same reality was/is constructed continuously by the subject in a manner *subject to certain constraints*.

The aspects of the past that cannot change are precisely these constraints, which exist although they are difficult to describe, even if this entails a need to accept the logical aporias resulting from the attempt to account for them in accordance with a criterion of absolute truth and not merely on the basis of intuition. For it must not be forgotten that this construction is subject to certain invariants and regularities, which stem from natural selection and ultimately from the physical coordinates that make life possible, and that its purpose is adaptive in nature, in the sense of a subjective but nevertheless effective recognition of a domain different from the mind. From the subject's point of view, the past can, paradoxically, be said to be no more closed than the present, but just as there are limits to the 'construction' of the present, so too there are limits to the recontextualization of the past.

It follows from this approach that the principle of viability, in the sense of appropriateness and/or adaptation, comes to be the indispensable frame within which the problems of temporality and causality must be addressed. The updated version of the concept of *Nachträglichkeit* – i.e. of a theory of memory as an activity of recategorization – is consistent with modern constructivist paradigms of the mind and of knowledge, and confirms the genius of Freud's insight. In these paradigms, versions of the past or present that are to a greater or lesser extent *true* do not exist, but only ones that are to a greater or lesser extent *viable*, or capable of being experienced. In place of the metaphysical conception of 'truth', Edelman has contributed inestimably to the final acceptance of the evolutionary criterion of *adaptation*, which is here understood in the sense used by von Glasersfeld – quoted in Ceruti 1986: 70 – not as 'progress towards a better match with the environment, but rather in terms of finding viable paths'.

Repetition, memory and categories of the traumatic

Arguing on similar lines to those of this chapter, Garella (1991: 534) holds that memory, as the 'almost indispensable function of recording variations in phenomena through time' and of neutralizing environmental disturbances, is necessary to the stability of psychic organization. Repetition is seen by this author as a 'regulative tie' (p. 542) and as such serves the purpose of conservation, thus assuming manifestly progressive significance. From this point of view, a relevant notion is the theoretical definition of the concept of categorial memories – that is, preverbal, non-representational memories, sensorimotor and affective schemata that constitute the precipitate of past experiences and at the same time appear as the containers of subsequent experiences.

Now if there is anything radically anti-conservative, an event that is the absolute antithesis of memory, it is trauma. The sudden irruption of painful affects thereby involved destabilizes the sense of self, the horizon of time and the logical order of events; it plunges the very possibility of producing meanings into crisis. By definition, trauma is aggression or a lacerating wound, with the risk of psychic collapse. It may on the other hand be wondered if its repetition, in accordance, precisely, with the model of categorial memories, might not in fact represent an attempt by the function of memory which the subject still somehow retains to become a memory (in the sense of something remembered) and to gain access to consciousness. Might this repetition not, in particular, bear witness to the tension of the ego directed towards repairing the breach that has occurred in the psychic envelope, towards incorporating the disorganizing event in a new semantic and affective context, towards integrating it in the subject's history, and towards providing a new opportunity (Kirshner 1994)? As such, repetition would in some cases be the only memory of the trauma, its 'zero level', outside the realm of any genuine cognitive or affective inclusion in the individual's personality and in the symbolic order, totally beyond the reach of the regulative capacity of the ego. In other cases, however, as can be observed in the treatment of the psychoses, it is precisely the persistence of 'high-fidelity' memories that demonstrates the failure of retranscription.

On the other hand, there must necessarily be some kind of mnemic activity, even if expressed in the form of pure repetition or hyper-saturated and hyper-luminous photographic memories, as otherwise the effects of the trauma would have been so irreversible as to set psychic life back to its zero point. In the majority of cases, this activity is manifested in a plurality of ways which are not mutually exclusive either synchronically or diachronically, and which are arranged on a gradient of expressiveness that extends from absolute disavowal to highly differentiated forms of awareness.[4]

For Edelman and Modell, a traumatic event can be conceived as something that cannot be recognized, assimilated and neutralized by the mind system, for which it remains as it were an alien psychic body – as an event that cannot be revised or retranscribed by memory in more *appropriate* ways, but can only be repeated. Because the repetition does not become recategorization, it remains repetition of the identical. The transition from perceptual trace to representation does not take place. The traumatic event does not succeed in entering into the reconstructions and stories devised by the subject in the constant attempt to link past and present, to preserve the continuity of the self and to undertake reality testing. In this sense, a trauma constitutes a caesura in the subject's history and, in its unchanged representation, is experienced as an eternal present, as timelessness.

In the more restrictive interpretation of *Nachträglichkeit* put forward by Laplanche and Pontalis (1967: 112), which could be contrasted with Lacan's wider view, it is not 'lived experience that undergoes a deferred revision but, specifically, whatever it has been impossible in the first instance to incorporate fully into a meaningful context. The traumatic event is the epitome of such unassimilated experience.' We now know that the work of rearrangement or recataloguing of memory is evidently much more pervasive.[5] If *Nachträglichkeit* is not limited to trauma and is conceived not only in terms of its pathogenic potential but also, in a wider sense, in adaptive terms, the decisive question inevitably arises as to the preconditions for and appropriateness of the retranscription. In this sense, it would perhaps be less ambiguous to consider, not so much that the traumatizing event cannot be rearranged, as if it were lost in a kind of *elsewhere* vis-à-vis the psyche, as that the attempt to assign new meaning, which in any case takes place unceasingly, and partly also by way of forms of 'mute', inert and non-transformative forms of repetition, does not so to speak produce satisfactory versions, of which more use can be made. However paradoxical it may seem, these very forms of repetition of trauma should be seen as possessing conservative value. Just as, according to the telling image presented by Janin (1995), a traumatic nucleus lies at the root of every psychic process, so an anti-traumatic tension is inherent in every search for the trauma. For this reason, it may be wondered whether it might not be appropriate to preserve, in a purely descriptive sense, the distinction between repetition as a biological function and the compulsion to repeat as ineffective repetition or as malfunctioning recontextualization.

Différance

In fact, surprisingly, it is in the field of philosophy and not of psychoanalysis that the concept of *Nachträglichkeit* has been received and utilized on a large scale, albeit in the name of a (creative) infidelity as the only form of true fidelity to the Freudian heritage (Derrida 1999)[6] and to its intrinsically subversive spirit. In Derrida's critical theory, *Nachträglichkeit*, retranscribed as 'différance', is presented as a conceptual intersection at which three things converge: the recognition of a filiation ('there is, and would have been, no Derrida without Freud' – Bennington 2000: 96); a theory of signification and of temporality; and, lastly, the reference to an anti-metaphysical position. In French, the word for difference (*différence*) is pronounced identically even if spelt with an *a* instead of an *e*. In this way, Derrida is alluding to the play of the signified and the nexus of arbitrariness that links it to the signifier. Two signifiers may differ but be pronounced in the same way and mean the same thing. At the same time, the signified depends on differences and is deferral – continuous postponement. Temporalization is constitutive of meaning. A differential economy governs both the unconscious text and, so to speak, the unconscious of the text. Derrida writes (1967a: 273f.):

The unconscious text is already a weave of pure traces, differences in which meaning and force are united – a text nowhere present, consisting of archives which are *always already* transcriptions. Originary prints. Everything begins with reproduction. Always already: repositories of a meaning which was never present, whose signified presence is always reconstituted by deferral, *nachträglich*, belatedly, *supplementarily*: for the *nachträglich* also means *supplementary*. The call of the supplement is primary, here, and it hollows out that which will be reconstituted by deferral as the present. The supplement, which seems to be added as a plenitude to a plenitude, is equally that which compensates for a lack (*qui supplée*) [. . .]. Let us note: *Nachtrag* has a precise meaning in the realm of letters: appendix, codicil, postscript. The text we call present may be deciphered only at the bottom of the page, in a footnote or postscript. Before the recurrence, the present is only the call for a footnote. That the present in general is not primal but, rather, reconstituted, that is not the absolute, wholly living form which constitutes experience, that there is no purity of the living present – such is the theme, formidable for metaphysics, which Freud, in a conceptual scheme unequal to the thing itself, would have us pursue.

Again, retrospectively, in a dialogue with Elisabeth Roudinesco exactly 30 years later (Derrida and Roudinesco 2001: 171), the same author comments as follows on his personal return to Freud:

My concern was to find, in a 'logic of the unconscious' [. . .] something with which to support a discourse that, from another place, according to another approach, I felt to be necessary. It was a question of the motifs of deferred action, delay, or 'originary' difference, everything that ruined or threatened the absolute phenomenological authority of the 'living present' in the movement of temporalization and the constitution of the ego or the alter ego, the presentation of sense, of life, and of the present in phenomenology.

Similarly, in the field of critical theory and literature, Brooks (1984) points out that in the two notes added to the 'Wolf Man' case history in 1918, Freud contemplates the possibility that the famous primal scene witnessed by the patient as a child might be nothing but a subsequent fantasy transferred on to the parents. In affirming this substantial undecidability between fiction and reality, between fantasy

109

and history, and in the seeming abandonment of the problem of origins, Brooks discerns 'one of the most daring moments of Freud's thought, and one of his most heroic gestures as a writer' (p. 277).

Just as the classical subject of philosophy, since Freud, has never been fully present to itself, no longer having a stable, defined centre in consciousness, so the concept of 'différance' brings about a similar deconstruction of so-called logocentrism — that is, of man's conceptions or narratives about himself which are based on a metaphysical or transcendental foundation or, in other words, originate outside a system of differences. The logic of the *après-coup* results in a shift in the weight and effect of the primal event. For this reason, every event is a 'sending', an automatic onward reference to its own effects deferred in time. It is immediately transformed into a trace, sign, stamp, indication or impression of what has been in the past and is no longer, and exists only in deferral and in an interpretation which, by its nature, cannot but be interminable. Representation comes into being as a fiction (Borutti 2006); it is an 'as if'; it can never aspire to a perfect identity or identification with the presence or thing-in-itself. There is no such thing as a given that can be defined as purely pre-categorial 'except as a retroactive effect of the categorial, as an effect of a request for further information (*Rückfrage*)' (Vergani 2000: 29, translated).

Drawing attention by the evocative title of *Mal d'archives* (1995) to his own discomfort with a certain static conception of memory, Derrida ultimately sets history against substantialist philosophical theses and at the same time philosophy against history's claims to truth (Culler 1982). The signified is a function of context, but context is not finite and limitable. It is this impossibility that renders the signified always unstable, revisable, under construction. Meaning is the product of differences between signs, and never comes to an end because the signifier is not reducible to a fixed signified. Their relationship is ultimately, as de Saussure teaches us, arbitrary and context-dependent. Furthermore, every statement alters the context and reinitiates the play of signification. There is a supplement: *Nachtrag* also means an addition, something that serves as a supplement, that integrates, that compensates for a lack, the 'lack' here denoting the inevitable unsaturated status of the sign in relation to the signified.

The Nietzschian antecedents of the concept are obvious, and indeed attention has been drawn to them by Eickhoff (2006: 1462), who attributes their discovery to Wolfgang Loch: 'Nietzsche had written of a "chronological reversal [. . .] so that the cause enters the consciousness later than the effect", and asked us to consider that "a piece of the external world that we became aware of is reborn after the effect which is exerted upon us from outside, is later projected as its cause".'

A missing concept?

Following the above review of certain present-day perspectives, which are admittedly heterogeneous and very diverse, as a starting point for reinterpretation of the concept of *Nachträglichkeit*, I shall now attempt a concluding summary. First of all, it is worth emphasizing the particular vicissitudes of regionalization to which *Nachträglichkeit* has been subject. The French analysts make liberal use of it, albeit with theoretical implications that vary from place to place. One not infrequently has the impression that its meaning is merely evocative or 'auratic'. It is a fact that Lacan, Laplanche and Pontalis, and, as we have seen, Derrida – to whom we ought to be a little 'fairer' – have established a strong theoretical tradition, of which Faimberg (2005) is currently the most authoritative protagonist.

In the United Kingdom, like Molière's character who, while speaking in prose, was convinced that he was expressing himself in verse, analysts are discovering a posteriori that they have always unwittingly used the concept of *Nachträglichkeit* through their way of interpreting the here-and-now of the session. That is why Sodré (2005) refers ironically to *Nachträglichkeit* as a non-concept, or rather as a concept that can be dispensed with, as indeed the British analysts do, partly because, in her opinion, it is reabsorbed into the concept of mutative insight. However, the impression is gained that she sees retranscription only as the possibility of access by the patient to an 'objective' truth of his history.

A more convincing approach is that of Birksted-Breen (2003), who reaches a similar conclusion by a different route: *Nachträglichkeit* is implicit in the idea that the here-and-now, although taking shape within a specific dyad, carries with it a past which determines its possible modes and plots, and is therefore not resolved into a pure present. Nor could that ever be the case. From a different theoretical perspective, can it not be said that the α-function – that is, the capacity to confer meaning on primitive sensory and emotional impressions – is so to speak history incarnate? However, this is an aspect

111

that should be borne in mind: there is no single way of conceiving interpretation in the here-and-now, because, as a technical device, this can presuppose either a classical conception of historical reality or a radically social or intersubjective perspective.

In the USA, Blum (1996) decisively consigns deferred action to the lumber room as an ambiguous, antiquated and abstract concept. The notion of 'deferred action' is indeed a misunderstanding of *Nachträglichkeit*, or merely one of its possible forms, because it denotes not the attribution of new meaning, but only an action delayed in time – the famous time bomb. Conversely, however, the idea of a retroactive causality or of an actual reversal of the line of temporality seems equally untenable. The subject can perfectly well conceive that what can change are the recordings in the dynamic archive of memory, but only from the point of view of what has been experienced, especially as regards the part of experience of which he is unaware; he has no choice but to espouse this past that is always in the throes of transformation and, so to speak, to abandon himself to illusion. Ultimately, the process described by *Nachträglichkeit* lies at the centre of the new models of therapeutic action (I. Fonagy 1999; P. Fonagy 1999).

In conclusion, given the radical role and extension assumed by this Freudian notion in the philosophy of Derrida, and in its surprising convergence with some of the more advanced findings of neuroscientific research, analysts should in my view carefully re-evaluate it, on account of its wide-ranging potential implications for key concepts such as truth, history, interpretation and transference. The resulting description of the complex relationship between fantasy and history, summed up by Freud in the incredible notes added to the case history of the 'Wolf Man' in 1918, appears, in a disenchanted age such as our own, extraordinarily modern (or, perhaps postmodern, if I may resort to an abused term), in so far as it compels us to realize that there is no such thing as interpretative closure, or a perfect archaeology or teleology of the psyche. *Nachträglichkeit* is instead identified as the incessant movement of assigning new meaning as the fundamental condition for any shaping of experience. Derrida's approach, furthermore, restores philosophical substance to Freud's oeuvre, confirms more than ever the present-day validity of his thought, and opens the way to the most innovative developments of Bion's thought.

6

Transference, USA

From the archives

'In view of the increasing emphasis, by present-day psychoanalysts, upon dynamic, interpersonal, "here-and-now" phenomena in the therapeutic situation – as contrasted to Freud's tendency to view the individual in *relatively* static, mechanistic, and historical terms – our theories concerning transference phenomena need to be constantly modified to serve as a vehicle for our changing concepts of a maximally effective psychoanalytic technique,' writes Searles (1979: 165f.), one of the most authoritative figures in North American psychoanalysis. In this paper, written in 1947–48, Searles emphasizes the projective nature of transference phenomena and the fact that they are invariably aroused by something in the 'present' emotional attitude of the analyst. One does not project into the void: 'The writer has very regularly been able to find some real basis in himself for those qualities which his patients – *all* his patients, whether the individual patient be most prominently paranoid, or obsessive-compulsive, or hysterical, and so on – project upon him' (p. 177). (It may be noted in passing that Searles no longer adheres to Freud's distinction between transference neuroses and narcissistic neuroses.) Transference distortions are seen only as quantitative in nature – a question of disproportion – rather than qualitative; in other words, they are not false in absolute terms.

As described, this concept of projection anticipates that of projective identification in the sense used by Ogden (2005b), who recently told us, among other things, of his experience of supervision with Searles; that is, it appears to be already situated in an interactive and relational dimension. Transference is characterized less as an intrapsychic and more as an interpsychic phenomenon (Bezoari 2002).

113

The two poles of the unreal and the real that were to maintain the tensional field within which subsequent reflections on the transference concept would be accommodated are already clearly delineated in Searles's text. In support of his position, he invokes a trio of authors: Silverberg, Rank and Rioch. From Silverberg (1948) he takes the critique of the definition whereby transference is seen as misunderstanding and false connection, as well as the graphic image that sums it up: in the classical model, transference is like a phonograph[1] that goes on playing because no one has remembered to switch it off. In other words, it constitutes 'blind, repetitive behavior, having no specific purpose (apart from resistance to therapy)'. Rioch (1943), an analyst of the Sullivan school, on the other hand, postulates that the therapeutic factor in analysis lies not so much in the faithful historical reconstruction of the infantile neurosis, as in the relational climate or 'new experience' that makes it possible. In present-day parlance, what matters in therapeutic terms is growth of the patient's capacity for thought or symbolization rather than bringing a buried past to light; for Fonagy (2003), the latter is merely a 'co-occurrence' and not a direct causal factor. Rioch also maintains that the idea of a 'magic' immediate curative effect of the recovery of repressed memories – the foreign bodies within the psychic system featuring in the first aetiological theory of the neuroses – is a residue of the cathartic method of hypnosis. According to Smith (2003), Strachey's (1934) idealization of mutative interpretation shares these origins. Transference, when considered as a strictly interpersonal experience, is ultimately also modelled on the analyst's personality. Again, as a 'proto-relationalist', Rank (1945) too is if anything radical in attributing patients' reactions not to the automatic repetition of their infantile neurosis, but to the quality and dynamics of a specific therapeutic situation.

That, then, is Searles's view. Nor is it insignificant. However, besides the content and the date of composition, the most interesting thing about this text is the fact that, having been rejected by *Psychiatry* and by the *Psychoanalytic Quarterly*, it was published only 30 years later, in 1979, thanks to Langs (at that time editor of the *International Journal of Psychoanalytic Psychotherapy*), who had become aware of it during an interview with Searles in 1977 (Langs and Searles 1980; Borgogno 2004). To put this situation in its historical context, it should be recalled that hardly a decade had elapsed since the end of the great wave of immigration of European analysts into the United States. The year 1939 saw the publication of Hartmann's *Ego Psychology and the Problem of Adaptation*, which ushered in the school of ego psychology and, with the subsequent systematization of the abstract and 'anti-clinical' Rapaport (Gedo 1973; Vegetti 1986), assured it of lasting and undisputed success. Lastly, Fenichel's (1945) treatise, which can be seen as the theoretical summa of Freudian orthodoxy, had appeared a few years earlier.

But then, what had happened in the 30 years between Searles's failed scientific and publishing début and Langs's lucky archive discovery, made only in 1979? What had changed to such an extent as to render totally up to date the revisionist[2] theses expressed in Searles's contribution, which was at this time a kind of ghost (revenant), a term I use also as an introduction to the theme of the 'spectrality' of the transference? And, finally, would the present editorial board of the *Quarterly* reject Searles's paper?

Spectres and spectra of the transference

The evolution of the concept of transference in North America can be summed up in the formula that the transference is born of spectres, becomes a spectrum of concepts, and, lastly, might well soon end up as the spectre of a concept. Let me explain.

It was when Freud returned for the last time to the matter of the transference neurosis in *The Question of Lay Analysis* in 1926 that the entire situation began to take on a somewhat spectral air. Transference was equated with 'evil spirits' summoned up by the witch-analyst, which he could then not refuse to combat 'to the best of [his] strength' (Freud 1926: 227). A few decades later, Loewald – and not Stephen King! – took up Freud's suggestion and developed it further:

> The transference neurosis, in the technical sense of the establishment and resolution of it in the analytic process, is due to the blood of recognition which the patient's unconscious is given to taste – so that the old ghosts may reawaken to life. Those who know ghosts tell us that they long to be released from their ghost-life and led to rest as ancestors. As ancestors they live forth in the present generation, while as ghosts they are compelled to haunt the present generation with their shadow-life. Transference is pathological in so far as the unconscious is a crowd of ghosts, and this is the

beginning of the transference neurosis in analysis: ghosts of the unconscious, imprisoned by defences but haunting the patient in the dark of his defences and symptoms, are allowed to taste blood, are let loose. In the daylight of analysis the ghosts of the unconscious are laid and led to rest as ancestors whose power is taken over and transformed into the newer intensity of present life, of the secondary process and contemporary objects.

(Loewald 1960: 28)

The second 'spectral' notion to be considered in this chapter, the 'spectrum of concepts (and phenomena)', which recurs surprisingly often – perhaps, one might say, 'symptomatically'? – in the literature on the transference, refers to the band of colours that appears when a light ray is refracted by a prism. According to the dictionary, spectral analysis 'establishes which substances go to make up a body from the number and position of the lines in the emission spectrum' (Zingarelli 1969: 1560, translated). The curious reader will then learn of the existence of the intriguing spectre of the Brocken, a mountain in Germany that is the scene of a 'strange phenomenon whereby images are projected on to the clouds by the refraction of light through fog' (ibid.); so we have spectres/spectra, clouds, fog, and strange phenomena.[3] This is most decidedly the lexical and semantic area of the transference. One is surely put in mind of the comments of so many authors – starting with Freud: 'this odd love-relationship' (1926: 225) – about the particularly ambiguous, confused and obscure character of this term, which gives rise to controversies no less convoluted than those featuring in the Augustinian and Thomist proofs of the existence of God (and if Gottlieb [1996] says so, it really must be true!), even if it is still deemed the most important concept of all.

If I had to draw a single line of separation between the opposing camps and the principal theories, I would trace it along the pair of opposites unreality vs reality of the transference, stemming from the crisis of Freud's seduction theory, and its equivalents false connection – inappropriate/appropriate reaction; new impression – copy/new edition; brought to the analysis/co-constructed (Bachant and Adler 1997); transference neurosis/transference-as-process; transference/extratransference interpretations; essentialism/relativism; temporal and structural regression; and extending to the infantile neurosis/transference-as-function; transference-as-displacement/transference-as-organization (Fosshage 1994); and so on.

In terms of this fault line, North American psychoanalysis divides, roughly speaking, into two camps. On the one hand, there are the heirs of ego psychology and, among them, the Freudian interactionists, a subgroup of 'liberal or "left-wing" ' Freudian analysts (Aron 1996: xv); and on the other, a 'relational' area that groups together the 'patrols' of relational analysts proper (Aron, Hoffmann, Greenberg, Mitchell, Orange, Ghent, Fosshage, Benjamin and Gill); intersubjectivist analysts (Stolorow, Lachmann and Atwood); interpersonalist analysts (Bromberg, Stern, Levenson, Wolstein and Zucker); social constructivist or 'dialectical' analysts (Hoffmann); post-Kohutian analysts (Bacal); object-relations theorists (Summers); etc.

All present-day conceptions of transference are said to find their anchor, starting point and legitimation in Freud himself. Again, terms that might seem to us to be interchangeable actually reflect non-homogeneous approaches and antagonistic political and institutional histories. However, this is not only the effect of distance. In the United States too, for example, bitter polemical debates rage on the true meaning of the term 'relational' as a category – is it a perspective, a complete theory, a set of affinities, or a theoretical approach (Benjamin 1995; Bachant *et al.* 1996)? – and on whether the relational field includes the interpersonal field or vice versa (Aron 1996).

With regard to the transference, each analyst puts together his own mixture of ingredients. For instance, following Aron (1996), Evelyne Schwaber's transference concept could be defined as perspectivist, post-Kohutian, non-constructivist and essentially based on a single-person psychology. One and the same author – e.g. Gill – can espouse different conceptions over time, and on each occasion passionately and categorically. Sometimes, too, one observes surprising theoretical convergences on individual points in authors who start from contrasting perspectives; or, conversely, unexpected divergences. Who would suspect the existence of an Ogden assigned to the *non-relational* clan (Benjamin 1995; Bachant *et al.* 1996), on account of the space he sets aside for the concept of unconscious motivational systems? Ultimately, then, any attempt at systematization is doomed to failure from the outset, if not on the basis of large-scale mapping.

Considered on a large scale, the vision of the transference that has developed over the years can be seen as embracing a 'spectrum' of phenomena that can range from a zero level – and it is quite common for psychoanalytic concepts to pass from psychopathology into psychology – to the classical form; that is to say, to avoid any misunderstanding, the form that focuses on the development of a neurosis proper with symptoms *consciously* centred on the analyst and the analytic situation. If the gamut of transference manifestations is widened to its maximum extent, the consequence is of course to blur the already unclear distinction between process and outcome. The process can admittedly be thought of as a ubiquitous phenomenon not specifically bound up with the treatment, functioning at one and the same time as both catalyst and lens; whereas the transference neurosis, by contrast, can be seen as resulting from the sum of the transferring process and the analytic setting. In fact, however, there is no discontinuity between the various transference phenomena. For this reason, the concept of the *reverse, masked, displaced transference* (Leites 1997) has gained acceptance. Not only is the process now unconscious, or, that is to say, invisible; its outcome too becomes latent. The spectres, having barely emerged into the light, are chased back into their shadowy life. The theorem that the parent stands behind the analyst in the classical transference neurosis (transference resistance) is turned on its head: behind the parent of the manifest discourse lurks the transference on to the analyst (resistance to the transference). More precisely, the play of transference and interpretation, which is initially unidirectional, is characterized by the fact that it systematically brings the patient back to the opposite transference pole to that expressed in the manifest text of the analysis.

As to the third point, the 'spectrum of a concept' – that is to say, glancing into a possible near future – the transference and the transference neurosis might have a 'spectral'[4] fate. To start with, both have often been seen as past their sell-by date. For Brenner (1982), the transference neurosis, whatever that may mean, is a term that should no longer be included in the vocabulary of psychoanalysis. Stolorow and Lachmann (1984), as (pseudo-)post-Kohutian intersubjectivists, refer to it as the 'future of an illusion'. Cooper (1987), already President of the American Psychological Association (APA), Vice-President of the International Psychoanalytical Association (IPA) and editor of the *International Journal of Psychoanalysis* for North America, would pension it off. Similarly, Schachter (2002) sees it as an albatross, a source of problems; while Sandler *et al.* (1973) regret its loss of precision.

The fact is that, as we know, spectres are not prepared simply to go away – it is not by chance that the French call them '*revenants*' – and they disturb the sleep of anyone who thinks he is master in his own house, or in his own conceptual house. Not only does the transference not allow itself to be dismissed as a theoretical concept by the most intransigent modernists; it also cannot, for the traditionalists, be 'resolved' in a technical sense at the end of the treatment – partly because it sometimes does not even show itself. As Napolitano (2007, translated) points out, 'rather than to the transference, the category of the fictitious must be applied to the vague dream-like atmosphere generated by the rule of the setting, but only until it catches fire' – that is, until something that also has the character of a 'real' event intervenes in the representation and thus reintroduces the inescapable ambiguity and paradoxicality of the transference. Furthermore, it 'follows that the transference must not – in fact, cannot – be *liquidated*', but that one can at most aim, when the patient is ready, for it to be conveyed, or restored, from the theatre of the analysis to the outside world – in a word, for a 'transference of the transference'.

However, to return to the first of the rhetorical questions arising out of Searles's (formerly) spectral paper: how did we arrive at a theoretical spectrum that is so complex as to put one in mind of the subtleties of medieval scholasticism?

The quiet revolution

At least since the Alexander controversy, the concept of the transference neurosis has assumed a strategic significance, and not only in the treatment, since it has become the dogma whose interpretation divides 'believers' from 'unbelievers', and the criterion upon which the latter base the distinction between psychoanalysis and psychotherapics. To limit regression, dependence and the malignant–growth-like excesses of the development of the transference neurosis, in the 1950s Alexander proposed the adoption of active techniques to manipulate the transference. Varying the rhythm of the sessions, interrupting the treatment, or tactically taking up a position opposite to that of the presumed 'pathogenic' parent were conceptualized as anti–iatrogenic measures. However, these techniques are not devoid of the element of suggestion and therefore profoundly alter the nature of the analytic process.

Vigorous opposition soon became organized within the psychoanalytic establishment. In the APA panel of 1954, which ultimately assumed a 'deliberative' character, Gill and Rangell identified the treatment with the very development of the transference neurosis. In its absence, the treatment could not be called psychoanalysis (Fischer 1997). With time, however, the polemical overreaction (Reed 1994) died down. The political need to lay the foundations of the theoretical edifice on a stratum of bedrock became less pressing. Unanimism (of ideology) gave way to open dissent. A plurality of opinions were expressed, even within so-called mainstream Freudian psychoanalysis, on the meaning of the transference and the indispensability of treatment on the basis of the transference neurosis. The change in theoretical climate occurred within the two decades (Gilmore 1996) separating the two APA panels on the transference (Blum 1971; Calef 1971a, 1971b; Harley 1971; Loewald 1971; Weinshel 1971; Shaw 1991).

Hence what amounts to a revolution occurred during the 30 years when Searles's paper remained buried in the archives. However, as Cooper (2005) felicitously puts it, it was a 'quiet revolution'. In 1971, Kohut, a 'modifier' not so distant from Alexander's concerns (Bergmann 1993), published *The Analysis of the Self: A Systematic Approach to the Psychoanalytic Treatment of Narcissistic Personality Disorders*. The book aroused enormous enthusiasm, polemical blasts and even some reactions expressed in tones bordering on excommunication (Stein 1979). Kohut's text not only represented a new starting point, but accommodated and organized theoretical tensions that had emerged and become consolidated over time (Cooper 2005) – namely, the role of pre-Oedipal psychological organizations; the importance attached to the first term in the pair *nurture/nature* (that is, the actual quality and vicissitudes of maternal care); critique of the mechanicist schemata of metapsychology; a more humanistic and romantic vision of human beings, contrasting with Freud's tragic and conflictual view; and a new attention to the therapeutic relationship ('the temperature is warmer and the weather is less stormy in Dr Kohut's office', according to Cooper's summing up [2005: 29f.]). Holding thus regained ground from interpretation. Second, the possibility was considered that a patient's negative transference might in fact be induced by non-empathic attitudes on the part of the analyst.

Some other things also occurred in that fateful year of 1971. Winnicott sent *Playing and Reality* to the printer. The minutes of the panel on transference held in Boston in 1968 were published. The various contributions included the one in which Loewald (1971: 66) includes the character neuroses among transference manifestations, these being seen as diffuse, insidious and opaque forms, in 'so-called normal' patients (often members of or trainees in psychology-related professions, in analysis for professional reasons), in whom a protective narcissistic screen filtered and tempered the passions that would otherwise have given rise to a full-blown transference neurosis. In the same contribution, moreover, Loewald redefines the transference neurosis as, rather than a clinical entity, an 'operational concept', an 'ideal construct', which serves to impose order, from a defined perspective, on events that would not otherwise be comprehensible. Shortly afterwards, Levenson (1972), the founding father of the 'heretical' American school of contemporary interpersonalism, published *The Fallacy of Understanding*. Gedo (1973: 427) immediately registered the change of climate: 'Currently, we are probably entering an era of revolutionary challenge to the dominance of ego psychology.'

Meanwhile, the influence was beginning to be felt of the independent neo-Kleinian British analysts (Bion, Meltzer, Joseph, Rosenfeld and Racker, for whom the relationship with the mother was a transference from the beginning and transference was the expression of unconscious phantasy, so that it was always present and active in the here-and-now), as well as that of the independent British object-relations theorists (Balint, Winnicott, Fairbairn and Guntrip).

In 1979, Ogden published his important contribution on the concept of projective identification. In the early 1980s, the influential publications of Greenberg and Mitchell (1983) – the latter being the founder of *Psychoanalytic Dialogues*, the journal that would over the years present some of the most innovative contributions in the psychoanalytic field, and the 'federator' of revisionist schools – and of Gill (1982) paved the way for the birth of the relational approach, whose progenitors are Rank and Ferenczi. Spezzano (1995: 23) characterizes the relational analysts as a kind of American Middle Group, intermediate between ego psychology and interpersonalism. To sum up, the historicist conception, the archaeological model and an epistemological approach broadly definable as positivist all faced a looming crisis – a crisis that led to a different perception of the role of the analyst in the psychoanalytic process. It no longer appeared acceptable to disregard the therapist's personality in the definition of clinical data.

Whereas the definition of analytic neutrality stemming from Anna Freud's (1936) remark on the need for the analyst to maintain an equal distance from the id, the ego and the superego was for a long time the benchmark of ego psychology (Smith 2003: 1020), and still is for those who identify with that theoretical current, the relationalists' reference parameter could be said, precisely, to be the theory of transference as non-distortion – at least, not in an absolute sense.

As always when a new paradigm becomes established (Kuhn 1962), it proves difficult to determine the significance of individual factors. The new zeitgeist appeared more as the outcome of complex and heterogeneous sets of events that finally came together in the critical point of the change of state. Contributing factors were idiosyncratic and original theoretical perspectives, complex institutional vicissitudes and far-reaching cultural turning points, such as the 'linguistic turning point', the 'rhetorical turning point', post-structuralism, deconstruction, or critical theory; and there was no lack of syntheses.

Let us now return to the second of our rhetorical questions: would the current editorial board of the *Quarterly* reject Searles's paper? I venture to suggest that the answer would be 'no' (although one never knows!). This is not only because, obviously, Searles has meanwhile become Searles, one of the most original and best appreciated authors on the world psychoanalytic stage, but also because I am relying on the content of an interesting contribution on the transference by the present Director of that journal, Henry Smith, a critic of the traditional model of the analyst as an opaque screen (Smith 2003). That is why one can try to play this game.

Intimate theatre

Smith (2003) distinguishes between a narrow and a broader definition of transference. The former mostly characterizes ego psychology and inherits the special emphasis placed in the United States on Anna Freud's recommendation that the transference of defences should be interpreted. In one formula, transference is an 'unconscious stereotype plate' (Freud 1926) applied by the patient to the objective reality of the analyst. However, not all authors identify with this theoretical model. Arlow (1987), for example, accepts the existence of an interactive component, resembling Sandler's concept of 'role responsiveness', a derivative of the Kleinian concept of projective identification.

The broader definition, due specifically to relational psychoanalysis, is openly influenced by Kleinian theory. It is as if, in the shift of emphasis from the drive paradigm to the relational paradigm, the Controversial Discussions were being replicated in the United States, and as if the pendulum of metapsychology were swinging back from the ego towards the id. The transference is also seen in its character as a 'new creation', as pervasive and omnipresent. The gap between transference and transference neurosis, as well as that between transference and the analytic relationship, is tending to close. What is deemed to be transferred is psychic reality in its totality, and not only a limited unconscious ideo-affective constellation corresponding to the infantile neurosis.

Having established his general framework, Smith builds his model of transference partly in agreement with and partly in opposition to that of certain authors chosen because they are particularly representative and influential in North America – namely, Gill, Schwaber and Gray, as well as the UK's Joseph. The result is nothing but a psychoanalytic melting pot: an ex-Freudian relational analyst, a post-Kohutian-non-constructivist-perspectivist, a representative of ego psychology, and a Kleinian analyst.

For Gill (1982), the author of a superb (and controversial) little book on the theory and technique of transference interpretation, the analytic situation inevitably assumes an interactive and interpersonal form. All the patient's communications have transference implications. Priority is given to interpretation of the transference in the here-and-now over extra-transference or genetic interpretations. The analyst weighs up the real components of his attitude that contribute to the transference, and monitors the effects of his interpretations on the patient. Particular importance attaches to interpreting resistance to awareness of the transference. The analyst is not the depository of any truth and does not a priori regard the patient's perceptions as distorted. Instead, he considers that there might be other possible interpretations. This is the attitude that promotes openness to new points of view in the patient. The only possible certainties, if indeed any exist, are those reached consensually, by negotiation. The omnipresence of the transference and the centrality of its interpretation are points of contact with the Kleinian school. However, Gill criticizes that school's excessive use of genetic or profound interpretations, those regarded by Strachey (1934) as 'exceedingly inaccessible' to the patient's ego, remote from the reality of an interaction that turns out to be entirely reabsorbed in the galaxy of the most primitive unconscious fantasies. The experience of analysis is indeed a new affective experience, but only secondarily, and not as a matter of deliberate policy as with Alexander.

Some ambiguity persists in Gill as to the role of the analyst as a possible judge of the plausibility of the patient's perceptions and of their basis in reality. Furthermore, his technique involves a recourse to interpretation of the transference in the here-and-now that runs the risk of being excessive, of hyperstimulating the ego, of 'awakening' the patient from the hypnoid climate of the session, of holding up the flow of free associations, and of acting out the very dynamic that is being interpreted. According to Smith, however, the therapeutic interaction always involves an important component of action that cannot be eliminated. Analyst and patient inevitably 'collude' in the enactment of the patient's fantasies, especially when the transference is intense. What justifies the asymmetry of the respective roles is the analyst's self-reflective competence, which is based partly on the preparation of the sophisticated stage of the setting, and his capacity to 'think' the experience while it is happening, or rather after the inevitable deferral of meaning denoted by the term *Nachträglichkeit*.

Unlike Gill, and on the basis of Kohut's bipersonal theory of resistance, Schwaber is more interested in discerning in the patient's transference the subjective elaboration of the analyst's involvement – his *perceptions* and not his *distortions*. In a word, the problem does not arise of determining whether the behaviour attributed by the patient to the analyst, to which the patient reacts in the transference, is to a greater or lesser extent realistic. To avoid the failure of empathy, the analyst must abandon his role as an arbiter of material reality, take psychic reality very seriously, and resist the tendency to slip away into the reassuring position of an external, out-of-context observer. Only thus can what might objectively appear as irrational and unrealistic demands assume the significance of profound and legitimate needs on the part of the patient. At any rate, Schwaber's psychology remains a single-person psychology, because the only experience considered is that which the patient has of the interaction. Smith (2003) comments that the opposing of distortion and perception is false, because every perception is in itself also a distortion, and he adds that not all distortions are the same – that one of the analyst's tasks is to distinguish between reality and illusion. In fact, however, he leaves the problem unsolved.

With regard to the patient's associations, Gray, on the other hand, gives priority to listening to the chains of drive derivatives with a view to discerning their defensive drifts, and in particular the expression of hostile impulses in the transference. Adopting the method of 'close process attention', the analyst is ready to seize on the 'apple-sorting' that signals the patient's defensive retreat from aggressive impulses. In a now classical contribution dating from 1973, Gray champions the technique of focusing exclusively on what is most affectively immediate for the patient–analyst couple – on what is analytically most significant 'in that session' and 'in that setting'. If the analyst's attention is diverted on to events of external reality, not seen in terms of their status as details from the patient's stream of consciousness, the result may be to intensify the patient's defences.

Lastly, in her close scrutiny of the analytic text, Joseph (1985), who is less interested in the level of the manifest text and the analyst's actual behaviour, relies more on her own countertransference and on attentive, instant-by-instant monitoring of the patient's unconscious reactions to the analyst's interpretations.

Except for Joseph, all the analysts considered by Smith, although having different models, share an 'empirical' approach to analytic interaction, as well as a concern for the detail and surface of what the patient brings, and in particular for the transference. This attention to the interaction might appear to some as a departure from the task of analysing unconscious fantasies and defences, but Smith (2003) shows persuasively in the clinical part of his contribution that he is able flexibly to integrate the various approaches according to the situation, without aspiring to reconcile them on the theoretical level at any price. Like Brenner (1982), with whom he shares the model of conflict and of psychic compromise, and unlike Sandler *et al.* (1973), Smith is convinced of the omnipresence of the transference. In his view, it is impossible to identify moments in an analysis that are completely transference-free. If all perceptions are influenced by unconscious fantasy – that is, expressed in a different language, if they cannot be precategorial – then all the patient's perceptions of the analyst are to a greater or lesser extent conditioned by an ongoing transference activity. The paradox of the unreality/reality of the transference, at one and the same time displacement/projection and new experience, must be tolerated.

Transference, like resistance, is organized on the basis both of the patient's intrapsychic structures and of the conflicts, real characteristics and behaviour of the analyst. It is a joint creation. As a moderate revisionist, Smith (2003) sees the concept of transference neurosis more than anything else as the phenomenological description of a particularly intense transference situation. The forms assumed by the transference can admittedly be extremely varied, and even subtle and not easy to identify, but this does not make them less amenable to analysis. For they all represent compromise formations – that is, they always contain opposing impulses. From this point of view, classifications into distinct types, such as negative, erotic, positive, or blameless, appear as mystifications.

Preparatory work is often necessary in order to arrive at a transference interpretation. Extra-transference interpretations sometimes come to play a similar part to those of unsaturated interpretations in Antonino Ferro's bi-personal field model. That is to say, the analyst is aware of the transference significance of these interpretations, which has not been made explicit or has been only alluded to, and of their possible defensive significance. In other cases, extra-transference interpretations, and not transference interpretations, may be the instrument of choice for the creation of a climate of immediacy and authenticity, which ultimately constitutes the analyst's tactical objective. In such clinical situations, reconstructions or genetic interpretations may serve to modulate the intensity of a transference experience.

As to the timing of interpretations (early or late), it is a matter of steering a course between the Scylla of intellectualization and acting out in the transference, or of the possibility of triggering excessive anxiety in the patient (here the influence of Kohut, who legitimized the narcissistic or self-object transference, is obvious), and the Charybdis of forgoing explicit interpretation of the unconscious dynamics, of the failure of the transference to develop, and of the reinforcement, in its place, of transference resistance and the therapeutic impasse. In this case, patient and analyst are like ships passing in the night, without ever seeing each other.

In Berlin in 1906, with a performance of Ibsen's *Ghosts*, Max Reinhardt created a form of intimate theatre in an enclosed space, without clear-cut boundaries between the audience and the small number of actors, and with plots involving psychological introspection and subdued dialogue rich in subtle nuance, entirely lacking in magniloquent scenery and sumptuous declamation. For Smith, like Searles 60 years before him, the play of transference and transference neurosis is rather like such an 'intimate theatre' (*Kammerspiel*), which brings the members of the audience back into the performance space, and bears very little resemblance to Silverberg's phonograph stuck in its groove.

'What about me?'

The problem of the transference and its definitions is so vast as to defy any attempt at synthesis. For this reason, I shall for the third time adopt the method of sampling, moving on from the eclectic Smith to more polarized theoretical perspectives and taking advantage of what presents itself as the most up-to-date scientific polemic on the subject. Among the more recent studies of transference, two volumes stand out: Gail Reed's *Transference Neurosis and Psychoanalytic Experience* (1994), and Joseph Schachter's *Transference: Shibboleth or Albatross?* (2002). The latter author, although writing after Reed, is completely ignorant of her work, and is subsequently the victim of biting criticism in her review of his book in the *International Journal of Psychoanalysis* (Reed 2004).

Reed's text is destined to become an essential theoretical reference. It takes the form of an extraordinary synopsis of explicit theoretical positions and implicit conceptual models, derivable from the reports of the practice 'in the field' of a small but highly representative group of analysts of the modern Freudian school, the principal current of North American psychoanalysis. The author presents and comments on extended extracts from conversations with 21 anonymous therapists, recorded and transcribed, and hence only paradoxically definable as 'off the record'. This stratagem guarantees the text a character of freshness and authenticity, as well as a total absence of academic pedantry both in the theoretical parts and in the wealth of clinical material presented. However, the theses of analysts outside this tradition are illustrated, if at all, only indirectly and with polemical rejection. This elusiveness, of which Reed is perfectly aware, can be seen as the necessary limit of the book.

None of the interviewees espouses a rigid model of transference neurosis or sees the success of an analysis as dependent on such a model. Sometimes, as one of the interviewees remarks, the transference does indeed gradually become 'warmer . . . warmer . . . warmer' (Reed 1994: 58), an intensification of character traits in the patient, for example, being noted, and the transference is then tantamount to a transference neurosis. In other cases, a transference neurosis can be said to exist only by 'stretching . . . stretching . . . stretching' (p. 61) the definition to breaking point.

In the elegant, classical definition given by Bird (1972: 281), the transference neurosis is a new edition of the patient's original neurosis, 'but with me [the analyst] in it'. However, given the experience that a textbook transference neurosis does not always arise in the treatment, and considering the on the whole still valid notion that the transference neurosis is the sine qua non of analysis, there can be few analysts who do not feel lost and, like A., ask themselves (Reed 1994: 233): 'What about me?!' This 'What about me?!' replicates the famous question that Freud (1901: 118) blames himself for not having put to Dora: ' "Have you been struck by anything about me or got to know anything about me which has caught your fancy, as happened previously with Herr K.?" '

Of the analysts questioned by Reed, two thirds consider the theoretical and technical concept of transference neurosis to be still valid; one third point out that it is inappropriate; but no one any longer thinks it absolutely necessary. A transference neurosis is likely to develop, and, all in all, the idea persists that it can lead to a productive analysis; however, more attention must be paid to the iatrogenic risks.

The transference neurosis expresses not only libidinal impulses but also aggressive ones, as well as components and conflicts stemming from more mature levels. A. makes the interesting observation that a precondition of a transference neurosis is always a countertransference neurosis. Surprisingly though, the precise distinction between transference-as-function and transference neurosis is blurred. Reed herself defines transference neurosis in more restrictive terms, tending to distinguish the process of transference from its result – its distillate or crystallization. This strategy enables her to illustrate a theory that, while resting on a sound classical basis, nevertheless makes a number of concessions to critics, striking a balance between resistance to the equating of transference neurosis with countertransference enactment and the conviction that the ultimate aim of analysis of the transference is to bring out its infantile origin (Gilmore 1996).

Among the various 'concessions', I shall enumerate those which seem to me to be most significant: the transference-as–process can give rise to a broad spectrum of results, from preconscious, latent manifestations to a full-blown neurosis in which the patient's symptoms become increasingly centred on the analysis and the analyst; the analyst contributes to the clinical expression of the transference; the use of silence as a method of cultivating the transference neurosis no longer seems acceptable (cf. Arlow 1987) ('Nor does the transference neurosis leap, full blown, into the silent analyst's lap' – Reed 1994: 16); the transference neurosis can no longer be regarded as a direct transposition of the infantile neurosis, nor can the pre-Oedipal levels or subsequent recastings be excluded; and Freud's initial bellicose rhetoric which predicted that the transference neurosis would be destroyed (*vernichtet*) is obsolete because its resolution is only partial.

At any rate, the transference neurosis develops on the basis of a logic internal to the subject. The analyst must only supply the appropriate climate (Reed 1994: 56), to which a flexible theory of transference neurosis itself also contributes. Proceeding via a relationship with characteristics of *intimacy, immediacy, involvement* and *closeness* to the analyst, which for this reason must have time to develop, the therapeutic process consists in the work of clarifying and distinguishing between the primitive objects and the analyst himself. In other words, there remains a trust in the possibility of veritative activity on the part of the analyst, in an objectivity deemed to be 'sufficient' or 'relative'.

In the final chapters of the book, Reed summarizes her position. The transference neurosis, she writes: 'can be conceived of as a mutable organization constituted simultaneously by the patient's affect-laden perception of the analyst as entwined with the core, organizing, unconscious fantasies (assumed to include relevant memories) from childhood and the gradual disengaging of the object representation of the analyst from those core fantasies' (p. 229). The author is, moreover, shrewd enough to emphasize that the aspect of the patient's conscious concern for the analyst, which may be more or less intense and long-lasting, should not be deemed an indispensable condition for analysis. Hence the transference neurosis can manifest itself consciously, in the form of enactment, or, alternatively, with a hostility that masks highly guilt-ridden positive feelings.

Reed substantially presents us with a revised and corrected – that is, relativized – archaeological model. The transference neurosis remains of central importance, but its phenomenology is changed; its connections with the infantile neurosis are loosened, the indispensable bond with the treatment is no longer so close, the reference to the Oedipus complex forfeits its central position, and the analyst's reactions as unconscious micro-adjustments that can gratify impulses of the patient are now seen as transference reactions, similar to

Sandler's role responsiveness and to be distinguished from the counter-transference.

Everything is extended and blurred. Everything, or nearly every-thing, may be and . . . not be. For instance, mobilization of the analyst's conflicts is often observed, but this should not form part of the defin-ition; in other words, it may be absent. There are no conflict-free areas of the ego or indeed conflict-free analysts, but there remains as a therapeutic factor the traditional objective of making the patient aware of his distorted perceptions, and not only secondarily. The definition of transference neurosis is claimed to be rigorous, but one is wisely asked to interpret it flexibly.

Again, from a certain point of view, Reed's text is self-deconstructive. In the last chapter, the reader is confronted with the author's summing up and also with her explicit recognition of the limits of the work (the idiosyncratic aspect of any psychoanalytic model; the avoidance of certain key points, including the problem of an iatrogenically based transference neurosis; the impossibility of neutral, unconditioned observation; the vagueness of other non-secondary theoretical concepts encountered in the attempt to focus sharply on even one concept; the reference to the experiential dimen-sion, which can be shared, but which nevertheless puts one in mind of the famous conclusion of Wittgenstein's *Tractatus*, etc.). However, even if enriched by a great deal of theoretical and clinical wisdom, that reader will have difficulty in escaping the confusion induced by the comments of the interviewees, who are often much more radical revisionists than the book's editor, however mainstream they are purported to be. Moreover, this is the case even if everyone, with differences of emphasis, recognizes the central importance of the transference neurosis, which many have disputed at least from the 1970s on.

Finally, it is paradoxical that the single most frequent element to be found in the definition of transference neurosis is a rhetoric of closeness and mutual affective involvement (immediacy, intimacy, emotional intensification, and so on), precisely on the part of analysts who claim to belong to a tradition that has theorized and practised distance in forms whose possible harmful effects are now debated. The opaque screen has in effect become humanized – or is it in fact a matter of a return of the repressed, which I have symbolized here by the spectre of Searles's paper?

Schachter's (2002) text, endorsed on the back cover by Wallerstein,

Grünbaum and Renik and avowedly owing much to 'late' Gill, takes a very different path from Reed's. Schachter rejects the aetiological implications of transference theory because he regards them as unvalidated, and with them, the traditional historical approach and the archaeological model. In his view, a continuity cannot be demonstrated between infancy and adult pathology, nor can any stability of character traits be shown to exist. The concept of resolution of the transference is invalid; nor is the recovery of repressed memories in itself therapeutic. Schachter criticizes the theory that the transference involves unrealistic, distorted experiences, and hence the version of the transference as false connection: there is no way that the analyst can be a reliable judge of what is and is not realistic in the transference. On the contrary, it is from an attentive reading of the interaction in the here-and-now that the analyst can derive plausible hints for the reconstruction of the past from the gradually emerging relationship patterns.

Schachter considers the very term 'transference' to be excessively compromised by the aetiologistic hypothesis, so that it should be replaced by the concept of 'human relationship patterns'. This formula could be seen as a provocation, were it not for its kinship with a number of concepts that, whether one likes it or not, cannot simply be dismissed – from Bowlby's 'internal working models' to the 'model scenes' of Lichtenberg, Lachmann and Fosshage; from Horowitz's 'person schemes' and Luborsky's 'core conflictual relationship themes' to Stern's 'moments of meeting'.

In her review of Schachter's book, Reed (2004) accuses its author of presenting a caricature of the classical analysts' research, of being a zealous revisionist, like 'bloodhounds on the trail of a criminal', of failing to distinguish between reasons for and causes of unexplainable symptoms or actions, of misunderstanding the particular nature of psychoanalytic knowledge and, ultimately, of being insufficiently scholarly. However, the curious and unexpected impression aroused by this review is that Reed is critical more of issues of style than of substance. Schachter is admittedly not original, but must be taken seriously. One is surprised to see only a peripheral attack where a powerful polemic might have been expected. This too can perhaps be deemed a symptom of crisis, or a token of theoretical convergences concealed behind doctrinal and political divergences.

Yet, as Reed again reiterates, 'the concept is muddy'; it counts for little that, more than any other concept, transference *is* psychoanalysis itself. To make it less muddy, one approach adopted by some is to try to reconceptualize transference-as-process, to start again precisely from the place in theory where most of the analysts interviewed appeared to be disorientated and 'puzzled' (p. 23).

Matrices of transference

Among the viruses carried by Freud on his journey to North America is one that seems, as soon as the weakened conditions of the theoretical body of psychoanalysis so allowed, to have become even more virulent. The year is 1909. In the fifth of his Clark University Lectures (Haas 1966: 422), Freud pronounced the following sentence: 'Transference arises spontaneously in all human relationships just as it does between the patient and the physician' (Freud 1909: 51). This point in Freud's American discourse marks the origin of the extension of the transference concept and at the same time the need for it to be redefined – an issue that has been surprisingly neglected in the literature, but which can no longer be avoided. No longer confined to a restricted area of the treatment or to a form of pathology, the transference is identified with a principle of mental functioning.

Considering again the turning point in American psychoanalysis, in 1972 Bird attempts such a redefinition, writing that transference is an ego function that is at all times active, present and significant in the analytic situation – a structure of the mind. Transference is close to or 'allied' with the drives because it acts as an antidepressant for the ego, which it permits to bring the past into the present. As such, transference is not created by analysis, nor can it be resolved: 'The content may be, but not the function' (Bird 1972: 298), he remarks, and it is always active in the analyst too. No reaction by the analyst to the patient can be deemed absolutely realistic; indeed, precisely when something appears to present a maximum of realism, one can be certain that it is conveying important aspects of the analyst's transference. In a word, transference ensconces itself precisely at the point where reality is most luminous.

A few years later, McLaughlin (1981) describes transference as a general psychological principle ('a central organizing mode'), of which psychic reality is an emanation. Every aspect of the secondary process is closely entangled with derivatives of the primary process (transference). The analytic relationship centres on a constant activity of negotiation of meaning. This perspective can be seen as the acceptable solution – perhaps just a little too optimistic, a little too Habermasian – to the epistemological problem on which Smith focuses, but which he fails to resolve:

> What becomes mutually accepted as experientially 'real' in the two-party system of privacy and isolation can only be a shared consensus wrung from prolonged testing and verification by both. The 'therapeutic alliance' is not then a pregiven for analytic work but rather a gradually shaped trust which patient and analyst build up about the reliability of their shared views of what goes on between them, a consensus and comfort that allow the deep explorations of psychoanalysis to transpire. In this sense the outcome of successful analysis reflects an evolving, mutual authentication of the psychic realities of the two parties in the analytic search.
>
> (McLaughlin 1981: 658)

Next, adopting an intersubjectivist and post-Kohutian approach, come Stolorow and Lachmann (1984), who criticize the archaeological model, in which transference is seen as displacement, regression, distortion and projection, in favour of a multidimensional model in which transference is principally an 'organizing activity' – 'an expression of the *continuing influence* of organizing principles and imagery that crystallized out of the patient's early formative experiences' (Stolorow and Lachmann 1984: 26). They are thus able to stress the dynamicized developmental dimension of the self-object or narcissistic transference. This type of transference enables the patient to rediscover, in the tie with the analyst, the possibility of not being retraumatized in relation to primitive needs.

If the analyst is sufficiently empathic – and here the transference becomes an intersubjective fact – the patient achieves a more secure sense of self. Abstinence as the active frustration of infantile needs is very different from neutrality as a willingness to abstain from judgement and instead to work with the patient to get to know and explore his points of view and subjective experiences. The self-object dimension of the transference transforms the analytic situation into a holding environment (Winnicott). The patient can relive in positive form archaic experiences of at-one-ness and fusion. It is this dimension, which is never absent even in an analysis based traditionally on the analysis of resistances, that gives interpretation its curative power. So much for another taboo – the 'transference cure', in the sense that a therapy which owes its positive effects to an unanalysed transference loses its pejorative connotation.

An avowed Hegelian, Ogden too published a contribution on transference in 1991. In line with the idea of a subject radically immersed in corporeality and in an intersubjective matrix, which makes him more of a phenomenologist (Reis 1999), and hence essentially preconscious, pre-reflective or pre-personal, Ogden portrays the transference as the product of dialectically interrelated basic modes whereby the ego experiences reality. Transference not only concerns the experience of internal objects in external objects, but is also 'a transferring of one's experience of the internal environment in which one lives on to the analytic situation' (Ogden 1991: 593). Conceived in this way, transference-as-displacement is impossible to disentangle from transference-as-function; indeed, it represents nothing but a disproportionate effect of the latter.

We now come to Fosshage (1994), who presents an organization-based model in contrast to the traditional view of transference, the displacement model. Transference is the unconscious pattern or principle whereby the subject elaborates and responds to the stimuli of internal and external reality in perceptual-cognitive-affective terms. The patterns are activated, not transferred. For this reason, the idea of a 'transference' from the past is misleading, because it obscures the pervasive continuity of a process that in fact calls to mind Piaget's concepts of assimilation and accommodation.

Like the intersubjectivist Fosshage but without citing him, Bachant and Adler (1997), from the classical Freudian camp, emphasize the adaptive significance of transference as a function of the mind and again invoke Piaget's paradigm of assimilation and accommodation. Transference is both the result of primitive intrapsychic conflicts and the factor that integrates immediate subjective experience. On the basis of these assumptions, the authors interpret the significance of the elaboration in the transference of real aspects of the analyst and of the interaction:

> Specific features of the analyst are magnified or globalized to provide the patient what is looked for in the object. It is not that the patient has found the 'reality' of the analyst; rather, the patient has constructed an object representation around some real

element of the analyst's character or demeanor that he or she needs to find.

(Bachant and Adler 1997: 1107)

To preserve the centrality of the transference neurosis in the treatment, Bachant and Adler distinguish an intrusive, unrealistic, archaic and pathological ('spectral') transference, corresponding to transference activity that has met with repression, from an unrepressed, non-intrusive and adaptive transference activity (transference as a function).

I should like to end this chapter by mentioning the contribution from the North American area that has perhaps impressed me most, both for its precision and rigour, and for its flexibility and ability to integrate a number of different aspects of the phenomenology of transference. 'Developments in Cognitive Neuroscience II. Implications for Theories of Transference', by Westen and Gabbard (2002), preceded by Gabbard (2001), is an attempt to base a theory of transference on the model of neural networks known as 'parallel distributed processing'. For these authors, a 'monolithic' concept of transference or transference neurosis is outdated. Transference has less to do with the transferring of libido on to the analyst or with the reactivation of old representations that were so to speak put to sleep in the past, than with the continuous construction and reconstruction of experience. The mind is engaged at all times in elaborating the stimuli that reach it in a given context. A number of networks (associative, hedonic and cognitive, conscious and unconscious) are activated in parallel with a view to 'online' integration of experiences of the past and experiences of the present. Transferences are therefore always *multiple* and *multidimensional*, and relatively analyst- and context-dependent. The intensity and typical asymmetry of the analytic relationship are the factors that activate the deeper patterns most involved in psychic suffering, but the mechanism is identical even in the most superficial contacts of ordinary life.

Surprisingly, and as a measure of the distance separating past notions from more recent conceptions – one need only think of the evocative power and suggestive theatricality of Freud's application of the image of fire to analysis of the erotic transference – the model of transference at its zero level offered by Westen in his lecture to the Milan Psychoanalysis Centre is that depicted in Figure 6.1, taken from McClelland *et al.* (1986: 8).

THE CAT

Figure 6.1 Transference at its zero level.

This illustrates an elementary (?) cognitive problem: specifically, how the mind succeeds in perceiving in the words 'THE' and 'CAT' one and the same character written in such a way as to resemble either an A or an H, and how it is thus able to resolve the ambiguity. As seen by these authors, transference is a process of attribution of meaning that makes use of searching for the already known, seeking to refind realities already experienced. An individual's adaptation to the facts of external and internal reality calls for continuous 'focusing' on the context, and transference is the relay in which the correspondence between present and past perceptual categorizations is constantly reviewed and categorial definitions are arrived at of objects concerning which the mind lacks a priori instructions. For this reason, there is no such thing as an appropriate or realistic reaction by the patient or the analyst that is in principle free of the shadow of unconscious fantasy.

7

Difference (a certain) identity transference

Difference

An extended theory of transference as a spectrum of multidimensional clinical phenomena can potentially resolve, or at least cast new light on, the network of antinomies (normal/pathological; real/fictitious; copy/new edition; relational/transference-related; unitary/multiple; etc.) in which this absolutely central concept of psychoanalysis has ultimately come to be entangled. However, that being the case, the problem arises of proposing a new definition for the concept, which, as Laplanche and Pontalis (1967: 456) recognize, is 'so difficult'. At zero (normal), or 'molecular', level, some authors see transference as a general, pervasive and ubiquitous psychological principle and, in accordance with Piaget's notions of assimilation and accommodation, as one of the mind's ways of organizing reality and adapting to it.

Together with a passage in which Freud appears to attribute the elementary mechanisms of the psyche to a general principle described by the 'more comprehensive concept of "contact" ', and with similarly unitary hypotheses of deconstruction and narratology, I take this approach as my starting point for this chapter. In it, I outline a possible model of the *weak* polarity of transference by analogy with Derrida's concept of *iterability*, with *metonymy* in linguistics, and with *displacement* in the rhetoric of dreams; all these concepts emphasize the role of context in the processes of assigning meaning. Clearly, what I am attempting is to achieve a dialogue between different languages, which are, however, not too remote from each other, considering, for example, Derrida's filial debt to Freud and the importance in Derrida's thought of de Saussure's idea of the arbitrary nature of the sign.

As a (seeming) digression, let me begin with a brief vignette from ordinary life,[1] since, as everyone, not least Freud (1925: 42), after all agrees, transference 'is a universal phenomenon of the human mind', which is relevant to all relationships between individuals.

I am talking to an English friend of mine. It is a Saturday morning – a time we set aside every so often for a chat. We are reviewing the translation of the abstract of a psychoanalytic paper and end up talking about the difficult and intriguing problems of translation. At one point, half-ironically and half-mischievously, my friend remarks on the problem, which non–analysts find it hard to understand, of the infinite range of conflicting interpretations in psychoanalysis. Perhaps also with the secret intention of putting him to the test, I there and then glimpse a possible line of defence: I recall something I read recently which aroused my curiosity and which seems to be just what is needed. Taking a piece of paper, I write the English word 'cat' twice in a column:

CAT
CAT

My opening gambit is to say that it is not only analysts who have a problem with interpretation: others too would not necessarily agree on a single solution. For example, I tentatively ask him, 'Here, for instance, how many words would you say I wrote?' The situation is clear. If he answers 'two', I shall point out that it is actually one word. If he says 'one', I shall tell him that there are two. Lastly, if he concludes that it is the same word repeated, I shall show him that, in reality, the second occupies a different space from the first, is situated in a changed context, and cannot therefore strictly speaking be identical. Moreover, this is not mere sophistry, considering also the extremely serious source[2] – as we shall see below – because the very possibilities of assigning meaning are involved in such issues. After all, a sign is such only if it can be repeated and reread outside the original context of its recording, emission or production – a context which therefore no longer saturates its conditions of intelligibility.

However, let us now return to what actually happened. My friend reflects for a moment, scenting a trap. I see his eyes light up. He then completely floors me with his answer: 'IN MY OPINION, YOU HAVE THERE A SIAMESE CAT AND A PERSIAN CAT!' All of a sudden we see in our mind's eye prototypical images of these two noble animals, and we burst into hearty laughter!

The 'transference' nature of this sentence lies in the fact that it contains the 'dream' of the emotions present at a given moment in the emotional field constituted by the two interlocutors and their relationship, so that the cats-as-characters in his remark can also be seen as transference vectors. The β-elements, proto-emotions and proto-sensoriality, as 'impressions' of an unknown but inescapable reality, are transformed into dreamlike cinematic frames or α-elements, and, combined in the form of available oneiric thoughts, become 'Lego pieces' for the construction of thought. It is as if the mind is basically unable to detach itself from the reality in which it is immersed, and is forced to process the stimuli of the here-and-now, as Ferro (2006: 154) seems to imply when he calls free associations 'obligatory', even if the narrative genres chosen are indeed absolutely free. The psychoanalytic concept of transference is equivalent to the discovery that we experience only the present moment or the remembered present: there is no experience of the present without the integration of the experience of the past. In other words, it is impossible to escape from the irresistible seduction exerted on thought and affects by the objects to which one is bound by relations of contiguity in a specific setting.

My interlocutor is ultimately perfectly aware that, despite appearances, he is faced with two different 'cats', which, however, share a certain identity, a certain property (an 'encyclopaedic marker', as Eco [1980] would say). In this case, this is a linguistic sign (but non-linguistic signs conform to the same logic: are not sensations and perceptions perhaps permeated by language too?) (de Man 1979; Bennington 1989; Butler 1997). Moreover, my friend's comment can already be regarded as the outcome of a whole series of elementary transferences[3] or transformations.[4] At zero level, there is a transference, which is in fact already quite complex, of certain properties in the transition from the first to the second sign. In other words, the perceptual and affective experience of the first word is displaced on to the second, which is recognized as similar on the basis of certain common qualities. The second word is then superimposed on the first. The movement is therefore in both directions, a to-and-fro movement rather than a transfer of properties or semes (minimum units of meaning), since the reverse transference can also be regarded as active – in other words, the retrograde deferral of determinations of meaning known as *Nachträglichkeit* (Derrida 1967a; Barale 1993). That is to say, the two terms constitute each other in accordance with a logic of differences and of bidirectional deferral of meaning. The one term cannot exist without the other.

When, subsequently to, or rather almost simultaneously with, the 'simple' reading of the letters written on the sheet of paper, the transferences of my friend (and myself) are broadened so as to include other meaningful elements of the context,[5] and he jokingly describes the cats, the cognitive and affective process is already much more complex and involves a number of dimensions. What is *transferred* – that is, by means of a series of unconscious operations, *substituted for or integrated with* the material signs on the paper, but in reality their mental representations (or rather, to use a term with fewer connotations of permanence, traces) – is an entire world of links, experiences, knowledge, and conscious and unconscious, declarative and procedural memories, as well as the pleasurable habitual climate of our Saturday morning meetings, with a certain use of humour, including scratching with claws. The two (?) signs-as-stimuli come to life and arouse in each of us representations of both real and fantasy cats, as well as, however, more complex emotions and memories.

The example in my vignette is taken from a text on deconstruction and speech acts (Halion 1989: 76), in which the author illustrates Derrida's principle of *iterability* or of its particular case called *citationality*. According to this principle, every sign or expression owes its very nature to the fact that it can be reiterated or repeated. However, since this can always only happen in a different context, which is immediately characterized by otherness, if only on account of the ego's irreducible state of slavery in its own house, a sign is the fruit both of identity and of difference. In other words, it can never be completely identical to itself. Authorial intention is limited by the unconscious. As soon as it is pronounced, a word is already structurally a quotation. This thesis is advanced by Derrida (1988) in *Limited Inc.* (the implicit homage to Freud is already obvious in the title, *Inc.* being the French abbreviation for the unconscious) against the presumption of Searle (1969), the author of *Speech Acts*, that it is possible to map the context of experience in all its elements, precisely to mark the sign of the speaker's intentionality – of a self-transparent consciousness not limited by the unconscious – and, ultimately, to disambiguate any statement. Derrida (1988: 53) writes:

> For the structure of iteration – and this is another of its decisive traits – implies *both* identity *and* difference. Iteration in its 'purest'

form – and it is always impure – contains *in itself* the discrepancy of a difference that constitutes it as iteration. The iterability of an element divides its own identity a priori, even without taking into account the fact that this identity can only *determine* or delimit itself through differential relations to other elements and that it hence bears the mark of this difference. It is because this iterability is differential, within each 'element' as well as between the 'elements,' because it splits each element while constituting it, because it marks it with an articulatory break, that the remainder [*restance*], although indispensable, is never that of a full or fulfilling presence.

Now *restance* means that which remains of any kind of communication, whether written or oral (Ramond 2001: 63); a neologism written in italics, as if to say: 'Watch out; proceed with caution'; it is not 'a sure thing [*de tout repos*]' as a 'concept', Derrida (1988: 53) concedes, somewhat encumbered as he is by his own jargon; a concept that, while surely paradoxical, serves to dispose of the traditional, widely accepted idea of permanence.

Hence the problem which I presented to my friend serves to illustrate the aporia of the impossibility of an absolute identity between nature, things themselves, and language, the dissemination or non-unequivocality of meaning, the 'fundamental distance at the centre of every human experience' (Saccone 1979: xxiii, translated). My point is that Derrida's ambition (and the reason for mentioning his theories, albeit on the margin of the vignette – a way of putting it in inverted commas and thus permitting myself a certain reticence concerning not strictly psychoanalytic matters) is to clarify, through a rereading of Austin (1962) and the ensuing vigorous dispute with Searle, the very structure of experience, the secret of the relationship between subject and object that Nietzsche (1873: 58) thought could be 'at most an *aesthetic* relation [. . .] a suggestive transference, a stammering translation into a completely foreign tongue'. What is this if not a transference process? In other words, can transference be thought of as the function charged with performing this translation or assimilation of external reality in terms of psychic reality, and as the matrix from which even the most complex and sophisticated forms of thought stem? In order to apply a certain transference dynamic to that text itself, I shall now quote a passage from *Limited Inc.* (Derrida 1988: 10) in which the concept of 'text' is strategically generalized so as to embrace all possible referents – the very experience of being – and hence so as to represent the basic conditions of signification:

> Let us consider any element of spoken language, be it a small or large unit [. . .] let us say that a certain self-identity of this element (mark, sign, etc.) is required to permit its recognition and repetition [. . .] Because this unity of the signifying only constitutes itself by virtue of its iterability, by the possibility of its being repeated in the absence not only of its 'referent', which is self evident, but in the absence of a determinated signified or of the intention of actual signification, as well as of all intention of present communication. This structural possibility of being weaned from the referent or from the signified (hence from communication and from its context) seems to me to make every mark, including those which are oral, a grapheme in general; which is to say [. . .] the nonpresent *remainder* [*restance*] of a differential mark cut off from its putative 'production' or origin. And I shall even extend this law to all 'experience' in general if it is conceded that there is no experience consisting of *pure* presence but only of chains of differential marks.

However, where have we already read virtually the *same* phrase, 'a certain [. . .] identity', and in what *different* context?

A certain [some] identity

On a famous page of 'Totem and Taboo' (Freud 1912–13: 85, my emphasis), which – oddly enough – discusses the way magical thought deals with past situations as if they were present, Freud uses almost the same words:

> It is further to be noticed that the two principles of association – similarity [*Ähnlichkeit*] and contiguity [*Kontiguität*] – are both included in the more comprehensive concept of 'contact' [*Berührung*]. Association by contiguity is contact in the literal sense; association by similarity is contact in the metaphorical sense. The use of the same word for the two kinds of relation is no doubt accounted for by *some identity* [*Eine . . . Identität*] in the psychical processes concerned which we have not yet grasped.

142

I found the coincidence intriguing. Starting from different vertices, Derrida and Freud use what is effectively one and the same phrase to sum up an essential, if problematic, quality of the mind that makes the creation of meaning possible. For Derrida, this quality is substantially equivalent to the concept of '*restance*' (but also to the trace, or 'a certain identity') which combines with 'difference' in iterability to reinitiate the cycle of signification each time. In the passage quoted, Freud, on the other hand, postulates the existence on the infralinguistic level of a central psychic mechanism, as yet undetermined, and does so by 'transferring himself' into the lexical field of linguistics or rhetoric. He therefore subordinates similarity (metaphor, from the Greek *metapheréin*, 'to transport') and contiguity (metonymy, from the Greek *metonymía*, 'change of name', although what is involved here is not so much the classical definition of the figure as the type of semantic relationship, based on its implied coexistence/proximity) to 'contact'. But when we say 'contact', are we not yet in fact also saying 'contiguity'? That is to say, are we not asserting the primary character of the second of the modes of relationship, contact 'in the literal sense'? Here we are assisted by the additional contribution of meaning afforded by etymology, which reveals the common root of the two terms in the Latin *contingere*. A point relevant to this argument, to which the above Freud quotation seems to allude, is that, notwithstanding irremediable disagreements, some authors in the field of linguistics consider that metaphor itself can be traced back to metonymy and placed under its hegemony. In this way, they believe that they can make metonymy the sole transformative device or trope[6] which can be thought of either as a general function of semiosis or as something involving a strategy of thought that cannot be further decomposed.

I shall now permit myself a second digression (or 'transference'?) with a view to – of course intuitively – interpreting Freud's phrase in terms of linguistics and narratology. Proust's description of the ability of involuntary memory to bring the past into the present in conscious scenes of extraordinary complexity is perhaps also the most impressive illustration, if considered at unconscious level, of the pervasive and potent action of transference. The following quotation from Proust is taken from Genette (1972: 57, translated); a certain play of quotations, or *iterations/alterations* of signs in this section, is also a direct or performative way of illustrating the proposition concerned: 'In that case as in all previous cases, the common sensation [. . .] had sought to recreate the old place *around itself* [. . .] the distant place begotten

143

around the common sensation [. . .] these resurrections of the past are so *total* that they *not only* compel our eyes [. . .] but force our nostrils [. . .] our will [. . .] our entire person [. . .]'. The emphasis is Genette's, and its aim is to underline, in the preselected text, the indications, interwoven as they are with chance and contingency, of the metonymic movement that lies at the origin of the analogical resolution, or short-circuit or magic of metaphor, which is presented as the antithesis of the usual character of necessity. Here is his extraordinary commentary:

> For there is seemingly nothing in the mechanism of reminiscence that is not purely analogical, since reminiscence is based on the identity of sensations experienced very far apart from each other in time and/or space [. . .] a single point of contact and communication [. . .] metaphor is here apparently lacking in any metonymy.
>
> It will not remain so for one more instant. Or rather, it never has been so, and it is only a process of analysis after the event that can enable us to assert that the reminiscence 'began' with what this analysis denotes as its 'cause'. The real experience in fact commences not with the grasping of an identity of sensation, but with a feeling of 'pleasure', of 'felicity', which initially appears 'without the notion of its cause' [. . .]. It will therefore be seen that the metaphorical relation is never perceived first, and that in most cases it even appears only at the end of the experience, as the key to a mystery played out entirely in its absence.
>
> But whatever the moment of manifestation of the role of what – since Proust himself refers to the 'explosion of memory' – one is inclined to call the analogical *detonator*, the essential point to be noted here is that this first blast is always, necessarily and immediately, accompanied by a kind of chain reaction which proceeds, no longer by analogy, but instead by contiguity, and which is, very precisely, the moment when the metonymic contagion (or, to use Proust's own term, the *irradiation*) takes over from metaphorical evocation [. . .]. It may be added that Proust himself, although giving the impression of considering only the metaphorical moment of the experience (perhaps because this moment is the only one he is able to *name*), insists again and again on the importance of this widening by contiguity.
>
> (Genette 1972: 55–57, translated)

So the first transition in these 'resurrections' of the past (Freud 1938: 174 also uses the term 'reincarnation' in relation to the transference) does not result, according to Genette, from the sudden kindling of the metaphorical image, but consists in the reawakening of *an unspecified affect*, not yet attracted by a particular object. The metonymic process then takes charge of the amplification of the contact point, which was seemingly based on pure analogy and is often only the choice and the bringing-into-the-present determined by the context of experience of one among a number of analogical virtualities: 'the difference is recorded in a system of similarity by contagion' (Genette 1972: 44, translated). That is why associations can be seen as in a sense rendered 'obligatory' by relations of 'coexistence'. Genette then associates the 'rhetoric of desire' with the phenomenon of metonymic *slippage*, which he regards as 'very well known in psychoanalysis' (p. 58, translated). Swann's passion for Odette causes him to frequent and appreciate a restaurant located near his beloved's house, and so on.

Based on the examination of certain cases of aphasia involving a crisis either of the combination aspect or of the selection aspect of language, Jakobson (1963), in an epoch-making contribution, denounced the hegemony of metaphor in favour of a diarchic system involving both metaphor and metonymy. Other, more radical, authors deconstruct (de Man 1979) or completely overturn the traditional hierarchy. Eco (1980: 222f., translated), for example, stresses the priority of metonymic contiguity: 'There are no reasons,' he writes, taking up the most extreme implications of his reading of Genette, 'why the taste of the *madeleine* should stand for *Combray* or indeed for time regained, other than that Proust's context intervenes to establish this relationship [. . .]; metaphors are metonymies that are unaware of each other and will one day become metonymies.' The primary role, therefore, is that of relationships of contiguity, of context and of history (as opposed to what might be, so to speak, timeless fantasies).

However open or inventive, then, metaphor proves to be a derivative of other preliminary operations. It cannot dispense with the pressures of a metonymic context,[7] of a 'rhizomatic fabric of cultural properties' (Eco 1980: 213f., translated), which decides which 'transfer features' (Weinrich 1976) are capable of being activated. The production of metaphors constitutes *work* calling for intertextual competence and the learning of a system of combination within a categorial index, encyclopaedia (potential reserve of information), or 'tree of implicitations'. The similarity is 'neither perceptual nor ontological, but semiotic' (Eco 1980: 229, translated).

Let us now return to the Freudian field. Transference as a function is to transference neurosis as the work of the karstic[8] stream of the activity of metonymy is to the – to paraphrase Wordsworth – stationary blasts of the waterfalls of metaphor. Just as metonymy proceeds from a feeling 'without any notion of its own cause', which cannot be explained except in terms of having been aroused by the immediate context of experience, so pleasurable or unpleasurable affects, inclinations or fears compel the subject to master the unknown and activate the play of signification (even if, of course, we are here introducing a teleonomic principle of the kind adduced ironically by Freud [1905: 59] in the form of Lichtenberg's *Witz*: 'He wondered how it is that cats have two holes cut in their skin precisely at the place where their eyes are'). The intensity of transference results from the extent of the affects aroused by the experience of reality. Ogden (1989: 209) expresses a similar concept: transference 'is a name we give to the illusion that the unknown object is already known [. . .]. As a result, no encounter is experienced as entirely new [. . .]. Without this illusion, we would feel intolerably naked and unprepared in the face of experience with a new person'. Moreover, it could be remarked that a *necessary* illusion becomes structural; it is no longer illusion as contrasted by the classical definition with the background of the possibility of an uncorrupted perception. The quest for similarities, for seemingly complete identities, united by the short circuit of metaphor, is a way of mastering experience. However, as we have seen, similarity is ultimately based on the perception of relationships of proximity and on the substitutions or displacements thereby permitted. Might this be the 'more comprehensive concept of "contact" ' or the 'some identity' postulated by Freud?

It is from these suggestions, which stem from Derrida, Freud and Genette, which have in common the centrality of the metaphor of the text[9] which is of course also shared by Bion and his alphabetical model, that I derive the key hypothesis advanced in this chapter, which is that of a substantial equivalence – of, precisely, *a certain identity* – between iterability in deconstruction, metonymy in language, displacement in the rhetoric of dreams and transference at its zero degree on the psychic level. These concepts refer to elementary mechanisms employed by the psyche for the generation of meaning. Inherent in all of them is an emphasis on the importance of the immediate context of experience (even if, in Derrida's case, it might be more correct to refer to the devaluation of the so-called real or historical, or 'originary', context, because it is not fully determinable, and to the re-evaluation of the immediate, unconscious context).

In the concept of unconscious narrative derivatives (Ferro), of waking dream thought (Bion), then, the productive convergence of (Freudian[10]) dream rhetoric and textual rhetoric (narratology) accounts for the status of the characters in the material brought by patients, thus affording a glimpse of the subterranean transference work in progress from the very first encounters, as well as in the smallest fragments of dialogue, as the clinical 'snapshots' presented in the following section will show.

The restricted field

The Romanian au pair

'The Romanian au pair,' Paola begins, 'asked me: "What does the word '*moroso*' mean? A lover, or boyfriend?" [A silence] . . . Sometimes when my dog is on the lead, Fluffy [the cat] comes close to him, OTHERWISE HE RUNS AWAY!!!'

Keeping interpretations on the lead, or even making less use of silence, seems to be essential to the development of a passionate transference.

Allergies

P: [Fluffy again] For a while he was allergic to tins of food. A youngish vet didn't understand that . . . Then we went to another one . . .

T: . . . Did he recommend a change of food . . .?!

P: Yes. And then the allergy went away!!

Interpretations are nourishing and fortunately there are some nice ones at the ready, or even pre-packed ones if you have neither the time nor will to cook – but watch out for allergies!

147

Scratches

Anna: Three months have gone by and my lymph nodes are still swollen. My doctor said it was because of the scratch I had from my cat, but I don't want to go and have the tests done. But if I start shivering and faint again, I might have to reconsider.

It can sometimes take a long time to correct mistakes.

The boyfriend

Eva: When R. and I make love, I feel like a woman. He makes me feel my body. I'm not a 'dead she-cat' any more, as my boyfriend always used to say.

Since Antonino Ferro described sexuality in analysis as a 'narrative genre', another way of reading remarks like the above is as an indication of the vitality of the therapeutic relationship.

The pet psychologist

P: Last night Cloe was absolutely off her head [Stefania tells me]. 'Yoooou, my friend, will have to go to a pet psychologist!!' I thought. I go along for my catty cuddle, but she takes it into her head to scratch me!

T: So . . . umm . . . the cat . . . scratched you!?

P: Yes, she scratched me! When she does that, it gets on my nerves. The fact is that she was the only cat in the house. Then the other one, the shaggy one, arrived. But she won't let anyone touch her . . . She is hysterical, quite crazy in fact, and runs away if anyone touches her. I said to Piero: 'Let's try to care just for her for a bit.' But so far we haven't been very successful.

An appropriate caption for the above might be 'an analyst-as-a-cat that scratches' – partly because an analytic little sister has been 'born' – instead of providing cuddly words and of 'looking after her' as suggested by Stefania, who is jealous and in retreat.

According to the classical, *restricted* definition, it would be difficult to deduce how the transference will develop from these micro-narrations. However, in an *extended* conception, they could be regarded as transparent (?) examples of how the interactive sequences of the analytic couple are structured at a precise instant. A first, hypothetical, level of meaning already appears on the surface. Each vignette contains plausible factual information: the au pair really exists; so does Fluffy; and the same applies to the boyfriend, to A., to S., to R., etc. Yet these characters can also be thought of as unconscious narrative derivatives of waking dream thought. Cats, catwomen, deer, foxes and chickens can each be seen as diffraction products of the transference or as condensation points of transference vectors activated by the couple's emotional field at a certain moment of their interaction – in the same way as metaphors are brought into the present by the metonymic context. The cats too, or rather the 'cats' as characters of the text of the analysis or as Freudian dream personifications, have a transference (certain inferences could also be drawn as regards real cats![11]). That is why, from the point of view of clinical work on the transference, it becomes important to abandon the position of an omniscient and neutral narrator looking down from on high, and instead humbly to ask oneself – in order to arrive at a 'vision with' the patient, a perspective known in narratology as internal focalization or 'restricted field' (Blin 1989) – what does the cat see?

Transference

The conceptual review presented in this chapter makes use of points of contact between various disciplines and between clinical and non-clinical settings in order to interpret the idea of the ubiquity and modularity or extensiveness of transference. According to this model, transference can vary over a very wide expressive range. The exchange of a trace of the object for, or its replacement by, another trace, in which the work of transference consists, is based on the irradiation of 'contact' elements which is originally triggered and then maintained by an affective wave (itself deposited in traces). Considered in these terms, a false connection, distortion, cliché, misunderstanding, *mésalliance* or mix-up (*quiproquo* is the word used by Neyraut 1974) – all of which are traditional synonyms of transference – can ultimately be attributed to a kind of zero (normal) degree of mental functioning.

The current status of the transference concept could therefore be defined as liquid or plural (Pontalis 1990). If transference is understood to mean a continuum of phenomena, the difference between transference at its minimum level and transference neurosis is a quantitative difference, a difference of degree and not of structure. This avoids the risk of an excessive loss of specificity and hence of the impossibility of using the concept itself for the purposes of theory or technique. The transference becomes a 'variable-geometry' phenomenon, which is depicted as a fractal, a figure composed, with an effect of *mise en abyme*, of parts which infinitely reproduce the complete figure at smaller and smaller scales and which conforms to a recursive algorithm. The most familiar example is a tree (see Figure 7.1, which is taken from a design by John Ruskin, 1858), in which the self-similar forms are repeated on various scales.[12]

As with non-mathematical fractals, there is a natural limit to transference too. This could be the level of mental functioning corresponding to 'metonymic contagion', to 'contact associations', or to the irradiation of memory traces. In discourse, this kind of functioning is reflected in tropes and rhetorical figures of increasing complexity, all of which, however, manifest the oscillatory mechanism that is the linchpin of transference/displacement according to the traditional definition of metonymy as substitution by contiguity, and also according to its less traditional definition as a metaphor-generating device, involving substitution by similarity. It is this mechanism that Freud (1901: 118) is invoking in his famous

Figure 7.1 Tree with self-similar forms repeated on various scales.

150

comment about Dora: 'It was clear that I was replacing her father in her imagination.'

The mental apparatus, then, seeks identity, but finds only traces. A trace is the mark of an object that is no longer 'present', the residue or evidence of something withdrawn from full presence, from perfect 'identification'. It is the part that can be displaced, translated or transferred, and that assumes responsibility for the substitution. Lastly, it is the marker that links the elements in a chain of associations. Transference is the process of recognition of both psychic and material reality, which consists in displacement from trace to trace, and each trace can be the meeting point of a number of associative lines – the actual metaleptic movement of thought. Being unable to come to rest in a perfect identity – that is, in a homeostasis that is never affected by any disturbance – in a state of perpetual 'once only-ness' (Niall 2004), the subject, in order to adapt to the flux of the world, has no choice but to function on the basis of tropes, of figures involving the exchange of one thing for another.

From this point of view, transference is the process that seeks what is already known to the subject so as to enable the subject to adapt to reality. Present perceptual categorizations are compared with those deposited in memory on the basis of criteria of similarity. In this way it becomes possible to know a world concerning which the mind does not possess pre-ordained instructions, and meaning is constructed.

By virtue of this play of identity and difference, every interpretation/reading becomes a misreading, another sign that can be interpreted in turn, because, in the longing for a perfect identity or correspondence or match between words and things, one ultimately finds only the outcome of a wearing away of the metaphor that is the matrix of the literal meaning, the ineliminable undecidability of the figurative, and the intrinsic closure of the system of language on to itself. Every word, as soon as it is spoken, carries with it a supplement of meaning to itself, which the subject is unable to control, and whose effects may be either immediate and visible, as in the hyperbolic case of a parapraxis, or totally outside the awareness of the subject and sometimes surprising.

Given that no one is immune from 'distortions', distortion after all being the rule (or rather a possibility inherent in the structure of communication), transference cannot be perceived and revealed by the analyst and resolved (solely) in utterances concerning the truth/ falsity of the relationship – that is, constative utterances. However, to an even greater extent, or additionally, interpretation inevitably takes the form of a doing, of a performative act – that is, of a statement that to some extent contributes to the production of what it describes, in order to modulate the patient's affective states and to negotiate the disproportion (the sign of an internal unbalance) that distinguishes a transference bordering on the pathological (the category 'pathological' being, moreover, cultural and social).

However, it must be repeated that, whereas the reading of reality is a necessary misunderstanding, a misinterpretation – the very precondition, in the view of Lacan, of an effective interpretation – we can nevertheless not evade a requirement of correctness, because, on the contrary, the awareness of the relative illegibility of reality (that is, of the fact that ultimate reality is inaccessible) makes the reading itself an ethical act (Hillis Miller 1987). But if the rules delimiting the relevant sphere of correctness are understood to be conventional and the fruit of an agreement, this will nevertheless be an agreement that cannot be confined to the couple and to the enclosed space of the analyst's consulting room. The only possible way of conceiving the situation is in fact as a centrifugal consensuality that on each occasion pushes beyond the perimeter of the virtually infinite series of communities to which each person belongs and their zones of intersection. Yet this consensuality can never optimistically be said to be complete or to attain truth in a transcendental sense.

To sum up, in an extended conception of transference, the most important aspect to be considered is the constant and necessary busy hum of its operation as the key mechanism of the dreamwork and alpha-function of the mind, and ultimately of thought. This function is performed, in proportion as the intimacy of the relationship grows, through the activation and dynamic, exponential and parallel enlistment of a large number of associative pathways – which Westen and Gabbard (2002), two authors who consider the traditional concept of transference to be no longer valid, equate in their model with neural networks. It involves the bidirectionality of transference vectors – that is, the twofold movement from patient to analyst and from analyst to patient, which has the consequence that there are no true copies or reprints of the transference, but only new editions; and an infinite dispersal of intensity, or wide spectrum of manifestations.

At the two extremes of this spectrum – the 'evil spirits' (Freud 1926: 227) awakened to new life in the transference neurosis, on the one hand, and the zero-degree transference as a bridgeman or 'general ferryman' (Ferruta 2006, translated), on the other – a term that alludes to both can perhaps again be found in Derrida's limiting concept of *restance*, which, together with that of difference, structures iterability. The *restance* (what remains of the play of identity and difference, or, according to Bion, of *invariances* and *transformations*) – the trace or resistance; what is reiterated and returns; a ghost or *revenant* – is a non-identity which, however, permits and at the same time represents a 'minimal idealization', 'a certain repeatable identity' – that is, the deposition of a mental trace or concept of the object (and hence once again in its absence).[13]

If we eschew the reintroduction of an absolute and already dis-carded notion of permanence (of full consciousness or presence-to-itself), while at the same time having to take account of the possibility of recognition inherent in the phrase 'a certain identity', a 'divided' or differential identity, then the *restance*, or *non-present restance* (a para-dox), not based on any decomposition or abyssal regression to stable sub-entities or essences, involves rather, as the minimum unit of experience, the mind's capacity to *categorize*, or to *construct* – as Freud (1895) would say, to *sieve* – experience.

In other words, the *restance* inherently carries with it the metonymic movement of temporalization, of the very possibility of reusing a sign; it is the movement of transference, of the same transference that, in the classical sense, is in fact connoted by a concept of permanence, of the timeless presence of the sign to itself, as something transferred, tendentially unchanged, from the past on to its new object. Vis-à-vis this already dominant model, a reversal of perspective is brought about by Bion: the objective of analysis is now less that of enabling the subject to relive the infantile neurosis than of listening to the way he organizes his immediate context of experience (partly) through the language of the past.

The recording of the mark or trace (or indeed of the visual picto-gram or α-element) could be conceived in the same way as Barthes (1980: 115) sees photography as 'a bizarre *medium*, a new form of hallucination: false on the level of perception, true on the level of time: a temporal hallucination, so to speak, a modest *shared* hallucin-ation (on the one hand "it is not there," on the other "but it has indeed been"): a mad image, chafed by reality'. A photograph always seems to carry with it the referent (what it represents); it is its 'weight-less, transparent envelope' (p. 5), while nevertheless bearing witness to the tautology of a system of perception or recording which is by its nature tendentious and actually reproduces the structure of its own chemical and physical 'transference' devices. Photography documents not the real, the object, but Time, 'the lacerating emphasis of the *noeme* ("*that-has-been*"), its pure representation' (p. 96). Subjectivity, in a word, emerges from a language[14] that precedes it, is determined by it and then also contributes to determining it.

The paradox of the transference is thereby perhaps merely shifted to a different level, and reality ultimately gives the impression, as it were, of dissolving into the insoluble problem of Time. Who, one might well ask, could better symbolize this removal of things from any metaphysical logic, from any firm grip on identity, than Alice's cat – if I may again engage in the play of the dissemination of meaning – a Cheshire cat, which disappears bit by bit leaving behind, quite conspicuous between the branches of a tree, nothing but its enigmatic grin?

8

More affects . . . more eyes
On postmodern issues and
deconstruction(s) in analysis

> There is *only* a perspective seeing, *only* a perspective
> 'knowing; and the *more* affects we allow to speak about
> one thing, the *more* eyes, different eyes, we can use to
> observe one thing, the more complete will our 'concept'
> of this thing, our 'objectivity,' be.
>
> (Friedrich Nietzsche, *On the Genealogy of Morals*,
> 1887)

Derridian cor/respondences[1]

'It is under this title [*Civilization and Its Discontents*] that Freud's provocative challenge to the folklore of modernity entered our collective consciousness and in the end framed our thinking about the consequences − both intended and unintended − of the modern adventure.' With these words, Zygmunt Bauman (1997: 1) begins his book *Postmodernity and Its Discontents* by paying tribute to Freud and placing the malaise, the crisis of modernity, that characterizes our age under the banner of psychoanalysis. As further evidence of the role of Freud's theories in moulding the new cultural climate that can broadly be described as postmodern, the Derridian theses subsumed in the concept of 'deconstruction' may be mentioned. These can indeed be seen as a radical version and development, in the sphere of philosophy, of certain themes of psychoanalytic thought.[2] In this connection, one need only mention the decentring of the subject; the

155

emphasis on the rhetoric of dreams; the central importance of the metaphor of the text; the intrinsic symptomaticity of language; the principle of self-reflexivity; and the pluralism of viewpoints surrounding the conscious/unconscious dichotomy. Further elements that may be adduced include the 'realization' of the psychic; the dislocation of reflective-rational thought in the rule of evenly suspended attention and in the (virtually) unlimited abandonment to the drift of free associations; the intersubjectivism implicit in the notions of transference and countertransference and in the non-objectivizing analytic attitude; or the constructivism of 'narrative' interpretations.

So it is surely impossible not to see the Freudian enterprise as involving a radical 'antirealism' (here understood in the sense of a critique of the immediate data of consciousness) within the outer shell of an epistemological continuity – that is, of a modernism or positivism progressively and inexorably corroded from within, and already 'marked' by the singular decision to pay attention to the rejected products of the ego, to what remains on the margins of rational thought, and for that reason alone constitutes grounds for scandal – namely, dreams, slips of the tongue, *Witze*, parapraxes, and symptoms. But at the same time, how else is this antirealism to be understood than as the search for a 'truer' sense of reality, as the tension directed toward the unmasking of an illusion, the referential illusion – the Montalean 'usual illusion' – and, ultimately, toward the erosion of the very 'principle of reality' (Vattimo 1989), and as the expression of an absolutely 'active' and ethical scepticism?

It is for this reason, owing to the pervasive presence of Freud-derived themes – that it has been possible to describe the work of Derrida as the 'psychoanalysis of philosophy', or rather of the neurosis of philosophy that has always been known as metaphysics. A century after the *Traumdeutung*, at the turn of a new millennium, 'deconstruction' can be seen as one of the most valuable collateral developments of psychoanalytic thought, and surely one of those that have most authentically absorbed the sense of the Freudian 'plague' – that element of the sulphurous, of a 'residue' that cannot be equated with totally normalized thought. In Derrida's passion, one may discern what Virgil calls *veteris vestigia flammae* – beyond the negligible aesthetizing aspects and the associated risks of narcissistic reflection, of the sterility of the manner, and of the asphyxia of non-inspiration – in the rigorous, stubborn shunning of the neutralization that would stem from institutionalization in a 'neo-' or 'post-ism', from the once-for-all reduction to the state of captivity of one ideology among others. This resistance to homologation is another feature of the affinity between psychoanalysis and deconstruction, which is justified by the obvious relationship of filiation (although other, no less decisive, influences are of course also at work, including in particular Nietzsche and Heidegger).

Analytic listening, in Derrida, becomes a slow and patient reading and rereading, an intimate conversation with the text aimed at detecting its most secret resonances – the faults, discontinuities and hiatuses that betoken its repressions, or, in other words, the effects of the relations of force that weave its subterranean fabric. The classical method of philosophical argumentation is transmuted into a 'style' of associative commentary, and the practice of thought thereby inaugurated, known as deconstruction, is called for short the 'transference' of meanings ('more than one language' is perhaps the only other formula by which Derrida was ever prepared to describe it), a 'therapeutic activity that makes demands on the text, just as an analyst speaks to a neurotic, inducing him to tell his story, in an interminable analysis that promises not to cure its disease but only to make it tolerable' (Ferraris 2003: 41, translated).

Deconstruction and psychoanalysis can be thought of as mutual inscriptions *en abîme* – to use an image dear to Derrida – that is, as each supplementing, or *en coeur* of, the other. Derrida is thus a Freudian against the purported 'return to Freud' of Lacan, who, in the guise of critical thought, establishes the tyranny of the letter (or literality) of the signifier – against the Lacan who deciphers and reveals the ultimate truth of Poe's 'The Purloined Letter'. He is a Freudian, too, against Foucault, who, in *Madness and Civilization*, sees psychoanalysis – not without ambiguity and some rethinking – as the *n*th insidious form of the 'Enlightenment-based' repression of everything the bourgeoisie relegates to the extraterritoriality of *unreason*. He is a Freudian, finally, in his radical refusal to elevate his own thought to the status of a system – as he explains in his splendid short contribution 'Some Statements and Truisms about Neologisms, Newisms, Postisms, Parasitisms, and other small Seismisms'[3] (Derrida 1990a) – a thought seen rather as a critical theory that is always *en cours*, in a state of flux, by definition unreconciled (as psychoanalysis is bound to be), as well as in his view that one thinks (if at all) and assumes responsibilities only if one has the courage to confront the aporias of reason and the inexpressible.

157

It would be impossible here to enumerate fully all the Freudian themes disseminated throughout the writings of Derrida, as well as, conversely, the deconstructionist concepts that have profoundly influenced contemporary psychoanalysis (Protter 1985; Leary 1994; Aron 1996; Elliott and Spezzano 1996; Holland 1999): antiessentialism; the critique of the structuralist paradigm; the turning to account of the materiality of language; the stressing of the hierarchies and value choices implicit in any discourse; the idea summarized in the concept of *différance*, according to which 'language, or any code, any system of referral in general, is constituted "historically" as a weave of differences' (Derrida 1972: 11f.); the thesis of the subordination of any experience of self or objects to semiotic mediation; the critique of the 'metaphysics of presence' or of the subject – that is, of the idea of a 'natural' construction; and so on. What matters is to draw attention to his non-symbiotic, non-instrumental but original and creative spirit in relation to Freud's oeuvre. Even a certain illegibility – a point that irritates some critics – reminds us, on the one hand, of the dilemmas of knowledge, the unbridgeable gap between the aspiration to dominate reality, to 'tell' the meaning, and the tragic inappropriateness and fallaciousness of our cognitive, emotional, perceptual and linguistic instruments, and, on the other, of the requirement of not saturating the sense, of offering a 'hospitableness to the reading of the other' (Derrida and Ferraris 1997: 32), of emphasizing the meaning of subjective experience, and of deconstructing the reassuring 'scientific' distance from the object. The sense is deferred (*Nachträglichkeit*, another Freudian legacy): it is always the pale remembrance of something that belongs to the past.

The phrasing of Derrida, who was recalled on the morrow of his death in the two largest circulation American dailies as the 'abstruse theorist' (Kandell 2004) and the founder of a 'diabolically difficult' philosophy (Sullivan 2004), is informed by an inexhaustible ethico-existential tension; it is full of pathos, always replete with a kind of amazed awe, but never cerebral or an end in itself, even in the most virtuosic of linguistic games. The tools with which he digs into words, the lexical innovations and graphic anomalies – bars, quotation marks and parentheses, frames or borders or margins: places of inclusion or exclusion, where the sense arises from the repression of everything outside – appear as elements of a skilful mixture of rhetorical choices. In this way, there are enacted in the text – often in a deliberately 'literary' style – the same contents as are then expressed in plain, direct form in more traditionally argumentative interludes, staging posts for the reader on a passionate but by no means easy journey. The philological precision, coupled with a kind of infinitesimal and radical displacement of meaning, the tangential homing in on concepts, and the 'micro-Finnegans Wakes' – that is, the lightning-swift, Joycean flights of certain syllabic condensations – may irritate, but then, every so often, we also encounter the unexpected epiphany of intuition, the shock of meaning.

The result is a textual practice that demystifies the 'natural' linguistic codes, challenges the stereotypes of a rationality whose movements are prefigured and constrained in its very categories, and seems at times to entrust itself to the generative ambiguity of poetic phrasing, without ever aspiring to a closure of sense, or succumbing to the illusion of being able to achieve such a closure – owing not to a *parti pris*, but to the painful consciousness of the intangibility of any ultimate truth. This consciousness is reflected in the rank and space accorded to rhetoric, which appears on the one hand as performative and directed toward persuasion, and, on the other, as a system of tropes, a device that deconstructs its own text. So the reading-cum-interpretation of a text boils down not so much to the extraction of a truth – a liquidation of the text through criticism – as to the writing, or production, of another text that is superimposed on the first, thereby bringing about numerous openings of sense in a process of 'doing'. Finally, then, deconstruction is a thought, a central aspect of which is the Oedipal metaphor of blindness as a prelude to insight (De Man 1971; Derrida 1990b), and which is perhaps definable by this *quasi-oneiric* aspect: that is the adjective that comes to mind, and with it the suggestion of another, obvious, Freudian correspondence and anticipatory vision. Does the relative opacity of consciousness not correspond, in analysis, to the intermittent blindness of the suspension of focused attention; to the temporary hypnosis of reflective logic; and to the darkness in the auditorium whereby the theatre of the unconscious can be illuminated?

The neo-rhetorical turn

In a celebrated drawing by Johann Heinrich Füssli, a man, head bowed, beside the magniloquent but now mutilated and scattered remains of the colossal statue of Constantine in the courtyard of the

Conservatory Palace in Rome's Campidoglio, weeps for the lost grandeur of antiquity; the fragmented body is surely one of the most telling figures of modernity. Prior to the work of Kuhn (1962) on the structure of scientific revolutions, standards of rationality were deemed to be totally timeless, ahistorical and a-ideological. The self-reflexivity of modern epistemologies and the attention paid to the procedural nature of cognitive activities, by contrast, entail mourning for any essentialism or foundationalism, and renunciation of the reassuring aspiration to a divine knowledge of the world and of a solid, eternal order. Knowledge has become uncertain, fickle, provisional, partial and untrustworthy. A turn of such proportions confronts us with the loss of our customary references and familiar certainties, and with a radical sense of quasi-vertiginous and uncanny (in Freud's sense) loneliness and disorientation.

Among those who have done most to plunge the certainties of the philosophy of science into crisis is Paul Feyerabend: it is easy to imagine the upheaval caused by the bursting of a Dadaist into the genteel salons of the 'laureate' epistemologists, from Vienna to Oxford. With his iconoclastic spirit, Feyerabend blew a breath of fresh air into the oppressive, musty atmosphere of 1960s epistemological imperialism. He showed persuasively how knowledge accretes through the proliferation of virtually incommensurable theories – theories that have ahistorical development, and depend on their context, as well as on the opportunism and pragmatism of scientists. The workshop of science is chaotic, disorderly and labyrinthine: rules are constantly violated, and seemingly absurd theses are stubbornly and impudently upheld in the teeth of all sensible evidence. The systematic effraction of method – perpetrated with cunning, imagination, rhetorical skill, dialectical capability and a sense of play – seems to be the only rule; 'there is only *one* principle that can be defended under *all* circumstances and in *all* stages of human development. It is the principle: *anything goes*' (Feyerabend 1975: 28). Scientific advances often mature in a chaotic climate, made up of backward steps, the forgoing of reason, deviations, errors and illogical sideways excursions: 'The ideas survived and they can *now* be said to be in agreement with reason. They survived because prejudice, passion, conceit, errors, sheer pigheadedness, in short because all the elements that characterize the context of discovery, *opposed* the dictates of reason *and because these irrational elements were permitted to have their way*' (p. 155).

The cardinal elements of Feyerabend's model are competition, persuasion, and history. From a methodological standpoint, what matters is the evolution of a theory over long periods of time and not the form it assumes at any given time. These ideas cannot fail to remind us of the passage in 'On Narcissism: An Introduction' where Freud writes that empirical interpretation 'will not envy speculation its privilege of having a smooth, logically unassailable foundation, but will gladly content itself with nebulous, scarcely imaginable basic concepts, which it hopes to apprehend more clearly in the course of its development, or which it is even prepared to replace by others. For these ideas are not the foundation of science, upon which everything rests [. . .]' (Freud 1914b: 77).

In recent years the human sciences have experienced several decisive turns: first the linguistic turn, then the hermeneutic turn, and lately the rhetorical turn (Simons 1990). It would not be wrong to see Feyerabend (together with Perelman, Rorty, and others) as one of the protagonists in the consolidation of this trend. A conviction shared by those involved, in various capacities, in this cross-current of ideas is that rhetoric can not only supply the instruments for a critical approach to the objectivistic claims of knowledge, but also constitute the foundation of a new theory of inquiry. Rhetoric proceeds in two directions: on the one hand, it deconstructs scientific discourse, which is presumed to be epistemologically strong and based on logic and sense data, drawing attention to its metaphorical, argumentative, and persuasive fabric and its attention to its audience; while, on the other, it informs us that these characteristics are not secondary, or emendable, or spurious, but that it is precisely in them that the very possibility of establishing any type of knowledge inheres.

In this way, the elements of arbitrariness, contingency, chance and creativity are highlighted in the rhetorical edifice of scientific argument. Non-algorithmic procedures, values and interests of the scientific community, intuition, aesthetic judgements and idiosyncrasies of every kind are involved in the construction of discourse. Texts are analysed, decentred and defamiliarized. The very 'facts' are seen as intimately bound up with the theories and context: for example, the aura of magic surrounding expressions such as 'statistical significance' or 'reliability' is clearly brought out. It is maintained that knowledge has no foundations, or that the foundations themselves are historically determined constructions; and that the strategic scientific debates in which each thesis drives its fellows up to higher levels of articulation, in a process of ongoing competition, have a deliberative character.

Rhetoric appears to lend itself better than hermeneutics to describing the sense of the practice of science, because it draws attention to the dialogic, persuasive and organizational character of empiricism itself. From the rhetorical point of view, what takes place is not discovery but creation. There is no longer any distinction between a context of discovery and a context of justification, and between observational and theoretical terms: the phases of discovery, creative imagination, justification and rational presentation overlap, each being directed towards a public, whether real or only imaginary. The principle inevitably espoused is of a truth based on a rational consensus rather than on purely logical knowledge and 'pure' empirical data – on the narrative paradigm, understood in terms of its two currents, namely, an argumentative, persuasive theme on the one hand, and an aesthetic, literary theme on the other.

The only apparently remaining foundation lies in intersubjectivity and dialogue, in accordance with the theories of Habermas and Gadamer. Forms of relativism are consolidated, their only corrective being the search for a consensus of opinion, which is never arrived at once and for all, but remains in a state of continuous negotiation. As Bion points out in *Cogitations* (1992), the heliocentric hypothesis, which had been known since antiquity, did not become scientific until it received a sufficient degree of approval on the part of the research community. It is the harsh Darwinian selection of ideas, the tension between competing theories and their relative persuasive strength, that decides what comes to be accepted in any given instance as a more or less accurate representation of reality.

From the point of view of a dialogic and intersubjective justification of scientific practice, rhetorical enunciations, then, are no longer seen as ornamental components, but as institutive elements of discourse itself. The rhetorical strategy governing discourse is distributed over various levels; it may be to a greater or lesser extent concealed, and certainly determines what is or is not accepted as empirical evidence. One of rhetoric's main tools is metaphor. Now declared metaphors, even in scientific discourse, are not accessories, devoid of meaning, or mere expedients, but clues located on the surface of the text to the existence of a highly complex labour of narration and imagination, and they therefore also constitute privileged pathways affording access to more abstract levels of argument. While it is true that images have meaning within the linguistic fabric in which they are embedded, an analytic-scientific text too may be said to aim for metaphors 'of its own', to presuppose and justify these, and to be resolved in them. Contemporary culture is extremely interested in the status of metaphor. This reflects the crisis of 'correspondentist' epistemologies: the tendency is to repudiate the ideal of a philosophical/scientific language unpolluted by figurative elements, and even the opposition of metaphor and concept. Indeed, conceptual-demonstrative or abstract language, with its univocal bias, is interwoven with metaphors, whose figurative sense has been lost: these are now dead, lexicalized, and have become 'necessary'. However, any text directed toward the acquisition of knowledge establishes within itself a renewed tension between unknown metaphors (concepts) and living metaphors. Again, the pair 'denotative/ connotative' calls to mind the opposition between 'cognitive' and 'emotional' − and it is not difficult to see that, even in psychoanalytic discourse, recovery of the emotional/aesthetic dimension is central to the process of knowledge. The dimension of metaphor cannot be limited to the single enunciation (which remains its minimum space), but extends to the text as a consistent set of enunciations.

With such a conception of knowledge, the problem arises, not as Spence (1994) seems to suggest, of purging scientific (in the present case, psychoanalytic) discourse of rhetoric, but of comparing a number of more or less accurate representations of reality and selecting the most convincing ones; of deciding in each case whether a representation possesses the character of arbitrariness or necessity, appropriateness, or internal and external consistency, and of justification in relation to the context. In Spence's critique, psychoanalytic discourse is seen as thoroughly pervaded by rhetorical elements (with reference to the use of metaphors and of *auctoritas*), understood in the common, negative sense of 'empty rhetoric'. Spence, for his part, advocates the adoption of the rules applied by the natural sciences and the establishment of a large-scale database containing a mass of empirical research by the techniques of data recording and computer processing. The concept of 'narrative truth' is adduced only to show it in the worst possible light, while the notion of the inevitable and contingent function of rhetoric in any scientific discourse is completely lacking. The presumption is somehow maintained that it is possible to define the nature of an element of clinical data and that, at some time in the future, the various psychoanalytic theories will be unifiable. Spence's critique of the use of metaphor ultimately suggests a belief in the possibility of a 'true', timeless science, corresponding to 'a world out there'.

Grünbaum (1984) disposed once and for all of the claim of psycho-analysis to the status of a natural science. Although he admittedly constructed his target ad hoc, without taking account of the history of Freud's theories and their evolution over time, his critique of the nature of the 'facts' of psychoanalysis should not be rejected on that account. Again, it seems impossible for psychoanalysis ever to be able to satisfy the criteria of a scientific empiricism, which has, in certain restricted circles, attained high levels of formalization – what can be expressed, in other words, as a virtually unanimous consensus among the research community on certain concepts, procedures and meth-odological principles (although even here one may note how readily idealizations and simplified visions of the theoretical and practical 'workshops' of others come to be accepted, and how much con-ceptual indeterminacy enters into the respective models the closer one approaches to their 'periphery').

The recent history of the relationship between theories of know-ledge and psychoanalysis is the history of a controversial relationship: judgements from which no appeal lies; defences that are weak rather than strong, or irritated, or over-optimistic; abstruse arguments; or simple repression of the problem. In a book on this subject, Strenger (1992) places psychoanalysis at the intersection of hermeneutics and science. Now the hermeneutic approach gives rise to the risk of philosophical-literary homogenization, of a psychoanalysis à la carte, which seemingly lacks the reference to the bedrock of the constraints imposed on psychic life by biology and hence by the drives. The 'nihilistic vocation' of hermeneutics (Vattimo 1994), the inevitable, albeit extremist and abstract, outcome on the theoretical level, con-jures up, for some, the ghost of unlimited semiosis and consequently of an absolute relativism. However, such a position – aside from the fact that it is contradictory in terms of its own logical premises, for not even the idea that nothing is knowable can aspire to be absolute! – would be limited by the obvious circumstance that not all the infinite versions or interpretations of the world are compatible with life: the paradoxes and aporias of reason do not dispense one from the obliga-tion of finding an effective form of practice, with which the treatment must be identified, and from submission to an ethical principle of responsibility. So, many of the anti-postmodern positions that ultim-ately converge in the charge of nihilism are based on the same mistake as is made by those who place the natural sciences in an ahistori-cal dimension and take an essentialist view of them.[4] It is as if

interpretative activity emerged from the void and were not conditioned, as it in fact is, by complex networks of constraints, by discursive and control strategies, and by the demands of consistency – as
if language itself were not rooted in a living world (the Heideggerian
Lebenswelt).

In fact, however, not all scientific theories meet with the same
degree of acceptance, and not all interpretations are equivalent. Yet,
uncomfortable as it may seem, there is no ahistorical, universal criterion for deciding whether, at a given historical moment, a specific
practice (e.g. exorcism – Strenger 1992) may be deemed correct and
efficacious. Rhetoric shows us what science and hermeneutics have
in common (the fact that both are based on a 'political' consensus)
and what divides them – namely, the differing degree of consensus,
which proves to be inversely proportional to the complexity of the
object and directly proportional to the possibility of manipulating it.

The practice of psychoanalysis is no different from that of other
scientific disciplines in predetermining its own theoretical conditions
of existence – that is, its postulates – in selecting its own opening on
to the world, in negotiating means of verification, and in holding to
the observance of certain operational constraints. This too points to a
consensus of opinion within the community of researchers who
share an interest in the same object of knowledge, on whose definition they agree – an object that, in this case, cannot tolerate excessive
reductionism owing to its hypercomplexity. The fact that the degree
of agreement may be less than in other communities does not detract
from the scientific nature – and perhaps one might say the 'rationality'
– of the procedure itself. In medical treatments too, we ask for the
rationale for the use of a drug, and not the absolute presumption of
a given effect. If, like certain authors – for instance, Meltzer – one
asserts that psychoanalysis is an art, this means only that one has opted
to emphasize an aspect of psychoanalytic procedures that is present in
every science: for the imagination will always find figures or models
that have certainly not been inferred empirically, but nevertheless
organize empiricism.

Given these premises – that is, the impossibility of drawing a clear
boundary between science and hermeneutics (or rather rhetoric) – it
might also appear quite futile and meaningless to ask whether psychoanalysis should be assigned to the former or the latter field. Yet psychoanalysis is faced with some formidable rivals. It therefore cannot
fail to take account of advances in neighbouring disciplines. It must

be capable of convincing. Even if its actual legitimacy is (perhaps) no longer in question, it must nevertheless demonstrate its superiority over other scientific theories and therapeutic practices, and possibly adopt a critical stance toward the ideology of the domination of technique and efficiency (Protter 1985).

It may be concluded that the founding principles of psychoanalysis cannot but be multiple and heterogeneous, and that the choices will either be dictated on each individual occasion by rhetorical strategies, or depend on chance and on the dynamic tensions arising out of the complex fabric woven by other disciplines and by alternative universes of discourse. The idea is gaining ground of a truth equivalent to the itinerary undertaken to attain it, and of a therapeutic action due no longer (solely) to the rewriting of the subject's history, but to the psychological growth permitted by the theatre of analysis and the play of the unconscious (Bollas 1999). It is obvious too that the 'linguistic game' of historical reconstruction contributes to this growth – and that, conversely, when a patient becomes more capable of symbolization, his vision of himself and of the course of his life is enriched and broadened – that is to say, it becomes 'truer' and more consistent.

The form of the content

In some recent articles I tried to revisit a few pivotal psychoanalytical concepts from the viewpoint of the analytic field (Ferro 1992; Gaburri 1997; Baranger 2005), which can be broadly referred to as 'postmodern' sensibility. Here, I am just synthesizing their essential themes.

It is no coincidence that Freud, who was the first to read his own case histories as 'short stories', preferred the term 'construction' to that of interpretation, arguing as follows (1937: 260f.): 'The analyst finishes a piece of construction and communicates it to the subject of the analysis so that it may work upon him; he then constructs a further piece out of the fresh material pouring in upon him, deals with it in the same way and proceeds in this alternating fashion until the end.' Hence the interpretation is structured like a narrative that actually contributes to the making of the text it is intended to illuminate, of which it eventually comes to form an integral part. The patient's text and the analyst's interpretation-cum-text are ultimately indistinguishable (Schafer 1992).

Now, the plots revealed by transference interpretation unfold on the stage of the unconscious. Precisely for this reason, transference interpretation may be deemed to give rise to the same modal shift (namely, the opening of access to another possible world) as the telling of a dream (Bal 1985; Nelles 1997; Genette 2004), and can thus be seen as an 'embedded' narrative, located by its very nature on a different narrative level – that is, within a different spatio-temporal frame.

That is not all. Within the text of the analysis in vivo, transference interpretation also brings about a *metalepsis*,[5] a transgression of the narrative framework (as in Woody Allen's film *The Purple Rose of Cairo*, when Tom Baxter walks off the screen to meet his devoted fan Cecilia): a reader (the analyst, listening as a flesh-and-blood person, who is therefore external to the text) enters into the patient's account in order in the latter's eyes (those of a real person) to demystify the narrator himself (the projection of himself in his autobiographical account), the other characters of the story and their actions. In the case of a clinical vignette, by contrast, the 'irruption' of the analyst, starting from a first level that is already internal to the text, shifts to a secondary level.

Metalepsis can thus be seen as the narrative device – which is intrinsically violent, as well as possessing a virtual capacity for transformation – that contributes to the production of the text of the analysis, while at the same time 'constructing' subjectivity on the basis of the category of an omitted, repressed or split-off causality. In the most frequent case, the antecedent – the story told by the patient – is taken to be the consequence of *another* story, held to be *truer*, which unfolds at unconscious level and concerns the relationship existing in the here-and-now of the consulting room. In this way, the patient and indeed also the analyst constantly (re)discover themselves as characters in a fiction, as well as, in turn, the fact that they are being 'narrated' by the unconscious (and by its discourse).

On each occasion, it is as if the analyst were remarking: 'What? Didn't you notice that outside the compartment window [an allusion to Freud's well-known image of the fundamental rule of free association], when you thought you were looking at x, y or z . . . you were actually seeing me?!' The golden rule of translation to be applied in transference interpretation then becomes (Roth 2001: 536): ' "When you say them you mean me". I am "them" '.

Significantly, all interpretation does is to draw attention, by continuous metaleptic slippage from one frame to another, to the importance of the frame itself (or the setting) – as well as to the fact that we live in more than one world at a time, so that there is no such thing as a single, fixed reality. Metalepses are essentially *transgressions* of the splits or disavowals on which identity is built. The subject is thereby deconstructed – that is, either relativized or strengthened in his degree of awareness of himself and the world.

In conclusion, attention to the narrative planes and frames of the analytic text, and in particular to the rhetorical device of metalepsis as a figure of the violation of diegetic levels, in accordance with the principles of narratology, can be a valuable conceptual instrument for delimiting the structure and function of interpretation. It can also throw light on the associated matters of narrative construction, factual reality and the conceptualization and communication of clinical facts.

Another way of trying to catch the meaning of the setting (its self-reflexive character) and the fictionality of the real is in rethinking dreams about the session as scenes *en abyme*, i.e. from the vantage point of one of the key rhetorical figures of postmodernity and meta-narrative strategies. Dreams in which the analyst appears undisguised almost always depict violations of the setting. Often experienced as special, epiphanic moments, they give a glimpse of an intense, emotional reaction to traumatogenic or otherwise significant events which have occurred during the session or in the most recent previous ones.

Probably, the essential aspect of these dreams can be found in the 'form of their content'. This may be paralleled by the narrative technique of 'mise en abyme' or mirror-text. The dream appears as a story within the main story and the scene of the analysis is reflected anti-illusionistically. The fictional structure of the setting is emphasized. Its self-consciously theatrical character is revealed at its best.

It can be postulated that the transformative, therapeutic value of these dreams derives from denouncing the referential illusion of 'concrete reality' and of 'what really happened'. For the analysand, they are an effective (i.e. emotionally intense) opportunity to discover the spatial articulations and the staggering refractions of the inside/outside, the textual/extra-textual, the psychic reality/material reality. In the continual comings and goings from one term to another, the work of symbolization is reactivated and the subject is constructed.

The dreams, in which the device of the cure itself is depicted, thus dramatize the manifold levels of reality and of the possible worlds we simultaneously live in. In these dreams a multiple and alternate play takes place between reinforcing and depotentiating the effect of the real in psychoanalytic narratives. In this way, they emphasize the narrative categories implicit in processes that guide observation, attribution of meaning and construction of the subject.

From this vertex, dreams about the session become a resource of modelling for the analytic work beyond the specific phenomenon which is referred to. They produce a global aesthetic effect: the intense feeling arising from the weird and stupefying transgression of narrative frames that also belongs – as we saw – to transference interpretation. What is more, they can be dignified as a model because they also link back to the oneiric paradigm of the cure.

Already an obvious Freudian principle, only in Bion's extended idea of 'waking dream thought' is the oneiric paradigm of the cure completely applicable. The hypothesis can be put forward that, by adopting this paradigm thoroughly, one can combine the radical antirealism which is expressed in the postulate by which all the patient's communications are transference connected (here meaning 'false connection' – i.e. as projection/displacement of elements of the patient's inner psychic world) with the 'reality' of the transference, that is to say with the conviction that the facts of the analysis are codetermined by the patient–analyst dyad and actually rooted in how they interact.[6]

Finally, the Freudian metaphor of the fire at the theatre can be reintroduced to suggest the crisis of the therapist's internal setting and capacity for reverie, which occurs when the irreducible ambiguity of the transference is resolved defensively, either on the patient's external reality or on his unconscious fantasy constellation. The Sirens' song of the external world in fact almost always serves the analyst's antalgic collusion and defensive splittings. Facts, understood as external events that only 'belong' to the patient, lend themselves to functioning as his 'thermal shields' (Ferro 1992: 107, 2003a), indispensable naturally when dealing with incandescent material. Clinical experience reveals, instead, surprising effects every time the demarcation line between setting reality and external/historical reality is gone over, even when extremely difficult, unavoidable and traumatic realities are being affronted: surprising for other possible meanings of the relationship and for the sense of immediacy and vitality that this assumes. From a fixed photographic image one passes in an instant, as in certain films, to a whole animated scene in which the characters gradually begin to move and talk, thus making themselves knowable. In this way 'an effect of the real' and of truth as emotional experience is recovered, but what counts above all is that keeping firmly in mind the connection between the actuality of the relationship and the facts of the session in every minimum detail seems to be the vertex that allows maximum trust in the modifiability of psychic facts.

At the 'Lio' (*l'Io?*) [7]

At the beginning of October, Giulio dreams of a bar in B called the *Lio* [something 'leonine', I wonder?]. He explains, 'It's a very fashionable place, where lots of university students meet. It's small, shabby, and smoky, located in a former industrial area that is now decaying, near the train station. Outside the bar is the railroad, with a grade crossing. The last train goes through at 8 o'clock. The bar opens at 8:30 [the time when all his sessions began in the first few months of treatment, and when two out of four still begin!]. So why not stop for a drink on the tracks? My brother and his friends used to meet in this bar in the past, and I was scared stiff of it – I had a real block. I never wanted to go because I knew quite a few of the people who might be there – people from my past, people I would be embarrassed to meet. It's quite a ritzy joint. Then I started going: I managed to overcome my fears to some extent. Evenings out often start there. The *Lio* in La Maddalena, in Sardinia, is also very small. It too is very trendy . . . This summer I felt a bit out of place. Aside from the name . . . the same feelings. Then people were making fun of me because I always carried my usual jute bag around with me, with my mobile charger (as well as other people's!) inside it. You couldn't go to this bar if you didn't feel perfectly all right. Well, some people go anyway. I go, but I feel I'm being watched.' I tell him he now seems to feel more at ease at the *Lio*. It has now become quite welcoming for him. The terror is gone and the criticisms are less important. He still has his bag to carry, but on the whole . . . what a relief! After a few minutes when he is lost in thought, he says, 'I remember that . . . when I got over my blockage about the *Lio*, it was because of Licia! It was our meeting place. And it was rather difficult, because her ex was around. So I was able to discover the good side of this bar, which, up to now, had meant nothing to me but anxiety and a sense of inadequacy. Oh, yes . . . Licia has helped me a lot.'

A few days later, he tells me that he has got to know an Argentinian girl in Pavia, with whom he has decided ('with the enthusiasm of a child') to take Spanish lessons [he is beginning, I tell myself, to move toward a more solar geography, further south than Sardinia – perhaps toward greater intimacy in the analytic relationship]. He would like to have conversation, but noticed right away that he also needed to brush up his grammar [. . . a bit of structure, I reflect].

At around the same time, prompted by his mother he recalls that, as a small child, he was afraid that she might die. It is as if submerged anxieties were able, through the medium of analysis, to begin to emerge. He goes to see a film, *La luce dei tuoi occhi* [The light of your eyes],[8] and discovers a character, a boy, who has the same fears as his own! He explains, 'The film tells the story of a very good person who falls in love with a woman and is close to her; he tries to help her in every possible way, even without her knowledge, and always with a smile, but she often treats him badly all the same.' It is a dull, rainy day, and thunder can be heard. Giulio associates: '. . . Thunder . . . I was afraid of it when I was small. My mother always came to see if we were awake, to reassure us with her presence. As I grew up, I remained fascinated by it. I like thunderstorms. I'm not afraid of thunder any more . . . my mother came without my having to call her.'

I comment, 'Like in the film . . . a guardian angel.'

The patient continues, 'I was very fascinated by this good character . . . Over and above his goodness, he's always able to find a solution . . . I'm also thinking of my room in B, in the attic: there are two windows in the roof. When it rains, the water beats down on the glass and I am in the warm, under my duvet.'

I say, 'It's your mother coming along silently to reassure you, to protect your sleep, that transforms the terror of the thunder into a natural spectacle to be contemplated without fear . . . and the same applies to emotional storms!'

He answers, 'But will I manage to trust my guardian angel? [After a few minutes' silence.] Afterwards, my father called me [he is referring to a heated discussion that had made him feel he was not understood, because his father wanted him to set about writing his thesis immediately]. He thanked me for the evening. I didn't know what to reply. I wanted to keep up a kind of harshness. I said to myself: "I don't know if he deserves it." Then I answered: "Thanks to *you*!" '

It is now mid-October. An evening at the *Lio*. He sees Licia again. 'Normally,' he tells me, 'I would have been afraid to get too attached, of coming over as tiresome . . . but she said we should meet again.

Even if we haven't seen each other a lot, we've bridged the gap that had opened up between us.' He then sends her a text message: '*It was great to see you again!*'

After missing a lesson with the Argentinian girl, which she had cancelled owing to another engagement, he comments, 'I felt bad. I am oversensitive to such situations: *my pap isn't ready!*' Then he tells me he has bought himself some boots. He did his best to hide them when taking them home, because his brothers were always pulling his leg about his choice of clothing. His brother notices. But this time, the reaction is very different from usual: 'You've bought the "amphibians" [boots]! . . . I thought I might get myself some too.' I tell him, 'So as to be okay in the dry and in the wet! When there's a "lesson" and when there isn't.' He adds, 'I fell in love with them. I put them on right away. It was raining . . . so they got some damnfool blisters! I was advised to soften them up a bit, to wear them for only a few minutes at a time.' It is as if he were asking me to give him time, to exercise more tact . . . Thinking of how difficult it must be for him to tolerate the absence of the other, moving around both on land and in water,[9] the 'intermittences of the field' as he called them – the manifest link is with the mobile phone network, but it is Proustian *intermittences du coeur* that are arousing emotions in him – I remark in a low voice, 'Well, on the whole, there's hardly anything that doesn't immediately give trouble . . . I recall a pair of *Doc Martens*! . . . But then, they're hard-wearing, you can walk for miles in them, and they're fine for winter and summer.' The patient exclaims: 'Mine were *Doc Marteeens*!!' It is quite obvious to me that he is well aware of the figurative sense of our conversation.

October is drawing to an end. They have been joined in the Pavia apartment by a new student, A., who is very different from his predecessor (but I find myself thinking of him as an emerging part of the patient's self, or as a new and different level of functioning between us – a more direct, less inhibited level). Giulio seems a little put out by the newcomer, but then a note of curiosity ensues. 'It's like this: if he sees a nice girl, he immediately tries to get to know her. He's more forward than me and my brother. He saw a female friend of ours around in the house and said: "What do you think of that one – would she or wouldn't she?" Then we usually make ourselves a big pasta. He grabs the first one, then the second one, and so on, and there are so many dishes to wash up! In the evenings, he goes out, saying something like: "It's nice and warm tonight, we should go

172

out." "It's nice and warm"!? *I* go out if I have something to do, not because "it's nice and warm" . . . PERHAPS HE WILL DO US GOOD!'

This brief clinical sequence, which condenses fragments of dialogue extending over a period of one month, readily lends itself to illustrating the narrative continuity that links the various sessions, provided that one is prepared to consider the multiform characters who appear in it as vectors that not only afford historical and factual clues and present characters from the patient's internal world, but also represent the dynamic tensions of the field and the state of the therapeutic relationship at a given point in time. From the patient's replies, which are of course organized in accordance with temporalities of variable amplitude, it is indeed possible to infer the degree of defamiliarization, insecurity and disorientation produced by interpretation, or alternatively the sense of discovery and the effect of reintegration to which it gives rise. In particular, listening to the narrative derivatives of waking dream thought (Ferro 1992) is one of the instruments capable of bridging the gap, to which Bader (1998) drew attention – see also Renik (1998) – between constructivist epistemologies and clinical operationality, between the space accorded to the analyst's subjectivity and attentive monitoring of field responses, of the confirmations or disconfirmations of interpretations – with a view to getting one's bearings among the numerous possible interpretations, discarding the implausible ones, and strictly detecting the patient-specific markers that might constitute reliable clues for validating the analyst's understanding and successive hypotheses.

In other words, the stage of the analysis comes to life if the analyst's internal setting establishes a vertex from which any event assumes meaning in the here-and-now, as an element – as one might say in Derridian semiotic jargon – of a differential system of signs in which nothing is *hors-texte*. The analyst gives credence to the multiple perspectives offered him by the patient through his personifications; he uses them to monitor the field, paying close attention to the 'fire alarms', to the effects of reality – 'strong' recourse to the register of reference – that may suspend the virtual theatre of the analysis. In this way he uses the self-reflexive functioning of the setting to maximum advantage: every narration is also a *mise en abîme*, a dream of the treatment – that is, a meta-narration.

In the clinical vignette, a certain progression in the degree of metalepsis will be noted in the analyst's interventions, which are inspired by a non-authoritarian principle. The interpretations are mainly elliptical and allusive, and respect the patient's text and the frame of his account. The risk of plunging the patient into cognitive disarray is taken only when it is felt that it will not be too destabilizing, and that it will be rewarded by the arousal of strong feelings rather than met with confusion.

Is this focus on the here-and-now detrimental to the patient's history and to a knowledge of his internal world? On the contrary: it is precisely the antirealistic vertex that lends substance to the historical reconstruction and to the mapping of the intrapsychic world, because what happens in the analyst's office gives rise to an effect of truth that reverberates positively on the re/construction of the subject's historical and psychological reality.

In these sessions, Giulio hints at his fear of meeting with the phantasms – or primitive fantasies – of the past, but also at the difficulties of trusting the analysis and the need to overcome his initial fears. The *Lio* is then *l'Io* [the ego], *the analyst's office* and *the bar* in B where he goes for a drink in the company of his friends, as well as the *out-of-place* location of the summer holidays, with his concern about telephones – that is, the distant voice of the analyst – and also the *attic* under whose roof he feels protected from his anxieties. Licia, the Argentinian girl, the mother whose mere presence affords reassurance when he is frightened by thunder, the brothers, the 'guardian angel', and the uninhibited, forward student who has come to live in the apartment, as well as inanimate objects such as the boots (but beware: these are DOCs,[10] and the minimalist self-disclosure strikes home because Giulio recognizes that they are precisely the same brand as his – that is, his *doctor* and his analysis!), can at one and the same time be seen as 'real' things or persons, as characters in the patient's internal world, or as functions of the analytic field. However, only by adopting this last position can the analyst find an ideal balance – which is by definition unstable – between interaction and immersion, and observe and activate the emotional transformations, reflected in narrations, toward which the treatment is directed.

The ethic of hospitality

Psychoanalysis is seeking a new paradigm. The theory of the analytic field is one of the models that are, in my opinion, capable of taking up the cultural challenge of the postmodern. 'By virtue of the field concept, the analyst's mind prepares itself for the study, not of a linear phenomenon, such as the dynamic of the transference in the classical theory, but of complex phenomena (vortices and turbulences, rather than laminar motion), for the understanding of which we perhaps lack even the appropriate theoretical instruments' (Goretti 1996: 399, translated). It is perhaps no coincidence that Derrida was so well received in literature departments (especially in the United States, and specifically by the 'Yale critics' – Bloom, Hillis Miller, De Man and Hartman), where the conceptual *instruments* of a sophisticated textual semiotics belong to the tools of the trade. It is now taken for granted by the narratologists – notwithstanding their differences over many theoretical issues – that in any narrative, including non-fictional ones, that portray reality, rhetorical mechanisms are at work, that objectivity is constructed, however counterintuitive this may be, and that, in the text, strategies of domination are deployed and unexpressed ideological assumptions lie concealed. Being invested with the power to dispense 'the violence of the interpretation' (Aulagnier 1975) and being conscious of all this ought to be one and the same thing. There is a radical difference between those who have this kind of consciousness and those who tend to make uncritical and unproblematic use of this power. In the former case, the interpretation takes a 'weak', unsaturated, open form (Ferro 1996, 2002b): it is a negotiable proposition or 'gift to the guest' (*xenia*), a dream or reverie that the analyst has about the patient's dream/account (Meltzer 1984); while in the latter – putting it in extreme form, for the sake of clarity – it not infrequently comes to resemble an oracular comment, or an instance of involuntary violation, to which the patient can only submit, or which he can at most resist. In the last, analysis, from a knowledge of the ideological grammars and genealogies and the rhetorical devices that organize discourse, it is possible to derive an absolutely ethical principle, and, from this, a respectful, kind way of being with the other and of offering him hospitality, without on that account lapsing into an uncritical oblatory mode. After all, there is violence and 'violence': hospitality and hostility have a common root in language *(hostis)*, and a certain demand to be counterinstitutional does not mean that one is *anti*-institutional (Derrida and Dufourmantelle 1997).

From the viewpoint of deconstruction, then, it will be simpler to consider the opposite aspect of the Babel[11] of psychoanalysis, and to appreciate the incredible vitality, depth and beauty of linguistic pluralism that are the obvious reflection of the very complexity of its object of study, the human mind. This does not on any account mean that 'anything goes' – because in fact conflictuality is only too readily unleashed and ideas face a harsh process of natural selection – except in the caricature of a misunderstood relativism drawn by 'saddened, *negative*, nostalgic, guilty, Rousseauistic' champions of essentialist models of knowledge (Derrida 1967a: 292) – of those toiling to tolerate a totally this-worldly, earthbound, and historical foundation of 'truth'.

Dialogue means not absolute relativism, but giving up the desire to impose oneself by force, and establishing shared rules even for scientific debate. The critique directed toward the metaphysical foundations of authority and toward dogmatism cannot lead to an abstract rhetoricism, or to the anarchism of 'anything goes', which is nothing but a fashionable slogan for placing the bewildering non-linearity of the progression of science in a historical perspective, and which can certainly not be elevated to nomothetic status. The antithesis of tyranny (including ideological tyranny) is democracy, civil converse and consensus; and it must be realized that democracy too creates its ghettos, and that even a concern for minorities, differences and political correctness can be perverted into violence, as Philip Roth (2000) tells us, with a touching sense of pietas, in *The Human Stain*. Just as the deconstruction of the non-neutrality of the sign and of the ideological codes present in language must necessarily be internal to language if we are not to lose ourselves in the myth of a linguistic degree zero, so the analyst cannot relinquish the authority and responsibility that stem from his role and competence, any more than a parent where children are concerned. Some, however – for instance Ferenczi – have drawn the attention of all of us to the real traumas and abuses perpetrated by parents and analysts alike. Again, just as deconstruction itself tends toward deconstruction*ism*, to institutionalization, and to the status of a system or supertheory, so too psychoanalysis experiences the inevitable but fertile tension between the aspiration to confirmation of its identity and the thrust toward change, between preservation and innovation, between immobilism and transgression.

The reason for condemning the so-called interpretative drift is often nothing but dismay at the ungraspability of a peremptory, ultimate and final meaning, and at the fact that the only 'truth' seems to be that of the quest for that truth, of the process, and that there is no actual end-point. After all, truth slips away at the very moment when one thinks one has pinned it down (an interpretation seizes on a detail and, at the same time, as a linguistic *act* – with its inevitable content of enactment – initiates a new cycle; it is recursive and always constitutes a form of a posteriori understanding), and its centre of gravity lies outside its cognitive content, in emotion and in an aesthetic theory (and not an aesthetizing theory, but in the 'successful antagonistic harmony of passion and reason' [Bodei 1999: 174, translated]!). Hence the only (provisional) foundation is shifting away from a transcendental centre of authority (in either a neo-Kantian or a theological sense), and the shift is also centrifugal, toward partially heterogeneous criteria as opposed to those of strictly logical-reflective thought – but is this appeal to affect not the mark of analysis?

An entomologist-analyst who cultivates an ideal of aseptic neutrality neglects to place himself on the level of the surface of the text, listening to the sense conveyed by the form, and not only by the content (but it is another misunderstanding to fail to see neutrality as a 'sweet' fruit of scepticism [Barthes 2002] and to forget that the primary meaning of the Greek *skeptikos* is meditative, observant, or reflective, rather than doubting!). Here, Derrida's hyperbolic – and, if you will, also provocative – emphasis on Freud's intuition of the importance of the signifier (as in *Non vixit/Non vivit*, or *You are requested to close the/an eye[s]*, and many similar examples) can be a lesson to us all, but only, of course, if pursued with rigour, courage and good sense. Some, however, when reminded of the role played by their own subjectivity in the definition of the clinical 'data', may feel that they themselves have been placed on the couch, and find it hard to endure the narcissistic wound of being denied – apart from the obvious asymmetry of the working situation – a special status, the marks of rank, or a perfect mastery of the field. Yet such mastery is in fact illusory and can only be recovered – if at all – after the event. It may indeed be uncomfortable to imagine oneself as being inexorably immersed in the twofold flow of projective identifications, and to think of pathology not only as something that *the* patient brings into the field, into the analyst's office, or unconscious fantasies *of* the patient that are expressed by themselves and that we can at most detect, but also as dysfunctions and unconscious fantasies *of the field*. If it is held that the analyst's task is to confront the analysand, to overcome resistances, and every so often to undergo negative therapeutic reactions, this may lead to constriction of the space of self-reflexivity. Clinging narrowly to the line of the transference–countertransference may be equivalent to limiting oneself to a restricted model of the transference as a false nexus, albeit bidirectional, with a constant reference to the *hors-texte* of the external world, to the historical reality of the infantile neurosis, and to seeing interpretation more as a revelation of truth *about* the patient than as an interpretative 'game'.

On the other hand, at the other end of the continuum of analytic styles lurks the risk of lapsing into a conception of naive realism, of squandering the Freudian gold of the concept of psychic reality, of placing one's trust in an almost pretechnical or preanalytic spontaneism, and of abandoning the hyperspecific method of evenly suspended attention and free association (a form of unconditional acceptance – *virtually unlimited availability for listening*, both diachronic and in terms of content – remains perhaps the simplest and most brilliant of Freud's discoveries!).

A relativism that seems more than anything to result from a misunderstanding of the postmodern critique of the concept of authority leads to the identification of a corrective to the figure of the over-detached and silent analyst in the form of pure emotional involvement, of the viscerality of the interaction, of a flow and counterflow of conscious exchanges, of a concentration on the real and on the secondary processes (even if a certain theoretical avant-gardism sometimes goes hand in hand with substantial orthodoxy of practice), and of the fiction of a symmetricality of the relationship.

If there is no longer a heteronomous centre from which legitimation may be derived, we are bound to return to a primacy of ethics and of dialogue, and to affirm the value of difference and of the pluralism of languages; to resist not rationality, but logocentrism (the authority of the linguistic); to oppose the subtle, insidious tendency of every discourse to set itself up as an absolute yardstick for the evaluation of any other discourse that differs from itself and to affirm its own will to power, sheltered by the utopian cloak that invariably conceals its totalitarian face, in the name either of some divinity or of a 'fact of nature'.

For psychoanalysis, then, *contamination* with some of the ideas of deconstruction (or of the so-called postmodern culture) may mean not the abstract, arid translation of the other's words, as some versions of this easily misunderstood term might suggest,[12] but instead the application of more than one code – the practice, with good sense and due proportion, of a certain theoretical nomadism, using interpretations as a gift of sense and an offer of hospitality, with absolute

178

simplicity and tact. In so doing, the analyst will rely on a rationality that, while defining itself as weak – 'a weakness that can transform itself into the greatest strength' (Derrida and Ferraris 1997: 63) – appears capable of assuming much heavier burdens of responsibility; as well as on a principle of tolerance (but beware the violence inherent in tolerance!) and a sense of compassion, sharing and solidarity with the other's suffering, born of respect for differences. However, in Freud (and Derrida), true hospitality means first and foremost the absolute acceptance of one's own numerous selves, of the constitutive otherness of the ego, and of everything human. Just as postmodern architectures, reacting to the excesses of the functionalist geometrism of the modern, have, precisely out of respect for the plurality and mixture of languages, once again become places for living in – *dwellings*[13] in the sense of stopping/pausing/residence/lingering/ slowness – so the acceptance of a 'weak' ontology, of course in the positive sense in which Vattimo (1985) uses the term, can have an *affirmative* character; and the 'feeling of not feeling at home', while disquieting, may also induce a sense of wonder and freedom. Freud's concept of *das Unheimliche* (1919) may be the best possible epitomization of the emotional and intellectual attitude suspended between perturbation and surprise, and the simultaneous sense of unease and intensity of feeling, that appears to be the dominant note of our time.

Notes

1 Fire at the theatre

1 Translated by Harriet Graham.
2 Translator's note: *Fatti fuori*, meaning 'to be killed' or 'done in' in Italian, here evokes the trauma of being thrown out (*fuori*) from his parent's/ analyst's room and that his recollections are pure facts (*fatti*).
3 A tradename which suggests an effect of reinvigorating and making you strong (in Italian 'forte'). The drug, generically known as etilefrine, is used to treat hypotension.
4 The word *intimissimo* in the original means not only lingerie but also 'very intimate'.
5 In Italian 'Armando' is not only the proper name of a person, in this case that of a parish priest (as the title 'Don' would suggest), but also the present gerund of the verb *armare*, meaning 'to arm', which only one letter, the 'r', distinguishes from another important gerund: *amando*, meaning 'loving'.
6 As usual, it is appropriate to turn to the poets, in this case, Eugenio Montale (1992 [1920–7]): 'Forse una mattina andando in un'aria di vetro, / arida, rivolgendomi, vedrò compirsi il miracolo: / il nulla alle mie spalle, il vuoto dietro / di me, con un terrore di ubriaco. / Poi come s'uno schermo, s'accamperanno di gitto / alberi case colli per l'inganno consueto. / Ma sarà troppo tardi, ed io me n'andrò zitto / tra gli uomini che non si voltano, col mio segreto.'

2 The symbiotic bond and the setting

1 Like the watercourses that flow through the karstic landscapes of the Yorkshire Dales in the UK or the provinces of Trieste and Gorizia in

north-east Italy, which disappear underground because of the geology of the area and then return to the surface in resurgences.

2   A difficulty confronting anyone who reads or discusses Bleger's writings is surely presented by the confusion resulting from his use of a number of terms as synonyms – namely, agglutinated, symbiotic, psychotic, undifferentiated, undiscriminated, syncretic and immature. For this reason, at the risk of repeating myself, I wish to point out that, for Bleger, the glischro-caric position is the *mode* of experiencing the reality that corresponds, in structural terms, to the state of fusion between ego and object, which he calls the 'agglutinated nucleus'. In adults, the *persistence* of this nucleus identifies the 'psychotic part of the personality'. The principal source of misunderstandings is the fact that this *residue* may undergo a variety of vicissitudes. Where a more differentiated ego can develop appropriately, the residue usually remains silent and is the guarantor of the *necessary* symbiotic links with the object and the non-human environment. If individual development has been deficient, it may give rise to a range of clinical forms dominated by ambiguity, extending from isolated personality traits to outright psychoses. In still other cases, it may, through regression of the more differentiated part, assume the role of a defensive organization. Symbiosis, or the symbiotic relationship or bond, is the *product*, which is non-apparent under basic conditions, of the 'psychotic part of the personality' on the behavioural level. This same part is sometimes referred to by the metaleptic expression – that is, one in which the antecedent is referred to by the consequent – of the 'symbiotic nucleus'.

From this point of view, the 'psychotic part of the personality' should not a priori be seen as a concept that expresses a pathological aspect of mental functioning, any more than certain other concepts initially used to denote strictly psychopathological phenomena (a long list of such concepts could be compiled). One may disagree with this choice of vocabulary, which is in any case essential for illustrating Bleger's model, but advantage can also be taken of a certain vagueness, including a conceptual vagueness, which in fact indicates that all psychic manifestations are actually situated along a continuum. This is by no means a trivial point, as a quick look back to Freud (1914b: 77) suggests: 'But I am of opinion that that is just the difference between a speculative theory and a science erected on empirical interpretation. The latter will not envy speculation its privilege of having a smooth, logically unassailable foundation, but will gladly content itself with nebulous, scarcely imaginable basic concepts, which it hopes to apprehend more clearly in the course of its development, or which it is even prepared to replace by others. For these ideas are not the foundation of science, upon which everything rests [. . .].'

3   According to Di Chiara (1971:55, translated), the setting 'must be made up of as few elements as possible', with 'the lowest feasible index of variability'. Searles (1960), too, attributes a vitally important role to the non-human environment as a harmonious extension of the self, on account of its major contribution to the subject's emotional security, sense of stability and continuity of experience, as well as to the development of personal identity.

4   Roussillon (1995: 36, translated) tellingly summarizes the questions with which the setting 'in pain' confronts the analyst:

> Certain chance breaches have the effect that the setting ceases to be 'silent', begins to 'weep' and thereby reveals its hitherto secret function of being the guardian of a split or disavowal. An analysis of the setting and its function thus appears not only necessary but essential. The difficulty arises when one wishes to determine how that function works. If the breach occurs by chance or spontaneously, it is quite likely that it can be analysed in the context of a restored setting, but where such a – temporary or localized – breach does not take place, what is to be done? The question arises particularly because what is 'deposited' or 'immobilized' in the setting remains inherently 'silent'. A deliberate breach of the setting by the analyst can scarcely be contemplated – what kind of breach would have a 'mobilizing' effect, and when? – and would in any case make the subsequent analysis of its impact very difficult.

The debate on this issue is long-standing: Bleger (1967b) already refers to contributions dating from the early 1950s, and comes out against the deliberate use of breaches of the setting as a technique. See also Ferro (1996); Stern *et al.* (1998); Rossi Monti and Foresti (2002); Ryle (2003).

5   'The concept of the "therapeutic alliance" arose within a theoretico-clinical model in which it was appropriate to see analysis as a war against unconscious resistances and in which it was therefore necessary to rely on a pact – an alliance, precisely – to be concluded with the healthy parts of the ego. This terminology and the associated concepts are somewhat anachronistic today, insofar as they are based on the drive model and on an approach that disregards the theoretical and clinical contributions of object relations. The idea of an analysis conducted by the ego in the form of a "war" against the resistances put up by the forces of the unconscious is connected with a conception of analysis that fails to take account of the kind of technique currently prevalent in the psychoanalytic community – a technique that was also largely forged in the treatment of seriously ill patients, in whom the defences to be considered are based not so much on repression [. . .], for which the model

of "war" and alliance is appropriate, as on splitting' (Ponsi 2002: 2, translated).

6 This term often has a negative connotation, even though, for example, it expresses the very essence of poetic language. Racamier (1992) and, among American authors, Kafka (1989) consider the experience of ambiguity to be essential to the acquisition and maintenance of the sense of reality.

7 Cf. Bleger (1967b: 55, translated): 'It is the concrete level on which symbiosis functions and stabilizes. What words generate in the other are not thoughts prior to action, but acts dissociated from the mental area and from its symbolic content. Communication is direct, literal from action to action. The mind is dissociated; it is at any rate present as a *spectator excluded* from the drama that is being played out.'

8 See also Civitarese (2006b).

9 Some people use autistic defences to prevent themselves from being moved. This is readily understandable in the light of the following statement by Bleger (1967b: 120n, my emphasis): '*affect and emotion are intrinsically object relations which remain undiscriminated in their structure, and which [. . .] always carry the risk of a loss of the boundaries between the ego and reality (i.e. the dissolution of identity).*'

10 'Now moments may occur when the traditional therapeutic frame risks being, or is, or should be, broken' (Stern *et al.* 1998: 912; see also Ryle 2003).

11 According to Bleger (1967b: 11), the 'mental phenomenon is a mode of behaviour, which in fact appears later than other modes, since the first undifferentiated, syncretic structures are fundamentally bodily relations', and continue to be so throughout life. This in effect means that the body remains the predominant theatre for the reproduction of the first object relations. In this connection, the following notes on the body appear relevant: the body is 'not only the limit but also the locus of the origin of mental life, its background, source and permanent "flesh" (mental life is not a "cognitive" life) [. . .]. Intersubjectivity, after all, takes the form of *intercorporeality* in the *tonic dialogue* with the other [. . .] this intercorporeal background is the place where attachment styles take shape and are organized [. . .]. It is the pre-representational matrix on the basis of which the subject can gradually become constituted, individuate and emerge with a greater or lesser degree of difficulty [. . .] this background is not "somewhere else"; it does not simply belong to our past. Nor does it come wholly to belong to the narration, open to constant remoulding by the mechanism of *Nachträglichkeit*, that is the subject's history. *It constitutes its silent matrix, which is operational and precategorial, and never fully mentalizable or thinkable*' (Barale and Ucelli 2000: 203f., translated; my emphasis).

3 Metalepsis, or the rhetoric of transference interpretation

1 Here I am departing from the traditional definition of this figure of speech, which is identified in classical rhetoric by a 'replacement of the lemma itself not by its direct metaphorical substitute, but by one or more indirect metaphors, via a series of gradual transitions' (De Mauro 2002: 1515, translated). My reference is instead to the modern, 'extended' reformulation due to Genette (2004), in whose sense metalepsis, now a concept midway between rhetoric and the theory of narration, denotes the paradoxical transgression of the boundaries between ontologically distinct narrative realities – e.g. the extra-textual world of the narrator and the world in which the narrator's characters live.

2 On a more abstract level, the concept of 'misreading' might also be relevant here: any reading is inevitably a misreading because the polysemy of the signifier and the discrepancy between the sign and the referent into which it insinuates itself, and of which the representation tells, make that representation not a linguistic mode among others or a marginal accessory, but instead the very paradigm of language. Considered in this light, an interpretation is inevitably ambiguous and decentred; it is not a transparent meaning or a deciphering, but another sign or text which in turn awaits interpretation (de Man 1979).

3 'The analyst producing the written text would be the historical author, but he would not be the general narrator, a fictional construct who addresses the transcription of the entire session to a general narratee. Embedded within this extradiegetic level, the patient and analyst (a fictional character who is not identical to the historical author) would take turns as intradiegetic narrator and narratee' (Nelles 2004).

4 She thus recites the end of the eighth Duino Elegy: 'Who's turned us around like this, / so that whatever we do, we always have / the look of someone going away? Just as a man / on the last hill showing him his whole valley / one last time, turns, and stops, and lingers – / so we live, and are forever leaving' (Rilke 1923: 59).

4 Immersion versus interactivity and analytic field

1 This chapter has been translated by Giovanna Iannaco.

2 See Birksted-Breen (2003) on the complex temporality inherent to the here-and-now of the session.

3 For the rhetorical–narratological concept of 'metalepsis', see Genette (2004).

4 Translator's note: In Italian: 'Lei', the polite form of 'you' but also the pronoun 'she'.

5   See Ovid (1995, vi, 10): 'occiderat mater'.
6   Translator's note: In Italian 'trama' denotes both 'plot' and 'warp', a set of lengthwise threads, which are intertwined with the threads of the weft to form the cloth ('tessuto'). 'Testo' ('text') derives etymologically from 'tessuto'.
7   Character of the famous television series *ER*.
8   See Civitarese (2007b).

5   Nachträglichkeit

1   Cf. Edelman (2004: 111): 'Much of cognitive psychology is ill-founded. There are no functional states that can be uniquely equated with defined or coded computational states in individual brains and no processes that can be equated with the execution of algorithms. Instead, there is an enormously rich set of selectional repertoires of neuronal groups whose degenerate responses can, by selection, accommodate the open-ended richness of environmental input, individual history, and individual variation. Intentionality and will, in this view, both depend on local contexts in the environment, the body, and the brain, but they can selectively arise only through such interactions, and not as precisely defined computations.'
2   Epigenesis refers to processes in which 'key events occur only if certain previous events have taken place [. . .] the connections among the cells are therefore not precisely prespecified in the genes of the animal' (Edelman 1992: 23).
3   According to Marcelli (1986: 64, translated), increasing meaning is a function of repetition: 'We believe that the first thought activity independent of perceptual or sensory activation is a thought about time. On the basis of this hypothesis, an infant's first thought – "thought" being understood as a neurocerebral activity not totally dependent on the sensory perceptions of the moment – could be formulated as follows: "After this, there will be something else".'
4   Laub and Auerhan (1993) describe the various forms assumed by the repetition of massive trauma: not knowing by means of denial, splitting, amnesia, derealization and depersonalization; fugue states as ways of reliving the traumatic experience in altered states of consciousness; compartmentalized memories of the experience (undigested fragments of perceptions that break into consciousness, decontextualized and deprived of meaning); fragments of memory relived in the transference, which insidiously distort the experience of the present or render it inappropriate and absurd; the irruption of memories without the element of time (overpowering narratives) – frozen images that impose

a burden on the present; pervasive life themes around which the subject's identity is organized; memories in which the ego recovers a function of witnessing, distance and perspective in relation to the event (witnessed narratives); and images and aspects of the trauma used as metaphor.

5   Cf. Barale (1989: 240, translated): 'The time of mental life, on the other hand – the time of the events that have access to the work of weaving and reweaving of meaning that is a memory – falls within the dimension of Freud's *Nachträglichkeit*, of revision "after the event", which is detached from the old idea that it constitutes an isolated phenomenon [. . .] and is instead understood in the radical sense of a moment of transition from memory as a function to a memory in the sense of something remembered, from an immediate, sensory apprehension of the object to the possibility of cathecting its symbolic substitutes. This is the time of mentalization, which has the effect that the meaning of events, including past events, is never given once and for all, as a perceptual quality of the events themselves.'

6   Derrida (1999: 60, translated) writes: 'If heritage consists simply in maintaining dead things or archives and in reproducing what was, then it is not what can be called heritage [. . .]. An unfaithful fidelity. Here again we find this twofold injunction which does not leave me.'

6 Transference, USA

1   Fonagy (2003: 504) uses a similar image in his polemic with Blum, to whom he attributes a 'naïve and unsustainable' notion of repressed memories, like photographs or video films that remain unmodified, unaffected by the work of retranscription of memory (*Nachträglichkeit*), whereas these memories, in his view, in all probability reflect the present relationship rather than the past.

2   According to Borgogno (2004: 171), the paper's original title was 'Two Suggested Revisions of the Concept of Transference. Comments Regarding the Usefulness of Emotions Arising During the Analytic Hour'.

3   '[Transference is] an event whose strangeness Freud never tired of emphasising' (Laplanche and Pontalis 1967: 456).

4   In Derrida, the concept of spectrality is linked to the radicalization of Freud's concept of a trace, to the idea that there can never be such a thing as a 'full' present that does not refer to an elsewhere, to the past or to otherness.

7 Difference (a certain) identity transference

1   Bion (1992: 180f.): 'Suppose I am talking to a friend who asks me where I propose to spend my holiday; as he does so, I visualize the church of a small town not far from the village in which I propose to stay. The small town is important because it possesses the railway station nearest to my village. Before he has finished speaking, a new image has formed, and so on.

'The image of the church has been established on a previous occasion – I cannot now tell when. Its evocation in the situation I am describing would surprise no one, but what I now wish to add may be more controversial. I suggest that the experience of this particular conversation with my friend, and this particular moment of the conversation – not simply his words but the totality of that moment of experience – is being perceived sensorially by me and converted into an image of that particular village church.

'I do not know what else may be going on, though I am sure that much more takes place that I am aware of. But the transformation of my sense impression into this visual image is part of a process of mental assimilation. The impressions of the event are being reshaped as a visual image of that particular church, and so are being made into a form suitable for storage in my mind.

'By contrast, the patient might have the same experience, the same sense impressions, and yet be unable to transform the experience so that he can store it mentally. But instead, the experience (and his sense impressions of it) remains a foreign body; it is felt as a "thing" lacking any of the quality we usually attribute to thought or its verbal expression.

'To the first of these products, that of dream-work-α, I propose to give the name, "α-element"; to the second, the unassimilated sense impression, "β-element".'

2   Searle and Derrida would disagree on the interpretation of this figure. Searle would say that two *tokens* of a single *type* are involved. In terms of *types* there is only one word; but if one is talking about *tokens*, then there are two. In fact, as Halion (1989) points out, noting that this reasoning has a somewhat disturbing effect, there may actually now be *three* things: one type and two tokens. In any case, there would be a centre, an ideal type – which is so to speak self-supporting – from which all the others are descended.

Derrida, for his part, rejects the antithesis *token/type* (as well as those of the *serious/non-serious*, *literal/metaphorical* or *normal/parasitic* use of language and the possibility of an unequivocal interpretation, to be anchored to an absolute centre), and would say that the two words are *at one and the same time* a *single* word because they are identical and *two* words because they are different; that is to say, each is an iteration of the other. A sign or word cannot exist as identical to itself, but comes into being only at the moment when it is replicated, in referring on to other traces – *to otherness* (!) – which are always present, if only in the virtual state. For this reason it is split, divided, from the beginning, a priori, constitutively; it is the residue of a play of identity and difference. Hence *the one, the category* and *permanence* must be deemed erroneous concepts.

3 Cf. Derrida (1967b: 292): 'an elementary transference'.

4 Cf. Bion (1965: 99): 'Carried to extremes, the term "cat" is merely a sign analogous to the "point" as the "place where the breast used to be" and should mean the "no–cat". Further denudation leads ultimately to the point which is merely a position without any trace of what used to occupy that position.' See also Bion (1997: 13): 'In analytic practice all statements must be regarded as transformations. Even a single word such as "cat", with its accompanying movements, intonation, and so forth, is a transformation of an emotional experience, O, into the final product Tβp.' Derrida absolutely agrees: the iterability of an expression in different contexts always entails a transformation.

5 See Derrida (1985: 4, translated) for the definition of context as a 'chain of possible substitutions'.

6 See States (1989: 8): 'Tropes involve "primitive" and "undecomposable" strategies of thought.'

7 The implications of the textual metaphor in Freud and of the transference function of the signifier have been explored most exhaustively by Lacan, who gives the following algorithm of the metonymic structure (1966: 181): $f(S \ldots S') S \cong S (-) s$. Here again, a primacy of metonymy could be conjectured from certain passages (p. 173 ibid.): 'The creative spark of the metaphor does not spring from the presentation of two images, that is, of two signifiers equally actualized. It flashes between two signifiers one of which has taken the place of the other in the signifying chain, the occulted signifier remaining present through its (metaphoric) connexion with the rest of the chain.'

8 See note in Chapter 2.

9 Forty years on, the essay 'Freud et la scène de l'écriture' read by Derrida to the Institut de psychanalyse at the Green seminar, still possesses extraordinary originality and density of content, accompanied by dazzling beauty of style.

10 Cf. Bion (1992: 137f.): 'To what extent are the mechanisms of dream-work evident elsewhere? [. . .] is it not possible that the mechanisms that Freud describes as peculiar to dream-work are in reality found to be operating over a wide area of the psyche and in a great number of

different functional fields?' What Bion means by 'dream' is 'a combination in narrative form of dream thoughts, which thoughts in
turn derive from combinations of alpha-elements' (1962: 16). The
narrativization of dream thoughts is governed by the mechanisms of
oneiric rhetoric featuring in classical theories ('they require no
elaboration beyond that which they have received in classical psychoanalytical theory' – Bion 1963: 23) – that is, condensation, displacement, representability and secondary revision. In fact, Bion initially calls
what was later to become the α-function 'dream-work-α', which
suggests that he had in mind the involvement of the rhetoric of dreams
even on this preliminary level.

When the apparatus for thinking thoughts is rudimentary, the
mother regulates the afflux of β by her own α-function, by her capacity
for reverie, by her permeability to the reception of projective identifications – in a word, by the way she places her capacity for symbolization at
the child's disposal. For Bion, this capacity is identified with waking
dream thought. Dreams are distinguished from the waking state only in
the variable degree of focalized attention. Rational thought, which cannot dispense with the micro-dreams represented by metaphors, whether
living or lexicalized, is a hyper-focalized dream.

More than anyone else after Freud, Bion carried psychoanalytic
reflection on dreams forward. Between the two, however, a profound
continuity can be discerned. Just as Freud liberated dreams from the
Ancients' mode of interpretation based on a fixed code and directed his
attention, along the lines of the rebus, to semantic relationships and to
the dreamwork, so Bion freed Freud's theory of dreams from the
encrustations of a psychoanalytic symbolism – a return to a view of
contents as static – and focused instead on the processes of signification,
the containing function, and thought; furthermore, by imagining an
unconscious and a conscious that are continuously *produced*, he released
them from the tendency to take on the contours of substances.

11 Indeed, this has already been done: 'Metonymy is not only the cognitive
means by which we experience the world, but basically almost all other
animals also employ the same means so far as they are able to experience
things' (Sugeno 1996).

12 Eco (1980) substantially bases his theory of metaphor on another tree,
which, however, is upside down – namely, Porphyry's tree, an ideal
model of a dictionary that organizes concepts in binary oppositions,
extending from the most universal genera to the most particular species.
Porphyry's tree is reminiscent of Freud's model of memory traces: a field
of forces or a system of differences without positive terms.

13 Cf. Bion (1965: 102f.): 'The problem is simplified by a rule that "a thing
can never be unless it both is and is not". Stating the rule in other forms:

"a thing cannot exist in the mind alone: nor can a thing exist unless at the same time there is a corresponding no–thing".'

14 Cf. Hobson (1988: 99): 'Language is just the possibility [. . .] of transference of a word or phrase out of one context and into another whose intentional field is hitherto unrelated.'

8 More affects . . . more eyes

1 'Cor' is both the Latin and the ancient Italian word for 'heart'.

2 Casey (1990) and Reisner (1999) refer respectively to a Freud who is *self-deconstructionist* and, in readings of his actual texts, *self-subversive*, while Thompson (2004) emphasizes his 'skeptical' temperament, drawing attention, with Barratt (1993), to a number of aspects of Freud's theories that can be seen as consistent with postmodern sensibility (the unconscious, interpretation, free association, neutrality, and the therapeutic ineffectiveness of purely rational discourse). Bass (1996) stresses the importance of Freud's late thinking about disavowal and ego splitting for postmodern psychoanalysis.

3 Significantly, the title of the Italian edition translates as 'How not to be Postmodern'.

4 Cf. Goldberg (2001: 124), for whom the critique of postmodern culture based on the assertion that it holds that 'anything goes' is 'an unfair and naïve comprehension of postmodern'. The same can be said of the unsophisticated, crudely pejorative use that is made of the term 'nihilism', in the same tone of scandalized censure as that adopted by Walter of Saint-Victor in denouncing the 'heresy of nihilianism' propounded by Peter Lombard and later condemned by Pope Alexander III in 1173 (Volpi 2004: 14); a similar emphasis may be discerned in the charges levelled at atheistic, materialistic psychoanalysis. Others, however – for instance Vattimo – see nihilism as a conceptual category that has dominated philosophical reflection for the past century at least, which is understood in positive, open terms as signifying antidogmatic, pluralist thought, 'closer to human finitude, joys, and sufferings than was traditional metaphysics' (p. 160, translated).

5 It was Genette (1972, 2004) who annexed the classical rhetorical concept of metalepsis to the field of narratology, in which it denotes transgression of the framework of the narration, subversion of ordinary narrative ontology and, typically, the irruption of the narrator into the textual universe in which his characters live.

6 For a comprehensive review of current conceptions on transference see Smith (2003).

7 Translator's note: A play on words: *l'io* means 'the ego'.

8 The film's actual title is *Luce dei miei occhi* [Light of my eyes]!

9 Translator's note: The Italian word for boots, *anfibi*, literally means 'amphibians'.

10 Translator's note: This is an allusion both to the Doc Martens and to the initial letters of the words indicating a registered designation of origin on Italian wine bottles – i.e. a mark of quality!

11 For Derrida (1996: 148), the Babel of 'languages' becomes a metaphor of renouncing the project of domination of a universal, absolute language in favour of 'a diversity of possible points of view [. . .]. Perhaps it is characteristic of postmodernism to take this failure into account. If modernism distinguishes itself by the striving for absolute domination, then postmodernism might be the realization or the experience of its end, the end of the plan of domination.'

12 See Johnson (1981: 5): '*Deconstruction* is not synonymous with *destruction*. It is in fact much closer to the original meaning of the word *analysis* itself, which etymologically means "to undo" – a virtual synonym for "to deconstruct" [. . .] If anything is destroyed in a deconstructive reading, it is not the text, but the claim to unequivocal domination of one mode of signifying over another. A deconstructive reading is a reading which analyzes the specificity of a text's critical difference from itself'.

13 The Italian word is 'dimora', from the Latin 'morari', which means to linger/delay/stay.

Bibliography

Abraham, K. (1923) The spider as a dream symbol. *International Journal of Psychoanalysis*, 4: 313–317.

Adams, L. (1990) The myth of Athena and Arachne: Some Œdipal and pre-Œdipal aspects of creative challenge in women and their implications for the interpretation of Las Meninas by Velazquez. *International Journal of Psychoanalysis*, 71: 597–609.

Alizade, A. M. (2002) Le cadre interne. Available HTTP <http://www.spp.asso.fr/Main/DebatsSansFrontiere/ApaSpp/2002/Discussions/texte2.htm> (accessed 22 September 2009).

Arlow, J. A. (1987) The dynamics of interpretation. *Psychoanalytic Quarterly*, 56: 68–87.

Aron, L. (1996) *A Meeting of Minds: Mutuality in Psychoanalysis*. Hillsdale, NJ: Analytic Press.

Aulagnier, P. (1975) *The Violence of Interpretation: From Pictogram to Statement*. Hove, UK: Brunner-Routledge, 2001.

Austin, J. L. (1962) *How to Do Things with Words*. Oxford: Clarendon Press.

Bachant, J. L. and Adler, E. (1997) Transference: Co-constructed or brought to the interaction? *Journal of the American Psychoanalytic Association*, 45: 1097–1120.

Bachant, J. L., Lynch, A. A. and Richards, A. D. (1996) On perspectives, theories, models, and friends. *Psychoanalytic Psychology*, 13: 153–155.

Bader, M. (1998) Postmodern epistemology: The problem of validation and retreat from therapeutics in psychoanalysis. *Psychoanalytic Dialogues*, 8: 1–32.

Bal, M. (1985) *Narratology: Introduction to the Theory of Narrative*. Toronto: University of Toronto Press.

Barale, F. (1989) Percorsi della memoria e del tempo nello psicotico e nel suo terapeuta. *Psicologia Generale e dell'Età Evolutiva*, 27: 235–249.

192

Barale, F. (1993) Transfert: dalle origini al caso di Dora. *Rivista di Psicoanalisi,* 39: 481–498.

Barale, F. (1999) Postfazione. In A. Ferro, *La psicoanalisi come letteratura e terapia* (pp. 149–61). Milan: Raffaello Cortina.

Barale, F. and Ucelli, S. (2000) Corpi estranei e corpi inclusi. Importanza e paradossi del corpo nella relazione terapeutica. *Psiche,* 8: 201–213.

Baranger, M. (2005) *Field Theory.* In S. Lewkowicz and S. Flechner (eds), *Truth, Reality, and the Psychoanalyst* (pp. 49–71). London: Karnac.

Baranger, M. and Baranger, W. (1961–62) La situación analítica como campo dinámico. *Revista Uruguaya de Psicoanálisis,* 4: 3–54.

Baranger, M., Baranger, W. and Mom, J. M. (1983) Process and non-process in analytic work. *International Journal of Psychoanalysis,* 64: 1–15.

Barratt, B. B. (1993) *Psychoanalysis and the Postmodern Impulse: Knowing and Being Since Freud's Psychology.* Baltimore, MD: Johns Hopkins University Press.

Barthes, R. (1970) *S / Z: An Essay.* New York: Hill and Wang, 1975.

Barthes, R. (1977) *Image, Music, Text.* New York: Hill and Wang, 1978.

Barthes, R. (1980) *Camera Lucida: Reflections on Photography.* New York: Hill and Wang, 1982.

Barthes, R. (1982) *L'obvie et l'obtus. Essais critiques III.* Paris: Seuil.

Barthes, R. (2002) *The Neutral: Lecture Course at the College de France (1977–1978).* New York: Columbia University Press, 2007.

Bass, A. (1996) Psychoanalysis and the Postmodern Impulse. Knowing and Being since Freud's Psychology: By Barnaby B. Barratt. Baltimore, MD/ London: Johns Hopkins University Press, 1993, 262 pp. *Psychoanalytic Quarterly,* 65: 629–635.

Bauman, Z. (1997) *Postmodernity and its Discontents.* New York: New York University Press.

Benjamin, J. (1995) Comment. *Psychoanalytic Psychology,* 12: 595–598.

Bennington, G. (1989) Deconstruction is not what you think. In A. Papadakis, C. Cooke and A. Benjamin (eds), *Deconstruction Omnibus.* London: Academy Editions.

Bennington, G. (2000) *Interrupting Derrida.* London: Routledge.

Bergmann, M. S. (1993) Reflections on the history of psychoanalysis. *Journal of the American Psychoanalytic Association,* 41: 929–955.

Berto, G. (1998) *Freud, Heidegger, lo spaesamento.* Milan: Bompiani.

Bezoari, M. (2002) La nevrosi di transfert come funzione del campo analitico. *Rivista di Psicoanalisi,* 48: 889–905.

Bezoari, M. and Ferro, A. (1989) Ascolto, interpretazione e funzioni trasformative nel dialogo analitico. *Rivista di Psicoanalisi,* 35: 1015–1051.

Bezoari, M. and Ferro, A. (1992a) L'oscillazione significati-affetti nella coppia analitica al lavoro. *Rivista di Psicoanalisi,* 37: 381–403.

Bezoari, M. and Ferro, A. (1992b) From a play between 'parts' to transformations in the couple: Psychoanalysis in a bipersonal field. In L. Nissim Momigliano and A. Robutti (eds), *Shared Experience: The Psychoanalytic Dialogue* (pp. 43–65). London: Karnac.

Bick, E. (1984) Ulteriori considerazioni sulle funzioni della pelle nelle prime relazioni oggettuali: Integrando i dati dell' 'infant observation' con quelli dell'analisi dei bambini e degli adulti. *Rivista di Psicoanalisi*, 30: 341–355.

Bion, W. R. (1962) *Learning From Experience*. London: Heinemann.

Bion, W. R. (1963) *Elements of Psycho-Analysis*. In W. R. Bion, *Seven Servants*. New York: Jason Aronson, 1975.

Bion, W. R. (1965) *Transformations: Change from Learning to Growth*. London: Heinemann.

Bion, W. R. (1970) *Attention and Interpretation. A Scientific Approach to Insight in Psycho-Analysis*. London: Tavistock.

Bion, W. R. (1992) *Cogitations*. London: Karnac.

Bion, W. R. (1997) *Taming Wild Thoughts*. London: Karnac.

Bird, B. (1972) Notes on transference: Universal phenomenon and hardest part of analysis. *Journal of the American Psychoanalytic Association*, 20: 267–301.

Birksted-Breen, D. (2003) Time and après coup. *International Journal of Psychoanalysis*, 84: 1501–1515.

Blass, R. B. and Simon, B. (1994) The value of the historical perspective to contemporary psychoanalysis: Freud's 'seduction hypothesis'. *International Journal of Psychoanalysis*, 75: 677–693.

Bleger, J. (1967a) Psycho-analysis of the psycho-analytic frame. *International Journal of Psychoanalysis*, 48: 511–519.

Bleger, J. (1967b) *Simbiosis y ambigüedad; estudio psicoanalítico*. Buenos Aires: Editorial Paidós.

Blin, G. (1989) *Stendhal et les problèmes du roman*. Paris: Josè Corti.

Blum, H. P. (1971) On the conception and development of the transference neurosis. *Journal of the American Psychoanalytic Association*, 19: 41–53.

Blum, H. P. (1996) Seduction trauma: Representation, deferred action, pathogenic development. *Journal of the American Psychoanalytic Association*, 44: 1147–1164.

Blum, H. P. (2003) Repression, transference and reconstruction. *International Journal of Psychoanalysis*, 84: 497–503.

Bodei, R. (1999) Le patrie sconosciute. Emozioni ed esperienza estetica. In T. Magri (ed.), *Filosofia ed emozioni* (pp. 167–195). Milan: Feltrinelli.

Bollas, C. (1995) *Cracking Up: The Work of Unconscious Experience*. New York: Hill and Wang.

Bollas, C. (1999) *The Mistery of Things*. London: Routledge.

Bolognini, S. (1994) Transference: Erotized, erotic, loving, affectionate. *International Journal of Psychoanalysis*, 75: 73–86.

Bolognini, S. (1995). Condivisione e fraintendimento. *Rivista di Psicoanalisi*, 41: 565–582.

Bolognini, S. (2002) *Psychoanalytic Empathy*. London: Free Association Books, 2004.

Bolognini, S. (2005) Il bar nel deserto. Simmetria e asimmetria nel trattamento di adolescenti difficili. *Rivista di Psicoanalisi*, 51: 33–44.

Bonaminio, V. (2003) La persona dell'analista: Interpretare, non-interpretare e controtransfert. In P. Fabozzi (ed.), *Forme dell'interpretare. Nuove prospettive nella teoria e nella clinica psicoanalitica* (pp. 25–59). Milan: Franco Angeli.

Borgogno, F. (2004) Esordio psicoanalitico di Harold F. Searles. *Rivista di Psicoanalisi*, 50: 171–174.

Borutti, S. (2006) *Filosofia dei sensi. Estetica del pensiero tra filosofia, arte e letteratura*. Milan: Raffaello Cortina.

Bottiroli, G. (1993) *Retorica. L'intelligenza figurale nell'arte e nella filosofia*. Turin: Bollati Boringhieri.

Boyer, L. B. (1999) *Countertransference and Regression*. Northvale, NJ: Jason Aronson.

Brazelton, T. B. and Greenspan, S. I. (2000) *The Irreducible Needs of Children: What Every Child Must Have to Grow, Learn, and Flourish*. Cambridge, MA: Perseus.

Brenner, C. (1982) *The Mind in Conflict*. New York: International Universities Press.

Briatte, K. (1997) Matériaux pour une rhétorique del l'hypertextualitè. *Strumenti Critici*, 85: 489–508.

Brooks, P. (1984) *Reading for the Plot: Design and Intention in Narrative*. New York: A.A. Knopf.

Butler, J. (1997) *The Psychic Life of Power: Theories in Subjection*. Stanford, CA: Stanford University Press.

Caffi, C. (2001) *La mitigazione. Un approccio pragmatico alla comunicazione nei contesti terapeutici*. Münster-Hamburg-London: LIT.

Calef, V. (1971a) Current concept of transference neurosis: Introduction. *Journal of the American Psychoanalytic Association*, 19: 22–25.

Calef, V. (1971b) Current concept of transference neurosis: Concluding remarks. *Journal of the American Psychoanalytic Association*, 19: 89–97.

Cartwright, D. (2005) β-Mentality in The Matrix trilogy. *International Journal of Psychoanalysis*, 86: 179–190.

Casey, E. S. (1990) The subdominance of the pleasure principle. In R. A. Glick and S. Bone (eds), *Pleasure Beyond the Pleasure Principle* (pp. 239–258). New Haven, CT: Yale University Press.

Ceruti, M. (1986) *Constraints and Possibilities: The Evolution of Knowledge and Knowledge of Evolution*. Lausanne: Gordon and Breach, 1994.

Chantraine, P. (1999) *Dictionnaire étymologique de la langue grecque*. Paris: Klincksieck.

Charles, M. (2001) Nonphysical touch: Modes of containment and communication within the analytic process. *Psychoanalytic Quarterly*, 70: 387–416.

Chianese, D. (2006). *Un lungo sogno*. Bologna: Franco Angeli.

Civitarese, G. (1998) Gioco delle parti e rapporto con la realtà nelle psicosi. *Rivista Sperimentale di Freniatria*, 122: 34–40.

Civitarese, G. (2003) Aspetti autistici nei disturbi schizofrenici. In G. Cardamone and G. Tagliavini (eds), *Ripensare le schizofrenie. Un dibattito italiano* (pp. 37–50). Milan: Edizioni Colibrì.

Civitarese, G. (2006a) Dreams that mirror the session. *International Journal of Psychoanalysis*, 87: 703–723.

Civitarese, G. (2006b) Discusiones: 'Vinculo simbiótico y encuadre'. *Revista de Psicoanálisis*, 63: 485–500.

Civitarese, G. (2007a) Sognare l'analisi. In A. Ferro, G. Civitarese and M. Collovà, G. Foresti, E. Molinari, F. Mazzacane and P.P.B. Boringhieri, *Sognare l'analisi. Sviluppi clinici del pensiero di W.R. Bion* (pp. 34–58). Turin: Bollati Boringhieri.

Civitarese, G. (2007b) Bion e a demanda da ambigüidade. *Revista de Psicanálise*, 14: 57–75.

Cooper, A. M. (1987) The transference neurosis: A concept ready for retirement. *Psychoanalytic Inquiry*, 7: 569–585.

Cooper, A. M. (2005) *The Quiet Revolution in American Psychoanalysis: Selected Papers of Arnold M. Cooper*. New York: Brunner-Routledge.

Culler, J. (1982) *On Deconstruction. Theory and Criticism After Structuralism*. Ithaca: Cornell University Press.

Damasio, A. (1999) *The Feeling of What Happens: Body and Emotion in the Making of Consciousness*. New York: Harcourt Brace.

de Man, P. (1971) *Blindness and Insight: Essays in the Rhetoric of Contemporary Criticism*. New York: Oxford University Press.

de Man, P. (1979) *Allegories of Reading: Figural Language in Rousseau, Nietzsche, Rilke, and Proust*. New Haven, CT: Yale University Press.

De Mauro, T. (2002) *Dizionario italiano*. Milan: Mondadori.

Derrida, J. (1967a) *Writing and Difference*. London: Routledge, 2001.

Derrida, J. (1967b) *Of Grammatology*. Baltimore, MD: Johns Hopkins University Press, 1976.

Derrida, J. (1972) *Margins of Philosophy*. Chicago: University of Chicago Press, 1985.

Derrida, J. (1978) *The Truth in Painting*. Chicago: University of Chicago Press, 1987.

Derrida, J. (1984) Pacific deconstruction, 2. Lettera a un amico giapponese. *Rivista di Estetica*, 17: 5–10.

Derrida, J. (1988) *Limited Inc*. Evanston, IL: Northwestern University Press.

Derrida, J. (1990a) Some statements and truisms about neologisms, mewisms, postisms, parasitisms, and other small seismism. In D. Carroll (ed.), *The States of 'Theory'. History, Art, and Critical Discourse* (pp. 63–94). New York: Columbia University Press.

Derrida, J. (1990b) *Memoirs of the Blind: The Self-Portrait and Other Ruins*. Chicago: University of Chicago Press, 1993.

Derrida, J. (1995) *Archive Fever: A Freudian Impression*. Chicago: University of Chicago Press, 1998.

Derrida, J. (1996) Architecture where desire can live: Jacques Derrida interviewed by E. Meyer. In K. Nesbitt (ed.), *Theorizing a New Agenda for Architecture: An Anthology of Architectural Theory 1965–1995* (pp. 142–149). New York: Princeton Architectural Press.

Derrida, J. (1999) *Sur parole. Instantanés philosophiques*. Paris: l'Aube.

Derrida, J. and Dufourmantelle, A. (1997) *Of Hospitality*. Stanford, CA: Stanford University Press.

Derrida, J. and Ferraris, M. (1997) *A Taste for the Secret*. Cambridge: Polity Press, 2001.

Derrida, J. and Roudinesco, E. (2001) *For What Tomorrow. . . . A Dialogue*. Stanford, CA: Stanford University Press, 2004.

Di Benedetto, A. (2000) *Before Words: Psychoanalytic Listening of the Unsaid Through the Medium of Art*. London: Free Association Books, 2005.

Di Chiara, G. (1971) Il setting analitico. *Psiche*, 8: 47–60.

Di Chiara, G. (1990) La stupita meraviglia, l'autismo e la competenza difensiva. *Rivista di Psicoanalisi*, 36: 440–457.

Di Chiara, G. (1992) Meeting, telling and parting: Three basic factors in the psychoanalytic experience. In L. Nissim Momigliano and A. Robutti (eds), *Shared Experience: The Psychoanalytic Dialogue* (pp. 21–41). London: Karnac.

Diodato, R. (2005) *Estetica del virtuale*. Milan: Mondadori.

Dubois, J. [Gruppo μ] (1970) *A General Rhetoric*. Baltimore, MD: Johns Hopkins University Press, 1981.

Eco, U. (1979) *The Role of the Reader: Explorations in the Semiotics of Texts*. Bloomington, IN: Indiana University Press, 1984.

Eco, U. (1980) Metafora. In *Enciclopedia* (pp. 191–236). IX, Turin: Einaudi.

Eco, U. (1990) *The Limits of Interpretation*. Bloomington, IN: Indiana University Press.

Eco, U. (1997) *Kant and the Platypus: Essays on Language and Cognition*. New York: Harcourt Brace, 2000.

Edelman, G. (1992) *Bright Air, Brilliant Fire: On the Matter of the Mind*. New York: Basic Books.

Edelman, G. (2004) *Wider Than The Sky: The Phenomenal Gift of Consciousness.* New Haven, CT: Yale University Press.

Eickhoff, F.-W. (2006) On Nachträglichkeit: The modernity of an old concept. *International Journal of Psychoanalysis,* 87: 1453–1469.

Elam, K. (1980) *The Semiotics of Theatre and Drama.* New York: Methuen.

Elliott, A. and Spezzano, C. (1996) Psychoanalysis at its limits: Navigating the postmodern turn. *Psychoanalytic Quarterly,* 65: 52–83.

Etchegoyen, H. (2000) Alcune riflessioni sull'interpretazione psicoanalitica. In E. Levis (ed.), *Forme di vita forme di conoscenza. Un percorso fra psicoanalisi e cultura* (pp. 38–40). Turin: Bollati Boringhieri.

Faimberg, H. (1996) Listening to listening. *International Journal of Psychoanalysis,* 77: 667–678.

Faimberg, H. (2005) Après-coup. *International Journal of Psychoanalysis,* 86: 1–6.

Fairbairn, W. R. D. (1952) *Psychoanalytic Studies of the Personality.* London: Tavistock.

Fenichel, O. (1945) *The Psychoanalytic Theory of Neurosis.* New York: Norton.

Ferraris, M. (2003) *Introduzione a Derrida.* Bari: Laterza.

Ferro, A. (1992) *The Bi-Personal Field: Experiencing Child Analysis.* London: Routledge, 1999.

Ferro, A. (1996) *In the Analyst's Consulting Room.* Hove, UK: Brunner-Routledge, 2002.

Ferro, A. (1999a) *Psychoanalysis as Therapy and Storytelling.* London: Routledge, 2006.

Ferro, A. (1999b) Interpretazioni, decostruzioni, narrazioni. Ovvero: le ragioni di Jacques. *Rivista di Psicoanalisi,* 4: 743–758.

Ferro, A. (2002a). Some implications of Bion's thought: The waking dream and narrative derivatives. *International Journal of Psychoanalysis,* 83: 597–607.

Ferro, A. (2002b) *Seeds of Illness, Seeds of Recovery.* London: Routledge, 2004.

Ferro, A. (2003a) Commentary on Ilany Kogan's 'On being a dead, beloved child'. *Psychoanalytic Quarterly,* 3: 777–783.

Ferro, A. (2003b). On: Kogan I. On being a dead, beloved child [commentary]. *Psychoanalytic Quarterly,* 72: 777–783.

Ferro, A. (2006) *Mind Works: Technique and Creativity in Psychoanalysis.* London: Routledge, 2008.

Ferro, A. (2007) *Evitare le emozioni, vivere le emozioni.* Milan: Raffaello Cortina.

Ferro, A., Pasquali, G., Tognoli, L. and Viola, M. (1986) L'uso del simbolismo nel setting e il processo di simbolizzazione nella relazione analitica. *Rivista di Psicoanalisi,* 32: 539–553.

Ferruta, A. (2006) Riflessione storico-critica sul concetto di transfert: il transfert tra le generazioni di analisti. Paper delivered at the Milan Centre of Psychoanalysis (CMP), 9 February.

Feyerabend, P. K. (1975) *Against Method: Outline of an Anarchistic Theory of Knowledge*. Atlantic Highlands, NJ: Humanities Press.

Fischer, N. (1997) Transference neurosis and psychoanalytic experience: By Gail S. Reed. Yale University Press, New Haven and London 1994, 240 pp. *Journal of the American Psychoanalytic Association*, 45: 257–261.

Fonagy, I. (1999) The process of remembering: Recovery and discovery. *International Journal of Psychoanalysis*, 80: 961–978.

Fonagy, P. (1999) Memory and therapeutic action. *International Journal of Psychoanalysis*, 80: 215–224.

Fonagy, P. (2003) Rejoinder to Harold Blum. *International Journal of Psychoanalysis*, 84: 503–509.

Fontanier, P. (1968) *Le figures du discours (1821–1827)*. Paris: Flammarion.

Fosshage, J. L. (1994) Toward reconceptualising transference: Theoretical and clinical considerations. *International Journal of Psychoanalysis*, 75: 265–280.

Fowles, J. (1969) *The French Lieutenant's Woman*. Boston: Little, Brown.

Freud, A. (1936) *The Ego and the Mechanism of Defence*. London: Hogarth Press.

Freud, S. (1895) A project for a scientific psychology. *SE* 1: 283–397.

Freud, S. (1900) The interpretation of dreams. *SE* 4: 1–338; *SE* 5: 339–625.

Freud, S. (1901) Fragment of an analysis of a case of hysteria. *SE* 7: 1–122.

Freud, S. (1905) Jokes and their relation to the unconscious. *SE* 8: 1–243.

Freud, S. (1909) Five lectures on psycho-analysis. *SE* 11: 3–55.

Freud, S. (1912) Recommendations to physicians practising psycho-analysis. *SE* 12: 111–120.

Freud, S. (1912–13) Totem and taboo. *SE* 13: 1–161.

Freud, S. (1913) On beginning the treatment (Further recommendations on the technique of psycho-analysis I). *SE* 12: 123–144.

Freud, S. (1914a) On the history of the psychoanalytic movement. *SE* 14: 1–66.

Freud, S. (1914b) On narcissism: An introduction. *SE* 14: 73–103.

Freud, S. (1915a) Observations on transference-love (Further recommendations on the technique of psychoanalysis III). *SE* 12: 159–171.

Freud, S. (1915b) On transience. *SE* 14: 303–307.

Freud, S. (1918) From the history of an infantile neurosis. *SE* 17: 7–122.

Freud, S. (1920) Beyond the pleasure principle. *SE* 18: 7–64.

Freud, S. (1925) An autobiographical study. *SE* 20: 3–70.

Freud, S. (1926) The question of lay analysis. *SE* 20: 179–250.

Freud, S. (1937) Construction in analysis. *SE* 23: 257–269.

Freud, S. (1938) An outline of psycho-analysis. *SE* 23: 141–207.

Friedman, L. (1995) La réalité psychique dans la théorie psychanalytique. *Revue Française de Psychoanalyse*, 59: 231–238.

Gabbard, G. O. (2001) What can neuroscience teach us about transference? *Canadian Journal of Psychoanalysis*, 9: 1–18.

Gaburri, E. (ed.) (1997) *Emozioni e interpretazione. Psicoanalisi del campo emotivo.* Turin: Bollati Boringhieri.

Garella, A. (1991) Coazione a ripetere e memoria. *Rivista di Psicoanalisi,* 37: 517–561.

Gedo, J. E. (1973) Kant's way: The psychoanalytic contribution of David Rapaport. *Psychoanalytic Quarterly,* 42: 409–434.

Genette, G. (1972) *Narrative Discourse: An Essay in Method.* Ithaca, New York: Cornell University Press.

Genette, G. (2004) *Métalepse: De la figure à la fiction.* Paris: Seuil.

Gill, M. (1982) *Analysis of Transference: Theory and Technique.* New York: International Universities Press.

Gilmore, K. (1996) Transference neurosis and psychoanalytic experience. *International Journal of Psychoanalysis,* 77: 628–632.

Goldberg, A. (2001) Postmodern psychoanalysis. *International Journal of Psychoanalysis,* 82: 123–128.

Goretti, G. (1996) La domanda dell'analista. *Rivista di Psicoanalisi,* 42: 393–403.

Gottlieb, K. I. (1996) Essential papers on transference. *Psychoanalytic Quarterly,* 65: 431–438.

Gray, P. (1973) Psychoanalytic technique and the ego's capacity for viewing intrapsychic activity. *Journal of the American Psychoanalytic Association,* 21: 474–494.

Green, A. (1983) *Narcissisme de vie, narcissisme de mort.* Paris: Minuit.

Green, A. (1983) The dead mother. In A. Green, *On Private Madness* (pp. 142–173). London: Hogarth Press, 1986.

Greenberg, J. R. and Mitchell, S. A. (1983) *Object Relations in Psychoanalytic Theory.* Boston, MA: Harvard University Press.

Grotstein J. S. (2007) *A Beam of Intense Darkness: Wilfred Bion's Legacy to Psychoanalysis.* London: Karnac.

Grünbaum, A. (1984) *The Foundations of Psychoanalysis: A Philosophical Critique.* Berkeley and Los Angeles, CA: University of California Press.

Haas, L. (1966) Transference outside the psycho-analytic situation. *International Journal of Psychoanalysis,* 47: 422–426.

Halion, K. J. (1989) *Deconstruction and Speech Act Theory: A Defence of the Distinction between Normal and Parasitic Speech Acts.* Available HTTP <http://www.e-anglais.com/thesis.html> (accessed 24 September 2009).

Handke, P. (1970). Nauseated by language (interview with Arthur Joseph). *Drama Review,* 15: 56–61.

Harley, M. (1971) The current status of transference neurosis in children. *Journal of the American Psychoanalytic Association,* 19: 26–40.

Hartmann, H. (1939) *Ego Psychology and the Problem of Adaptation.* New York: International Universities Press.

Hillis Miller, J. (1987) *The Ethics of Reading*. New York: Columbia University Press.

Hobson, M. (1998) *Jacques Derrida: Opening Lines*. London: Routledge.

Hoffman, I. (1983) The patient as interpreter of the analyst's experience. *Contemporary Psychoanalysis*, 19: 389–422.

Holland, N. (1999) Deconstruction. *International Journal of Psychoanalysis*, 80: 153–162.

Imbasciati, A. (2005) *Psicoanalisi e cognitivismo*. Rome: Armando.

Imbeault, J. (1997). *Mouvements* [Movements]. Paris: Gallimard.

Jakobson, R. (1963) *Essais de linguistique générale*. Paris: Minuit.

Janin, C. (1995) La réalité, entre traumatisme et histoire. *Revue Française de Psychoanalyse*, 59: 115–131.

Johnson, B. (1981) *The Critical Difference: Essays in the Contemporary Rhetoric of Reading*. Baltimore, MD: Johns Hopkins University Press.

Joseph, B. (1985) Transference: The total situation. *International Journal of Psychoanalysis*, 66: 447–454.

Kafka, J. (1989) *Multiple Realities in Clinical Practice*. New Haven, CT: Yale University Press.

Kandell, J. (2004) Jacques Derrida, abstruse theorist, dies in Paris at 74. *New York Times*, 10 October. Available HTTP. <http://query.nytimes.com/gst/fullpage.html?res=9E01E0DA133BF933A25753C1A9629C8B63> (accessed 24 September 2009).

Kern, J. W. (1987) Transference neurosis as a waking dream: A clinical enigma. *Journal of the American Psychoanalytic Association*, 35: 337–366.

Kirshner, L. A. (1994) Trauma, the good object, and the symbolic: A theoretical integration. *International Journal of Psychoanalysis*, 75: 235–242.

Kluzer, G. (1988) Elementi costitutivi latenti della fase iniziale della relazione analitic. *Rivista di Psicoanalisi*, 34: 316–345.

Kohut, H. (1971) *The Analysis of the Self; A Systematic Approach to the Psychoanalytic Treatment of Narcissistic Personality Disorders*. New York: International Universities Press.

Kuhn, T. S. (1962) *The Structure of Scientific Revolutions*. Chicago: University of Chicago Press.

Lacan, J. (1966) *Écrits*. New York: Norton, 2005.

Landow, G. P. (1992) *Hypertext: The Convergence of Contemporary Critical Theory and Technology*. Baltimore, MD: Johns Hopkins University Press.

Langs, R. J. (1971) Day residues, recall residues, dreams: Reality and the psiche. *Journal of the American Psychoanalytic Association*, 19: 499–523.

Langs, R. J. (1978) Validation and the framework of the therapeutic situation – thoughts prompted by Hans H. Strupp's 'Suffering and psychotherapy'. *Contemporary Psychoanalysis*, 14: 98–124.

Langs, R. J. and Searles, H. F. (1980) *Intrapsychic and Interpersonal Dimensions of Treatment: A Clinical Dialogue.* New York: Jason Aronson.

Laplanche, J. (1998) *Problématiques, tome 5: Le Baquet, transcendance du transfert.* Paris: Presse Universitaire de France.

Laplanche, J. and Pontalis, J.-B. (1967) *The Language of Psychoanalysis.* New York: Norton, 1974.

Laub, D. and Auerhahn, N. C. (1993) Knowing and not knowing massive psychic trauma: Forms of traumatic memory. *International Journal of Psychoanalysis,* 74: 287–302.

Leary, K. (1994) Psychoanalytic 'problems' and postmodern 'solutions'. *Psychoanalytic Quarterly,* 63: 433–465.

Le Guen, C. (1982) L'après-coup. *Revue Française de Psychoanalyse,* 46: 527–534.

Le Guen, C. (1995) Le principe de réalité psychique. *Revue Française de Psychoanalyse,* 59: 9–25.

Leites, N. (1997) Transference interpretations only? *International Journal of Psychoanalysis,* 58: 275–287.

Levenson, E. A. (1972) *The Fallacy of Understanding: An Inquiry into the Changing Structure of Psychoanalysis.* New York: Basic Books.

Loewald, H. W. (1960) On the therapeutic action of psycho-analysis. *International Journal of Psychoanalysis,* 41: 16–33.

Loewald, H. W. (1971) The transference neurosis: Comments on the concept and the phenomenon. *Journal of the American Psychoanalytic Association,* 19: 54–66.

Lothane, Z. (1983) Reality, dream, and trauma. *Contemporary Psychoanalysis,* 19: 423–443.

Lucco, M. (1998) San Girolamo penitente. In D. A. Brown, P. Humphrey and M. Lucco (eds), *Lorenzo Lotto. Il genio inquieto del Rinascimento* (pp. 102–104). Milan: Skira.

McClelland, J. L., Rumelhart, D. E. and Hinton, G. E. (1986) *Parallel Distributed Processing: Explorations in the Microstructure of Cognition.* Cambridge: MIT Press.

McLaughlin, J. T. (1981a) Transference, psychic reality, and countertransference. *Psychoanalytic Psychology,* 50: 639–664.

McLaughlin, J. T. (1981b) Clinical and theoretical aspects of enactment. *Journal of the American Psychoanalytic Association,* 39: 595–614.

Malina, D. (2002) *Breaking the Frame: Metalepsis and the Construction of the Subject.* Columbus, OH: Ohio State University Press.

Marcelli, D. (1983) Réflexion sur une conduite particulière de l'enfant autiste: Prendre la main. *Neuropsychiatrie de l'Enfance et de l'Adolescence,* 31: 259–261.

Marcelli, D. (1986) *Position autistique et naissance de la psyché.* Paris: Presse Universitaire de France.

Masson, J. M. (1985) *The Complete Letters of Sigmund Freud to Wilhelm Fliess, 1887–1904*. Cambridge, MA, and London, UK: Belknap Press of Harvard University Press.

Meltzer, D. (1984) *Dream-life: A Re-Examination of the Psycho-analytical Theory and Technique*. London: Karnac.

Meltzer, D., Bremner, J., Hoxter, S., Weddell, D. and Wittenberg, I. (1975) *Explorations in Autism: A Psycho-analytical Study*. London: Karnac.

Milner, M. (1952) Aspects of symbolism in comprehension of the not-self. *International Journal of Psychoanalysis*, 33: 181–195.

Mitrani, J. L. (1992) The survival function of autistic manoeuvres in adult patients. *International Journal of Psychoanalysis*, 73: 549–560.

Modell, A. H. (1989) The psychoanalytic setting as a container of multiple levels of reality: A perspective on the theory of psychoanalytic treatment. *Psychoanalytic Inquiry*, 9: 67–87.

Modell, A. H. (1990) *Other Times, Other Realities: Toward a Theory of Psychoanalytic Treatment*. Cambridge, MA: Harvard University Press.

Montale, E. (1992 [1920–7]) *Cuttlefish Bones* (W. Arrowsmith, Trans.). New York: Norton.

Mortara Garavelli, B. (1988) *Manuale di retorica*. Milan: Bompiani.

Napolitano, F. (2007) Transfert. In F. Barale, V. Gallese, S. Mistura and A. Zamperini (eds), *Psiche. Dizionario storico di psicologia, psichiatria, psicoanalisi, neuroscienze*, II (pp. 1107–1112). Turin: Einaudi.

Nelles, W. (1997) *Frameworks: Narrative Levels and Embedded Narrative*. New York: Peter Lang.

Nelles, W. (2004) Personal communication.

Neri, C. (1985) Contenimento fusionale e oscillazione contenitore-contenuto. *Rivista di Psicoanalisi*, 31: 316–325.

Neyraut, M. (1974) *Le transfert: Étude psychanalytique*. Paris: Presse Universitaire de France.

Niall, L. (2004) *A Derrida Dictionary*. Oxford: Blackwell.

Nietzsche, F. (1873) On truth and lie in an extra-moral sense. In C. Cazeaux (ed.), *The Continental Aesthetics Reader* (pp. 53–62). London: Routledge, 2000.

Nietzsche, F. (1887) *On the Genealogy of Morals/Ecce Homo* (W. Kaufmann and R. J. Hollingdale, Trans. W. Kaufmann, Ed.). New York: Vintage Books, 1989.

Ogden, T. H. (1979) On projective identification. *International Journal of Psychoanalysis*, 60: 357–373.

Ogden, T. H. (1989) *The Primitive Edge of Experience*. Northvale, NJ: Jason Aronson.

Ogden, T. H. (1991) Analysing the matrix of transference. *International Journal of Psychoanalysis*, 72: 593–605.

Ogden, T. H. (1994) The concept of interpretive action. *Psychoanalytic Quarterly*, 63: 219–245.

Ogden, T. H. (1997) *Reverie and Interpretation: Sensing Something Human.* Northvale, NJ: Jason Aronson.

Ogden, T. H. (2003a) On not being able to dream. *International Journal of Psychoanalysis*, 84: 17–30.

Ogden, T. H. (2003b) What's true and whose idea was it? *International Journal of Psychoanalysis*, 84: 593–606.

Ogden, T. H. (2005a) On psychoanalytic writing. *International Journal of Psychoanalysis*, 86: 15–29.

Ogden, T. H. (2005b) On psychoanalytic supervision. *International Journal of Psychoanalysis*, 86: 1265–1280.

O'Neill, P. (1994) *Fictions of Discourse: Reading Narrative Theory.* Toronto: University of Toronto Press.

Ovid (1995) *The Metamorphoses* (A. Mandelbaum, Trans.). Orlando, FL: Harvest/HBJ Books.

Pallier, L. (1985) Fusionalità, agora- e claustro-fobia e processi schizo-paranoidei. *Rivista di Psicoanalisi*, 31: 299–306.

Petrella, F. (1985) *La mente come teatro.* Turin: Centro Scientifico Torinese.

Petrella, F. (1993) *Turbamenti affettivi e alterazioni dell'esperienza.* Milan: Raffaello Cortina.

Pier, J. and Schaeffer, J.-M. (2005) *Métalepses: Entorses au pacte de la représentation.* Paris: Ehess.

Ponsi, M. (2002) Alleanza terapeutica. Interazioni collaborative. Regolazione della relazione. Paper delivered at the Milan Centre of Psychoanalysis (CMP), 15 March.

Pontalis, J.-B. (1990) *La force d'attraction.* Paris: Seuil.

Protter, B. (1985) Toward an emergent psychoanalytic epistemology. *Contemporary Psychoanalysis*, 21: 208–227.

Proust, M. (1993 [1913–1927]) *In Search of Lost Time: The Captive / The Fugitive* (C. K. Scott Moncrieff and T. Kilmartin, Trans.). London: Vintage Random House.

Proust, M. (1998 [1913–1927]). *In Search of Lost Time: Swann's Way* (C. K. Scott Moncrieff and T. Kilmartin, Trans.). London: Vintage Random House.

Puget, J. (1995) La rèalité psychique: Son impact sur l'analyste et le patient aujourd'hui. *Revue Française de Psychoanalyse*, 59: 251–259.

Puget, J. (1995) Psychic reality or various realities. *International Journal of Psychoanalysis*, 76: 29–34.

Quinodoz, D. (2002) *Words That Touch: A Psychoanalyst Learns to Speak.* London: Karnac, 2003.

Racalbuto, A. (2004) Le parole scritte e lette in psicoanalisi. Lavori che seducono, lavori che annoiano. *Rivista di Psicoanalisi*, 50: 389–400.

Racamier, P.-C. (1992) *Le génie des origines: psychanalyse et psychoses.* Paris: Editions Payot.

Ramond, C. (2001) *Le vocabulaire de Derrida.* Paris: Ellipses.

Rank, O. (1945) *Will Therapy: An Analysis of the Therapeutic Process in Terms of Relationship (1936).* New York: Knopf.

Reed, G. S. (1994) *Transference Neurosis and Psychoanalytic Experience.* New Haven and London: Yale University Press.

Reed, G. S. (2004) Transference: Shibboleth or albatross? By Joseph Schachter, 2002. *International Journal of Psychoanalysis*, 85: 539–542.

Reik, T. (1933) New ways in psycho-analytic technique. *International Journal of Psychoanalysis*, 14: 321–334.

Reis, B. E. (1999) Thomas Ogden's phenomenological turn. *Psychoanalytic Dialogues*, 9: 371–393.

Reisner, S. (1999) Freud and psychoanalysis: Into the 21st century. *Journal of the American Psychoanalytic Association*, 47: 1037–1060.

Rella, F. (1999) *Pensare per figure. Freud, Platone, Kafka.* Bologna: Pendragon.

Renik, O. (1998) Who's afraid of postmodernism? Commentary on Bader's paper. *Psychoanalytic Dialogues*, 8: 55–60.

Rilke, R. M. (1923) *Duino Elegies and the Sonnets of Orpheus* (A. Poulin, Jr., Trans.). New York: Mariner Books.

Rioch, J. M. (1943) The transference phenomenon in psychoanalytic theory. *Psychiatry*, 6: 147–156.

Riolo, F. (1983) Sogno e teoria della conoscenza in psicoanalisi. *Rivista di Psicoanalisi*, 29: 279–295.

Riolo, F. (1999) Il paradigma della 'cura'. *Rivista di Psicoanalisi*, 45: 7–27.

Rossi Monti, M. and Foresti, G. (2002) L'ineludibile aspecificità tecnica degli strumenti di lavoro dello psicoanalista. Paper delivered to the National Meeting of the Italian Psychoanalytic Society (SPI), Trieste.

Roth, P. (2000) *The Human Stain.* Boston, MA: Houghton Mifflin.

Roth, P. (2001) Mapping the landscape: Levels of transference interpretation. *International Journal of Psychoanalysis*, 82: 533–544.

Roussillon, R. (1995) *Logiques et archéologiques du cadre psychanalytique.* Paris: Presse Universitaire de France.

Ruskin, J. (1903–12) *The Works of John Ruskin* (E. T. Cook and A. Wedderburn, eds). London: Allen.

Ryan, M.-L. (1991) *Possible Worlds, Artificial Intelligence and Narrative Theory.* Bloomington, IN: Indiana University Press.

Ryan, M.-L. (2001) *Narrative as Virtual Reality: Immersion and Interactivity in Literature and Electronic Media.* Baltimore, MD: Johns Hopkins University Press.

Ryle, A. (2003) Something more than the 'Something more than interpretation' is needed: A comment on the paper by the Process of Change Study Group. *International Journal of Psychoanalysis*, 84: 109–118.

Saccone, E. (1979) Pratica e teoria della lettura. In P. de Man, *Allegorie della lettura* (pp.viii–xlv). Turin: Einaudi, 1997.

Sandler, J., Dare, C. and Holder, A. (1973) *The Patient and the Analyst: The Basis of the Psychoanalytic Process*. New York: International Universities Press.

Schachter, J. (2002) *Transference: Shibboleth or Albatross?* Hillsdale, NJ: Analytic Press.

Schafer, R. (1992) *Retelling a Life. Narration and Dialogue in Psychoanalysis*. New York: Basic Books.

Searle, J. R. (1969) *Speech Acts: An Essay in the Philosophy of Language*. Cambridge: Cambridge University Press.

Searles, H. F. (1960) *The Nonhuman Environment, in Normal Development and in Schizophrenia*. New York: International Universities Press.

Searles, H. (1975) The patient as therapist to his analyst. In P. L. Giovacchini (ed.), *Tactics and Techniques in Psychoanalytic Theory* (pp. 95–151). Northvale, NJ: Jason Aronson.

Searles, H. F. (1979) Concerning transference and countertransference. *International Journal of Psychoanalytic Psychotherapy*, 7: 165–188.

Segal, H. (1978) On symbolism. *International Journal of Psychoanalysis*, 59: 315–519.

Shaw, R. R. (1991) Panel: Concepts and controversies about transference neurosis. *Journal of the American Psychoanalytic Association*, 39: 227–240.

Silverberg, W. V. (1948) The concept of transference. *Psychoanalytic Quarterly*, 17, 303–321.

Simons, W. H. C. (ed.) (1990) *The Rhetorical Turn. Invention and Persuasion in the Conduct of Inquiry*. Chicago: University of Chicago Press.

Smith, H. F. (2003) Analysis of transference: A North American perspective. *International Journal of Psychoanalysis*, 84: 1017–1041.

Soavi, G. C. (1985) Fusionalità contro fusionalità e altri argomenti. *Rivista di Psicoanalisi*, 31: 307–315.

Sodré, I. (2005) 'As I was walking down the stair, I saw a concept which wasn't there . . .' Or, après-coup: A missing concept? *International Journal of Psychoanalysis*, 86: 7–10.

Spence, D. (1994) *The Rhetorical Voice of Psychoanalysis: Displacement of Evidence by Theory*. Cambridge, MA: Harvard University Press.

Spence, D. P. (1982) *Narrative Truth and Historical Truth: Meaning and Interpretation in Psychoanalysis*. New York: Norton.

Spezzano, C. (1995). 'Classical' versus 'contemporary' theory – the differences that matter clinically. *Contemporary Psychoanalysis*, 31: 20–46.

States, B. O. (1989) *The Rhetoric of Dreams*. Ithaca, NY: Cornell University Press.

Stein, M. H. (1979) The restoration of the self. *Journal of the American Psychoanalytic Association*, 27: 665–680.

Steiner, J. (1993) *Psychic Retreats. Pathological Organisations in Psychotic, Neurotic and Borderline Patients*. London: Routledge.

Stern, D., Sander, L., Nahum, J., Harrison, A., Lyons-Ruth, K., Morgan, A., *et al.* (1998) Non-interpretive mechanisms in psychoanalytic therapy: The 'something more' than interpretation. *International Journal of Psychoanalysis*, 79: 903–921.

Stolorow, R. D. and Lachmann, F. M. (1984) Transference: The future of an illusion. *Annual of Psychoanalysis*, 12: 19–37.

Strachey, J. (1934) The nature of the therapeutic action of psychoanalysis. *International Journal of Psychoanalysis*, 15: 127–159.

Strenger, C. (1992) *Between Hermeneutics and Science: An Essay on the Epistemology of Psychoanalysis*. Madison, CT: International Universities Press.

Sugeno, T. (1996) Metonymy as the primary trope. *Poetica*, 46: 101–118.

Sullivan, P. (2004) Jacques Derrida dies; deconstructionist philosopher. *Washington Post*, Washington, DC: 10 October, p. C.11. Available HTTP <http://www.washingtonpost.com/wp-dyn/articles/A21050-2004Oct9.html> (accessed 23 September 2009).

Tagliacozzo, R. (1985) Angosce fusionali: Mondo concreto e mondo pensabile. *Rivista di Psicoanalisi*, 31: 290–298.

Thomä, H., Cheshire, N. and Cheshire, U. (1991) Freud's Nachträglichkeit and Strachey's 'deferred action': Trauma, construction and the direction of causality. *International Journal of Psychoanalysis*, 18: 407–428.

Thompson, M. G. (2004) Postmodernism and psychoanalysis: A Heideggerian critique of postmodernist malaise and the question of authenticity. In J. Reppen, J. Tucker and M. A. Schulman (eds), *Way Beyond Freud: Postmodern Psychoanalysis Observed* (pp. 173–202). London: Open Gate.

Tustin, F. (1972) *Autism and Childhood Psychosis*. London: Hogarth Press.

Tustin, F. (1986) *Autistic Barriers in Neurotic Patients*. London: Karnac.

Vattimo, G. (1985) *The End of Modernity: Nihilism and Hermeneutics in Postmodern Culture*. Baltimore, MD: Johns Hopkins University Press, 1991.

Vattimo, G. (1989) *The Transparent Society*. Baltimore, MD: Johns Hopkins University Press, 1992.

Vattimo, G. (1994) *Beyond Interpretation: The Meaning of Hermeneutics for Philosophy*. Stanford, CA: Stanford University Press, 1997.

Vegetti, S. (1986) *Storia della psicoanalisi. Autori opere teorie 1895–1985*. Milan: Mondadori.

Vergani, M. (2000) *Jacques Derrida*. Milan: Mondadori.

Viderman, S. (1970) *La construction de l'espace analytique*. Paris: Denoël.

Viderman, S. (1979) The analytic space: Meaning and problems. *Psychoanalytic Quarterly*, 48: 257–291.

Volpi, F. (2004) *Il nichilismo*. Bari: Laterza.

Wachowski, L. and Wachowski, A. (1999) *The Matrix*. Warner Bros, USA.

Weinrich, H. (1976) Dispute sulla metafora. In H. Weinrich (ed.), *Metafora e menzogna: La serenità dell'arte* (pp. 115–132). Bologna: Il Mulino.

Weinshel, E. M. (1971) The transference neurosis: A survey of the literature. *Journal of the American Psychoanalytic Association*, 19: 67–88,

Westen, D. and Gabbard, G. O. (2002) Developments in cognitive neuro-science. II. Implications for theories of transference. *Journal of the American Psychoanalytic Association*, 50: 99–134.

Winnicott, D. W. (1956a) On transference. *International Journal of Psychoanalysis*, 37: 386–388.

Winnicott, D. W. (1956b) Primary maternal preoccupation. In D. W. Winnicott, *Through Paediatrics to Psycho-Analysis* (pp. 300–305). New York: Basic Books, 1975.

Winnicott, D. W. (1963) The development of the capacity for concern. In D. W. Winnicott, *The Maturational Processes and the Facilitating Environment* (pp. 73–82). New York: International Universities Press, 1965.

Winnicott, D. W. (1971a) *Therapeutic Consultations in Child Psychiatry*. London: Hogarth Press.

Winnicott, D. W. (1971b) *Playing and Reality*. New York: Basic Books.

Wolfreys, J. (1998) *Deconstruction – Derrida*. New York: St. Martin's Press.

Yeats, W. B. (1974) *The Collected Works of W.B. Yeats, Vol. 1: The Poems*. New York: Scribner, 1997.

Yehoshua, A. B. (1989) *Mr. Mani*. New York: Doubleday, 1992.

Zingarelli, N. (1969) *Vocabolario della lingua italiana*. Bologna: Zanichelli.

Index

abandonment, pain of 86
Abraham, K. 85
abreaction 97
abyss, as moment in analysis 20 [clinical vignette: Carla 11–15]
Adams, L. 85
adaptation 60, 100, 105, 106
adhesive identification 26, 28, 32
adhesiveness 26–29, 33, 38, 43, 101; autistic 29; primitive 43; to second skin [clinical fragment: Bruno] 37–38
Adler, E. 116, 134, 135
aetiopathogenesis of neuroses 96, 103
affective blockage 25
affective hologram 78
agglutinated/glischroid object 23
agglutinated nucleus 24–25, 32, 40–45, 181; loss of, catastrophic effect of 29
agglutinated object(s) 23, 27, 44
agglutination 25
aggregates, primitive 27
Alexander, F. 119, 120, 124
Alexander III, Pope 190
alexythymic mental functioning 94
Alizade, A. M. 95
Allen, W. 51, 167
alpha: -elements 9, 139, 187, 189; -function 9, 10, 43, 93, 111, 152, 189; screen 9
ambiguity and glischro-caric position 38–41

ambivalence 17, 40
American Middle Group 121
amnesia 185
amphibian state of mind 95
analysand: *see* patient/analysand
analysis: dialectical 117; as differential system of signs [clinical vignette: Giulio 170–174]; discourse of 72; as field of fantasy(ies) 72; as illusionary/as if area 19; as imaginary space 19; interpersonalist 117; intersubjectivist 117; like receiving and transmitting system of telephone 73; relational 117, 121; of resistances 134; text of, focus points internal to 89
analyst/therapist: absence of, consequences of [clinical fragment: Stefano] 34–35; antalgic collusion of 15, 169; blank-screen 19; close process attention of 125; dream of, about patient's narration 55; evenly suspended/floating attention of 14, 77, 91, 156, 178; failure of neutrality of 59; internal setting of 2, 4; maternal role of 6; participation of, in transference 3; and patient, psychic space between 43; reverie of 48, 78, 90, 169, 175 [as amphibian state of mind 92, 95]; role of, in psychoanalytic process 121; symbiotic connection with 33

209

211

function of 48; unconscious fantasy of 47

Füssli, J. H. 159

Gabbard, G. O. 135, 152
Gaburri, E. 9, 72, 166
Gadamer, H.-G. 162
Garella, A. 106
Gedo, J. E. 115, 121
genetic interpretations 123, 126
Genette, G. 50, 55, 57, 58, 143–146, 167, 184, 190
Gestalt psychology 42
Ghent, E. 117
Gill, M. 14, 117, 119–124, 131
Gilmore, K. 120, 128
glischro-caric position 22–24, 38, 40, 41, 49, 181
glischroid /agglutinated object 23
global positioning systems (GPS) 11
Goldberg, A. 190
Goretti, G. 175
Gottlieb, K. I. 116
granular ego 24, 40
Gray, P. 123, 124, 125
Green, A. 85
Greenberg, J. R. 117, 121
Greenspan, S. I. 48
Grünbaum, A. 131, 164
Guntrip, H. 121

Haas, L. 132
Habermas, J. 162
Halion, K. J. 140, 187
hallucination(s) 153; olfactory 46; shared 153; temporal 153
Handke, P. 80
Harley, M. 120
Harrison, A. 19, 47
Hartmann, H. 115
Heidegger, M. 157, 165
heliocentric hypothesis 162
here-and-now of session 20, 34, 57, 73, 78, 79, 86, 91–97, 104, 111–113, 121–124, 131, 139, 167, 173, 174, 184
hermeneutics 74, 162, 164, 165
Hillis Miller, J. 152, 175

Hinton, G. E. 135
historical reconstruction 11, 13, 114, 166, 174
Hobson, M. 190
Hoffman, I. 20, 117
Holder, A. 118, 125
holding environment 133
Holland, N. 158
homeostasis 151
homologation 157
Horowitz, M. J. 131
hospitality, ethic of 174–179
Hoxter, S. 26
hypertext, metaphor of 75–79
hypochondria 25, 34
hypochondriacal anxieties 34, 37; and symbiotic area of setting [clinical vignette: Silvia] 34

id 121, 123
identification: adhesive 26, 28, 32; primary 24; projective 113, 121, 122
identity: construction 27, 68: differentiation 52: and self, rent in continuity of [clinical fragment: Matteo] 35–36; transference 137–154
illusionary/as if area, analysis as 19
illusory transference 43
imaginary space, analysis as 19
Imbasciati, A. 100
Imbeault, J. 3
immobilization 23, 47
incest 87, 90
infantile autism 26
infantile development, and touching 26–29
infantile neurosis 7, 114, 116, 123, 129, 153, 178
infantile seduction theory 96
infantile sexual traumas 97
inner world, consciousness of reality of 72
insomnia as moment in analysis 20 [clinical vignette: Alberto, 4–11]
intentionality 27, 28, 38, 77, 99, 102, 140
interactionists, Freudian 117
interactivity vs immersion 72–95

McClelland, J. L. 135
McLaughlin, J. T. 132, 133
Malina, D. 57
Malle, L. 68, 69
Marcelli, D. 25–29, 39, 41, 185
Masson, J. M. 96
materiality of language 158
maternal behaviour, ritualization of 27
maternal care 32, 120; discontinuity of,
    effects of 32
maternal discourse 58
maternal negligence 85
maternal role of analyst 6
matrix(ces) of transference 132–135
meaning(s): assignment of 137, 138;
    bidirectional deferral of 140
Meltzer, D. 2, 9–11, 13, 26, 29, 93, 121,
    165, 175
memory(ies) (*passim*): associative
    character of 100; categorial, concept
    of 106; categories of traumatic
    106–108; and desire, Bionian precept
    of 8; dynamic model of 74; explosion
    of 144; fallibility of 96; as higher level
    organizing principle of consciousness
    or recategorization 98–102; intensely
    clear 66; involuntary 70, 143;
    neurophysiological mechanisms of
    99; replicative 100; retranscription of
    96–98; trace 101, 102
meningitis 86
mentalization 44, 186
meta-ego 23–25, 33, 38–43, 46, 47, 49,
    66; /non-ego 24, 42
metalepsis 50–71, 167–168, 173, 184,
    190
metaphor(s) 1, 10, 23, 39, 56, 79,
    143–146, 149, 150–151, 156, 169; of
    fire at theatre 8, 73, 169; Freud's, for
    analytic work 1; hypertext 75–79;
    Oedipal, of blindness 159; of spider
    83–89; tool of rhetoric 162–163
metaphysics 58, 105, 109, 156, 158, 190;
    of presence 105, 158 [and of
    'originary' 105]
metapsychology 80, 120, 123
metonymic slippage 145

metonymy(ies) 56, 137, 143–146, 151,
    188
Middle Group, American 121
Milan Psychoanalysis Centre 135
Milner, M. 67
mind, topographical model of 23
Minkowski, E. 23
minus K 19
Mitchell, S. A. 117, 121
Mitrani, J. L. 32
Möbius ribbon 93
Modell, A. H. 22, 45, 67, 102, 107
Molière 111
Mom, J. M. 97
moments of encounter 49
Montale, E. 180
Morgan, A. 19, 47
Mortara Garavelli, B. 56
mother: –child interaction 28; dead 85,
    86
mothering object, pre-consciousness of
    27
mourning for what is not 77
mutative interpretation 114

Nachträglichkeit/après-coup 73, 96–112,
    124, 139, 158, 183, 186
Nahum, J. 19, 47
Napolitano, F. 119
narcissistic neuroses 113
narcissistic nuclei 41
narcissistic screen 121
narcissistic transference(s) 41, 133
narcissistic wound 177
narration, definition 78
narrative, interpretation structured like
    53, 166
narrative derivatives 11, 70, 92, 147, 149,
    173; unconscious 92, 147, 149
narrative interpretations 49, 78, 156
narrative ontology, subversion of 57,
    190
narrative truth 163
narrative or unsaturated interpretation
    67
narratology 51, 54–57, 68, 137, 143, 147,
    149, 168, 190

216